MATHEMATICAL ELEMENTS
FOR
COMPUTER GRAPHICS

MATHEMATICAL ELEMENTS
FOR
COMPUTER GRAPHICS

DAVID F. ROGERS
Aerospace Engineering Department
United States Naval Academy

J. ALAN ADAMS
Mechanical Engineering Department
United States Naval Academy

McGraw-Hill Book Company

New York St. Louis San Francisco Auckland
Düsseldorf Johannesburg Kuala Lumpur London
Mexico Montreal New Delhi Panama Paris
São Paulo Singapore Sydney Tokyo Toronto

MATHEMATICAL ELEMENTS
FOR
COMPUTER GRAPHICS

7890 HDHD 8432

Library of Congress Cataloging in Publication Data

Rogers, David F   1937-
    Mathematical elements for computer graphics.

    Includes bibliographical references and index.
    I. Computer graphics. I. Adams, James Alan 1936-, joint author.
    II. Title
T385.R6   001.6'443   75-29930
ISBN 0-07-053527-2

CONTENTS

FOREWORD

Since its inception more than a decade ago, the field of computer graphics has
captured the imagination and technical interest of rapidly increasing numbers of
individuals from many disciplines. A high percentage of the growing ranks of
computer graphics professionals has given primary attention to computer-oriented
problems in programming, system design, hardware, etc. This was pointed out by
Dr. Ivan Sutherland in his introduction to Mr. Prince's book, "Interactive
Graphics for Computer-Aided Design," in 1971 and it is still true today. I
believe that an inadequate balance of attention has been given to application-
oriented problems. There has been a dearth of production of useful information
that bears directly on the development and implementation of truly productive
applications. Understanding the practical aspects of computer graphics with
regard to both the nature and use of applications represents an essential and
ultimate requirement in the development of practical computer graphic systems.
Mathematical techniques, especially principles of geometry and transformations,
are indigenous to most computer graphic applications. Yet, large numbers of
graphic programmers and analysts struggle over or gloss over the basic as well
as the complex problems of the mathematical elements. Furthermore, the full
operational potential of computer graphics is often unrealized whenever the
mathematical relationships, constraints, and options are inadequately exploited.
By their authorship of this text, Drs. Rogers and Adams have recognized the
valuable relevance of their background to these practical considerations.

Their text is concise, is comprehensive, and is written in a style unusually conducive to ease of reading, understanding, and use. It exemplifies the rare type of work that most practitioners should wish to place in a prominent location within their library since it should prove to be an invaluable ready reference for most disciplines. It is also well suited as the basis for a course in a computer science education curriculum.

I congratulate the authors in producing an excellent and needed text, "Mathematical Elements for Computer Graphics."

S. H. "Chas" Chasen
Lockheed Georgia Company, Inc.

PREFACE

A new and rapidly expanding field called "computer graphics" is emerging. This field combines both the old and the new: the age-old art of graphical communication and the new technology of computers. Almost everyone can expect to be affected by this rapidly expanding technology. A new era in the use of computer graphics, not just by the large companies and agencies who made many of the initial advances in software and hardware, but by the general user, is beginning. Low-cost graphics terminals, time sharing, plus advances in mini- and microcomputers have made this possible. Today, computer graphics is practical, reliable, cost effective, and readily available.

The purpose of this book is to present an introduction to the mathematical theory underlying computer graphics techniques in a *unified* manner. Although new ways of presenting material are given, no actual "new" mathematical material is presented. All the material in this book exists scattered throughout the technical literature. This book attempts to bring it all together in *one* place in *one* notation.

In selecting material, we chose techniques which were fundamentally mathematical in nature rather than those which were more procedural in nature. For this reason the reader will find more extensive discussions of rotation, translation, perspective, and curve and surface description than of clipping or hidden line and surface removal. First-year college mathematics is a sufficient prerequisite for the major part of the text.

After a discussion of current computer graphics technology in Chapter 1, the manipulation of graphical elements represented in matrix form using homogeneous coordinates is described. A discussion of existing techniques for representing points, lines, curves, and surfaces within a digital computer, as well as computer software procedures for manipulating and displaying computer output in graphical form, is then presented in the following Chapters.

Mathematical techniques for producing axonometric and perspective views are given, along with generalized techniques for rotation, translation, and scaling of geometric figures. Curve definition procedures for both explicit and parametric representations are presented for both two-dimensional and three-dimensional curves. Curve definition techniques include the use of conic sections, circular arc interpolation, cubic splines, parabolic blending, Bezier curves and curves based on B-splines. An introduction to the mathematics of surface description is included.

Computer algorithms for most of the fundamental elements in an interactive graphics package are given in an appendix as BASIC* language subprograms. However, these algorithms deliberately stop short of the coding necessary to actually display the results. Unfortunately there are no standard language commands or subroutines available for graphic display. Although some preliminary discussion of graphic primitives and graphic elements is given in Appendix A, each user will in general find it necessary to work within the confines of the computer system and graphics devices available to him or her.

The fundamental ideas in this book have been used as the foundation for an introductory course in computer graphics given to students majoring in technical or scientific fields at the undergraduate level. It is suitable for use in this manner at both universities and schools of technology. It is also suitable as a supplementary text in more advanced computer programming courses or as a supplementary text in some advanced mathematics courses. Further, it can be profitably used by individuals engaged in professional programming. Finally, the documented computer programs should be of use to computer users interested in developing computer graphics capability.

ACKNOWLEDGMENTS

The authors gratefully acknowledge the encouragement and support of the United States Naval Academy. The academic environment provided by the administration, the faculty, and especially the midshipmen was conducive to the development of the material in this book.

---

*BASIC is a registered trade mark of Dartmouth College

No book is ever written without the assistance of a great many people. Here we would like to acknowledge a few of them. First, Steve Coons who reviewed the entire manuscript and made many valuable suggestions, Rich Reisenfeld who reviewed the material on B-spline curves and surfaces, Professor Pierre Bezier who reviewed the material on Bezier curves and surfaces and Ivan Sutherland who provided the impetus for the three-dimensional reconstruction techniques discussed in Chapter 3. Special acknowledgment is due past and present members of the CAD Group at Cambridge University. Specifically, work done with Robin Forrest, Charles Lang, and Tony Nutbourne provided greater insight into the subject of computer graphics. Finally, to Louie Knapp who provided an original FORTRAN program for B-spline curves.

The authors would also like to acknowledge the assistance of many individuals at the Evans and Sutherland Computer Corporation. Specifically, Jim Callan who authored the document from which many of the ideas on representing, preparing, presenting and interacting with pictures is based. Special thanks are also due Lee Billow who prepared all of the line drawings.

Much of the art work for Chapter 1 has been provided through the good offices of various computer graphics equipment manufacturers. Specific acknowledgment is made as follows:

Fig. 1-3   Evans and Sutherland Computer Corporation

Fig. 1-5   Adage Inc.

Fig. 1-7   Adage Inc.

Fig. 1-8   Vector General, Inc.

Fig. 1-11   Xynetics, Inc.

Fig. 1-12   CALCOMP, California Computer Products, Inc.

Fig. 1-15   Gould, Inc.

Fig. 1-16   Tektronix, Inc.

Fig. 1-17   Evans and Sutherland Computer Corporation

Fig. 1-18   CALCOMP, California Computer Products, Inc.

David F. Rogers
J. Alan Adams

In this second printing all the known errors have been corrected. We continue to solicit suggestions for improving this book to meet your needs.

David F. Rogers
J. Alan Adams
Annapolis, April, 1979

CHAPTER 1

INTRODUCTION TO COMPUTER GRAPHIC TECHNOLOGY

Since computer graphics is a relatively new technology, it is necessary to clarify the current terminology. A number of terms and definitions are used rather loosely in this field. In particular, computer aided design (CAD), interactive graphics (IG), computer graphics (CG), and computer aided manufacturing (CAM) are frequently used interchangeably or in such a manner that considerable confusion exists as to the precise meaning. Of these terms CAD is the most general. CAD may be defined as *any* use of the computer to aid in the design of an individual part, a subsystem, or a total system. The use does not have to involve graphics. The design process may be at the system concept level or at the detail part design level. It may also involve an interface with CAM.

Computer aided manufacturing is the use of a computer to aid in the manufacture or production of a part exclusive of the design process. A direct interface between the results of a CAD application and the necessary part programming using such languages as APT (Automatic Programmed Tools) and UNIAPT (United's APT), the direction of a machine tool using a hardwired or softwired (minicomputer) controller to read data from a punched paper tape and generate the necessary commands to control a machine tool, or the direct control of a machine tool using a minicomputer may be involved.

Computer graphics is the use of a computer to define, store, manipulate,

interrogate, and present pictorial output. This is essentially a passive operation. The computer prepares and presents stored information to an observer
in the form of pictures. The observer has no direct control over the picture
being presented. The application may be as simple as the presentation of the
graph of a simple function using a high-speed line printer or a time-sharing
teletype terminal to as complex as the simulation of the automatic reentry and
landing of a space capsule.

Interactive graphics also uses the computer to prepare and present pictorial material. However, in interactive graphics the observer can influence the
picture as it is being presented; i.e., the observer interacts with the picture
in real time. To see the importance of the real time restriction, consider the
problem of rotating a complex three-dimensional picture composed of 1000 lines
at a reasonable rotation rate, say, 15°/second. As we shall see subsequently,
the 1000 lines of the picture are most conveniently represented by a 1000 x 4
matrix of homogeneous coordinates of the end points of the lines, and the rotation is most conveniently accomplished by multiplying this 1000 x 4 matrix by
a 4 x 4 transformation matrix. Accomplishing the required matrix multiplication
requires 16,000 multiplications, 12,000 additions, and 1000 divisions. If this
matrix multiplication is accomplished in software, the time is significant. To
see this, consider that a typical minicomputer using a hardware floating-point
processor requires 6 microseconds to multiply two numbers, 4 microseconds to
add two numbers, and 8 microseconds to divide two numbers. Thus the matrix
multiplication requires 0.15 seconds.

Since computer displays that allow dynamic motion require that the picture
be redrawn (refreshed) at least 30 times each second in order to avoid flicker,
it is obvious that the picture cannot change smoothly. Even if it is assumed
that the picture is recalculated (updated) only 15 times each second, i.e.,
every degree, it is still not possible to accomplish a smooth rotation in software. Thus this is now no longer interactive graphics. To regain the ability
to interactively present the picture several things can be done. Clever programming can reduce the time to accomplish the required matrix multiplication.
However, a point will be reached where this is no longer possible. The complexity of the picture can be reduced. In this case, the resulting picture
may not be acceptable. Finally, the matrix multiplication can be accomplished
by using a special-purpose digital hardware matrix multiplier. This is the
most promising approach. It can easily handle the problem outlined above.

With this terminology in mind the remainder of this chapter will give an
overview of computer graphics and discuss and classify the types of graphic
displays available. The necessary considerations for development of a software system for the fundamental drawing, device-control, and data-handling

aspects of computer graphics is given in Appendix A.

1-1 Overview Of Computer Graphics

Computer graphics as defined above can be a very complex and diverse subject. It encompasses fields of study as diverse as electronic and mechanical design of the components used in computer graphics systems and the concepts of display lists and tree structures for preparing and presenting pictures to an observer using a computer graphics system. A discussion of these aspects of interactive computer graphics is given in the book by Newman and Sproul (Ref. 1-1). Here we will attempt to present only those aspects of the subject of interest from a user's point of view. From this point of view, computer graphics can be divided into the following areas:

Representing pictures to be presented

Preparing pictures for presentation

Presenting previously prepared pictures

Interacting with the picture

Here the word "picture" is used in its broadest sense to mean any collection of lines, points, text, etc., to be displayed on a graphics device. A picture may be as simple as a single line or curve, or it may be a fully scaled and annotated graph or a complex representation of an aircraft, ship, or automobile.

1-2 Representing Pictures To Be Presented

Fundamentally the pictures represented in computer graphics can be considered as a collection of lines, points, and textual material. A line can be represented by the coordinates of its end points (x_1,y_1,z_1) and (x_2,y_2,z_2), a point by a single-coordinate triplet (x_1,y_1,z_1), and textual material by collections of lines or points.

The representation of textual material is by far the most complex, involving in many cases curved lines or dot matrices. However, unless the user is concerned with pattern recognition, the design of graphic hardware, or unusual character sets, he or she need not be concerned with these details, since almost all graphic devices have built-in "hardware" or software character generators. The representation of curved lines is usually accomplished by approximating them by short straight-line segments. However, this is sometimes accomplished using hardware curve generators.

1-3 Preparing Pictures For Presentation

Pictures ultimately consist of points. The coordinates of these points are generally stored in a file (array) prior to being used to present the picture. This file (array) is called a data base. Very complex pictures require very complex data bases which require a complex program to access them. These complex data bases may involve ring structures, tree structures, etc., and the data base itself may contain pointers, substructures, and other nongraphic data. The design of these data bases and the programs which access them is an ongoing topic of research, a topic which is clearly beyond the scope of this text. However, many computer graphics applications involve much simpler pictures for which the user can readily invent simple data base structures which can be easily accessed.

Points are the basic building blocks of a graphic data base. There are three basic methods or instructions for treating a point as a graphic geometric entity: move the beam, pen, cursor, plotting head (hereafter called the cursor) to the point, draw a line to that point, or draw a dot at that point. Fundamentally there are two ways to specify the position of a point: absolute or relative (incremental) coordinates. In relative or incremental coordinates the position of a point is defined by giving the displacement of the point with respect to the previous point.

The specification of the position of a point in either absolute or relative coordinates requires a number. This can lead to difficulties if a computer with a limited word length is used. Generally a full computer word is used to specify a coordinate position. The largest integer number that can be specified by a full computer word is $2^{n-1} - 1$, where n is the number of bits in the word. For the 16-bit minicomputer frequently used to support computer graphic displays, this is 32767. For many applications this is acceptable. However, difficulties are encountered when larger integer numbers than can be specified are required. At first we might expect to overcome this difficulty by using relative coordinates to specify a number such as 60,000, i.e., using an absolute coordinate specification to position the cursor to (30000, 30000) and then a relative coordinate specification of (30000, 30000) to position the beam to the final desired point of (60000, 60000). However, this will not work, since an attempt to accumulate relative position specifications beyond the maximum representable value will result in the generation of a number of opposite sign and erroneous magnitude. For cathode ray tube (CRT) displays this will generally yield the phenomena called wraparound.

The way out of this dilemma is to use homogeneous coordinates. The use of homogeneous coordinates introduces some additional complexity, some loss in speed, and some loss in resolution. However, these disadvantages are far outweighed by the advantage of being able to represent large integer numbers with

a computer of limited word size. For this reason as well as others presented
later, homogeneous coordinate representations are generally used in this book.

In homogeneous coordinates an n dimensional space is represented by n + 1
dimensions, i.e., three-dimensional data where the position of a point is given
by the triplet (x,y,z) is represented by four coordinates (hx,hy,hz,h), where
h is an arbitrary number.

If each of the coordinate positions represented in a 16-bit computer were
less than 32767, then h would be made equal to 1 and the coordinate positions
represented directly. If, however, one of the Eucledean or ordinary coordinates
is larger than 32767, say, x = 60000, then the power of homogeneous coordinates
becomes apparent. In this case we can let h = 1/2, and the coordinates of the
point are then defined as (30000, 1/2y, 1/2z, 1/2), all acceptable numbers for
a 16-bit computer. However, some resolution is lost since x = 60000 and x =
59999 are both represented by the same homogeneous coordinate. In fact resolution is lost in all the coordinates even if only one of them exceeds the maximum expressable number of a particular computer.

1-4 PRESENTING PREVIOUSLY PREPARED PICTURES

With these comments about data bases in mind it is necessary to note that
the data base used to prepare the picture for presentation is almost never the
same as the display file used to present the picture. The data base represents
the total picture while the display file represents only some portion, view, or
scene of the picture. The display file is created by transforming the data
base. The picture contained in the data base may be resized, rotated, translated, or part of it removed or viewed from a particular point to obtain necessary perspective before being displayed. Many of these operations can be
accomplished by using simple linear transformations which involve matrix multiplications. Among these are rotation, translation, scaling, and perspective
views. As we shall see later, homogeneous coordinates are very convenient for
accomplishing these transformations.

As will be shown in detail in Chapters 2 and 3, a 4 x 4 matrix can be used
to perform any of these individual transformations on points represented as a
matrix in homogeneous coordinates. When a sequence of transformations is
desired, each individual transformation can be sequentially applied to the
points to achieve the desired result. If, however, the number of points is
substantial, this is inefficient and time consuming. An alternate and more
desirable method is to multiply the individual matrices representing each
required transformation together and then to finally multiply the matrix of
points by the resulting 4 x 4 transformation matrix. This matrix operation is

called concatenation. It results in significant time savings when performing compound matrix operations on sets of data points.

Although in many graphics applications the complete data base is displayed, frequently only portions of the data base are to be displayed. This process of displaying only part of the complete-picture data base is called windowing. Windowing is not easy, particularly if the picture data base has been transformed as discussed above. Performance of the windowing operation in software generally is sufficiently time consuming that dynamic real-time interactive graphics is not possible. Again, sophisticated graphics devices perform this function in hardware. In general there are two types of windowing - clipping and scissoring. Clipping involves determining which lines or portions of lines in the picture lie outside the window. Those lines or portions of lines are then discarded and not displayed; i.e., they are not passed on to the display device. In the scissoring technique, the display device has a larger physical drawing space than is required. Only those lines or line segments within the specified window are made visible even though lines or line segments outside the window are drawn. Clipping accomplished in hardware is generally more advantageous than scissoring; e.g., clipping makes available a much larger drawing area than scissoring. In scissoring, those lines or segments of lines which are not visible in the window are also drawn. This, of course, requires time, since the line generator must spend time drawing the entire data base whether visible or invisible rather than only part of the data base as in the case for clipping.

In two dimensions a window is specified by values for the left, right, top, and bottom edges of a rectangle. Clipping is easiest if the edges of the rectangle are parallel to the coordinate axes. If, however, this is not the case, the rotation of the window can be compensated for by rotating the data base in the opposite direction. Two-dimensional clipping is represented in Fig. 1-1. Lines are retained, deleted, or partially deleted, depending on whether they are completely within or without the window or partially within or without the window. In three dimensions a window consists of a frustum of vision, as shown in Fig. 1-2. In Fig. 1-2 the near (hither) boundary is at N, the far (yon) boundary at F, and the sides at SL, SR, ST, and SB.

As a final step in the picture presentation process it is necessary to convert from the coordinates used in the picture data base called user coordinates, to those used by the display device, called display coordinates. In particular, it is necessary to convert coordinate data which pass the windowing process into display coordinates such that the picture appears in some specified area on the display, called a viewport. The viewport can be specified by giving its left, right, top, and bottom edges if two-dimensional or if three-dimensional by also specifying a near (hither) and far (yon) boundary. In the

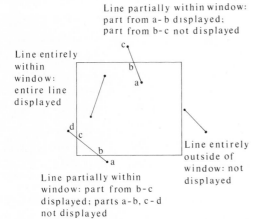

Line partially within window:
part from a-b displayed;
part from b-c not displayed

Line entirely
within
window:
entire line
displayed

Line entirely
outside of
window: not
displayed

Line partially within
window: part from b-c
displayed; parts a-b, c-d
not displayed

Figure 1-1 Two dimensional
windowing (clipping).

Figure 1-2 Three-dimensional
frustum of vision window.

most general case conversion to display coordinates within a specified three-dimensional viewport requires a linear mapping from a six-sided frustum of vision (window) to a six-sided viewport.

An additional requirement for most pictures is the presentation of alphanumeric or character data. There are in general two methods of generating characters - software and hardware. If characters are generated in software using lines, they are treated in the same manner as any other picture element. In fact this is necessary if they are to be clipped and then transformed along with other picture elements. However, many graphic devices have some kind of hardware character generator. When hardware character generators are used, the actual characters are generated just prior to being drawn. Up until this point they are treated as only character codes. Hardware character generation is less flexible since it does not allow for clipping or infinite transformation, e.g., only limited rotations and sizes are generally possible, but it yields significant efficiencies.

When a hardware character generator is used, the program which drives the graphic device must first specify size, orientation, and the position where the character or text string is to begin. The character codes specifying these characteristics are then added to the display file. Upon being processed the character generator interprets the text string, looks up in hardware the necessary lines to draw the character, and draws the characters on the display device.

1-5 INTERACTING WITH THE PICTURE

Interacting with the picture requires some type of interactive device to communicate with the program while it is running. In effect this interrupts the program so that new or different information can be provided. Numerous devices have been used to accomplish this task. The simplest is, of course, the alphanumeric keyboard such as is found on the teletype. More sophisticated devices include light pens, joy sticks, track balls, a mouse, function switches, control dials, and analog tablets. We shall examine each of these devices briefly.

A simple alphanumeric keyboard as shown in Fig. 1-3 can be a useful interactive device. Precise alphabetic, numerical, or control information can be easily supplied to the program. However, it is not capable of high rates of interaction, expecially if the user is not a good typist.

Perhaps the best known interactive device is the light pen. The light pen contains a light-sensitive photoelectric cell and associated circuitry. When positioned over a line segment or other lighted area of a CRT and activated, the position of the pen is sensed and an interrupt is sent to the computer. A schematic of a typical light pen is shown in Fig. 1-4. Figure 1-5 shows a light pen in use for menu picking.

The joy stick, mouse, and track ball all operate on the same principle. By moving a control, two-dimensional positional information is communicated to the computer. All these devices are analog in nature. In particular, movement of the control changes the setting of a sensitive potentiometer. The resulting signals are converted from analog (voltages) to digital signals using an analog to digital (A/D) converter. These digital signals are then interpreted by the computer as positional information. A joy stick is shown in Fig. 1-6. Joy sticks, mouses, track balls, and similar devices are useful for particular applications. However, they should not be used to provide very precise positional information.

Control dials as shown in Fig. 1-7 are essentially sensitive rotating potentiometers and associated circuitry such that the position of the dial can be sensed using analog to digital conversion techniques. They are particularly useful for activating rotation, translation, or zoom features of hardware and software systems.

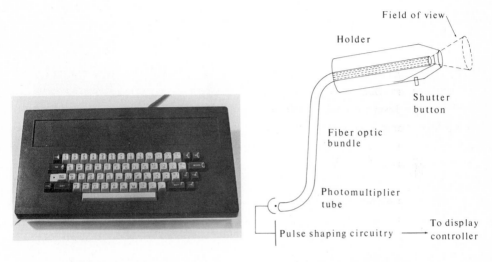

Figure 1-3 Alphanumeric keyboard.

Figure 1-4 Schematic of a light pen.

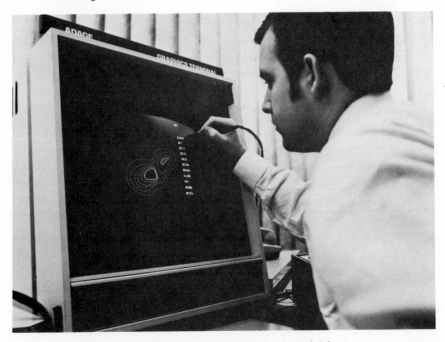

Figure 1-5 Light pen in use for menu picking.

Figure 1-6   Joy stick.   Figure 1-7   Control dials.

Function switches, shown in Fig. 1-8, are either toggle or push-button switches whose position can be determined by the graphics program. Lights indicating which switch or switches are active are also usually provided.

The analog tablet is the most versatile and accurate device for communicating positional information to the computer. Properly used, the analog tablet can perform all the functions of a light pen, joy stick, track ball, mouse, function switches, or control dials. Associated with the tablet is a pen which can be moved over the surface and whose position can be sensed. It is also possible to sense whether or not the pen is in close proximity to the tablet surface. Positional information with accuracies of $\pm$ 0.01 inch are typical of many tablets, and tablets with accuracies of $\pm$ 0.001 inch are available. Typical analog tablets are shown in Fig. 1-9. The position of the pen and its relative location in the picture-display area are tied together by means of a cursor (a small visible symbol) whose motion on the picture display area is in concert with that of the pen on the tablet. The analog tablet has two distinct advantages over the light pen. Namely, when the analog tablet is used to perform a pointing function, the indication occurs in the data base and not in the display file. Thus, the programming is simplified. Also, drawing or sketching or pointing using an analog tablet which is on a horizontal surface is more

natural than performing the same operation with a light pen in a vertical
orientation.

An analog tablet can be implemented
in hardware by using a variety of elec-
tromagnetic principles. Some of these
are discussed in Ref. 1-1 in more detail.
Except in unusual environments the user
need not be concerned with the precise
operating principle.

1-6 DESCRIPTION OF SOME TYPICAL GRAPHICS DEVICES

There are a large number of different types of graphics devices available,
far too many to describe them all here.
Therefore only a limited number of devices representative of those available
will be considered. In particular,
three different types of CRT graphics

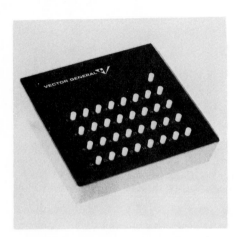

Figure 1-8   Function switches.

devices - storage tube, refresh, and raster scan; a pen and ink plotter; and
a dot matrix plotter - will be described. Additional devices and more detail-
ed descriptions are provided in Ref. 1-1.

The three types of CRT (cathode ray tube) devices are direct view storage
tube displays, refresh displays, and raster scan displays. The direct view
storage tube display, also called a bistable storage tube display, can be
considered as similar to an oscilloscope with a very long persistence phosphor.
A storage tube display is shown in Fig. 1-9. A line or character will remain
visible (up to an hour) until erased by the generation of a specific electrical
signal. The erasing process requires about 1/2 second. Storage tube displays
have several advantages and disadvantages. Some of the advantages are: the
display is flicker free, resolution of the display is good (typically 1024 x
1024 addressable raster points in an approximate 8 x 8 inch square), and cost
is low. Further, it is relatively easy and fast to obtain an acceptable hard
copy of the picture, and conceptually they are somewhat easier to program and
more suited to time-sharing applications than refresh or raster scan displays.
The principal disadvantage is that the screen cannot be selectively erased;
i.e., in order to change any element of a picture the entire picture must be
redrawn. Because of this the display of dynamic motions is not possible. In

Figure 1-9 Analog tablet.

addition, this characteristic results in the interaction between the user and
the display being somewhat slower than with a refresh display.

A refresh CRT graphics display is based on a television-like cathode ray
tube. However, the method of generating the image is quite different. Television uses a raster scan technique (see below) to generate the required picture, whereas the traditional refresh CRT graphics display is of the calligraphic
or line-drawing type. A refresh CRT graphics display requires two elements in
addition to the cathode ray tube itself: a display buffer and a display controller. In order to understand the advantages and limitations of a refresh
display it is necessary to conceptually understand the purpose of these devices.

Since the phosphor used on the cathode ray tube of a refresh display fades
very rapidly, i.e., has a short persistence, it is necessary to repaint or reconstruct the entire picture many times each second. This is called the refresh
rate. A refresh rate that is too low will result in a phenomenon called flicker.
This is similar to the effect which results from running a movie projector too
slow. A minimum refresh rate of 30 times per second is required to achieve a
flicker-free display. A refresh rate of 40 times per second is recommended.
The function of the display buffer is to store in sequence all of the instruc-

tions necessary to draw the picture on the cathode ray tube. The function of
the display controller is to access (cycle through) these instructions at the
refresh rate. Immediately, a limitation of the refresh display is obvious:
The complexity of the picture is limited by the size of the display buffer and
the speed of the display controller. However, the short persistence of the
image can be used to advantage to show dynamic motion. In particular, the picture can be updated every refresh or, say, every other refresh cycle if double
buffering is used. Further, since each element or instruction necessary to
draw the complete picture exists in the display buffer, any individual element
can be changed, deleted, or an additional element added; i.e., a selective
erase feature can be implemented. One additional disadvantage of a refresh CRT
graphic device is the relative difficulty of obtaining a hard copy of the picture. Although refresh CRT graphic displays are generally more expensive than
storage tube displays, the above characteristics make them the display of choice
when dynamic motion in real time or very rapid interaction with the display is
required.

A raster scan CRT graphics display uses a standard television monitor for
the display console. In the raster scan display the picture is composed of a
series of dots. These dots are traced out using a dual raster scan technique,
i.e., as a series of horizontal lines. Two rasters as shown in Fig. 1-10 are
used to reduce flicker. The basic electrical signal used to drive the display
console is an analog signal whose modulation represents the intensity of the
individual dots which compose the picture. In using a raster scan display console it is first necessary to convert the line and character information to a
form compatible with the raster presentation. This process is called scan conversion. Once it is converted the information must be stored such that it can
be accessed in a reasonable manner. With the advances in data storage techniques this is becoming more feasible. In considering a raster scan CRT graphic
display, the advantages and disadvantages are similar to those for line-drawing
displays, with some additional considerations. Namely, they are generally somewhat slower, the selective erase feature is more difficult to implement, and
they may be directly interfaced to closed-circuit television systems.

Digital incremental pen and ink plotters are of two general types - flat-
bed and drum. Figure 1-11 shows a flat-bed plotter and Fig. 1-12 shows a drum
plotter. Most drum and flat-bed plotters operate in an incremental mode; i.e.,
the plotting tool, which need not be a pen, moves across the plotting surface
in a series of small steps, typically 0.001 to 0.01 inch. Frequently the number of directions in which the tool can move is limited, say, to the eight
directions shown in Fig. 1-13. This results in a curved line appearing to be
a series of small steps. In a flat-bed plotter the table in generally station-

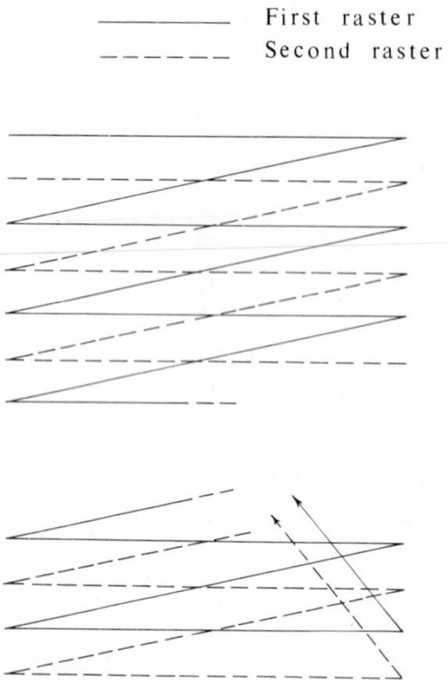

ary and the writing head moves in two dimensions over the surface of the table. A drum plotter uses a somewhat different technique to achieve two-dimensional motion. Here the marking tool moves back and forth across the paper while the lengthwise motion is obtained by rolling the paper back and forth under the marking tool.

————— First raster

— — — — — Second raster

Digital incremental plotters can provide high-quality hard copy of graphical output. Compared to CRT graphics devices they are quite slow. Consequently they are not generally used for real-time interactive graphics. However, where large drawings are normally required for a particular application, a flat-bed plotter can be utilized as a combination digitizer and plotter and an interactive computer graphic system successfully developed (see Ref. 1-2).

Figure 1-10   Raster scan technique.

The electrostatic dot matrix printer/plotter operates by depositing particles of a toner onto small electrostatically charged areas of a special paper. Figure 1-14 shows the general scheme which is employed. In detail, a specially coated paper which will hold an electrostatic charge is passed over a writing head which contains a row of small writing nibs or styli. From 70 to 200 styli per inch are typical. The styli deposit an electrostatic charge onto the special paper. Since the electrostatic charges are themselves not visible, the charged paper is passed over a toner which is a liquid containing dark toner particles. The particles are attracted to the electrostatically charged areas, making them visible. The paper is then dried and presented to the user. Very high speeds can be obtained, typically from 500 to 1000 lines per minute.

The electrostatic dot matrix printer/plotter is a raster scan device; i.e., it presents information one line at a time. Because it is a raster scan device it requires a substantial amount of computer storage to construct a complete picture. This plus the fact that the device is useable for only passive graphics are the principle disadvantages. A further disadvantage is relatively low accuracy and resolution, typically $\pm$ 0.01 inch. The principal advantages are the very high speed with which drawings can be produced and an excellent reliability record. Figure 1-15 shows an electrostatic dot matrix printer/plotter

Figure 1-11 Flat-bed plotter.

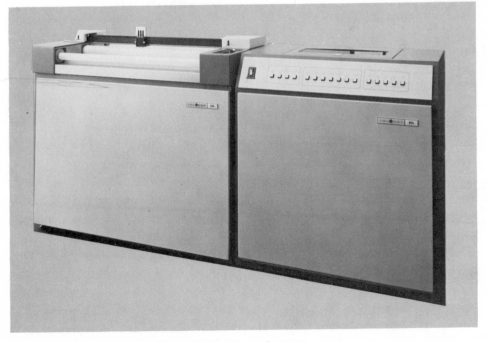

Figure 1-12 Drum plotter.

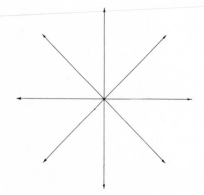

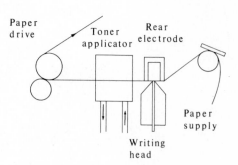

Figure 1-13 Directions
for incremental plotters.

Figure 1-14 Conceptual
description of electrostatic
dot matrix printer/plotter.

and typical output.

1-7 CLASSIFICATION OF GRAPHICS DEVICES

There are a number of methods of classifying computer graphics devices.
Each method yields some insight into the sometimes confusing array of possible
devices. We will discuss several different methods.

First let's consider the difference between a passive and an active graphics
device. A passive graphics device simply draws pictures under computer control;
i.e., it allows the computer to communicate graphically with the user. Examples
are a teletype, a high-speed line printer, and an electrostatic dot matrix
printer, pen and ink plotters, and storage tube cathode ray tube (CRT) and refresh CRT devices. Examples of some of these devices and the typical pictures
that they might generate are shown in Fig. 1-10, 1-12, and 1-15 through 1-20.
The reader might wonder about considering the teletype and the high-speed line
printer as graphics devices. However, they have been used to draw simple
graphs or plots for a number of years.

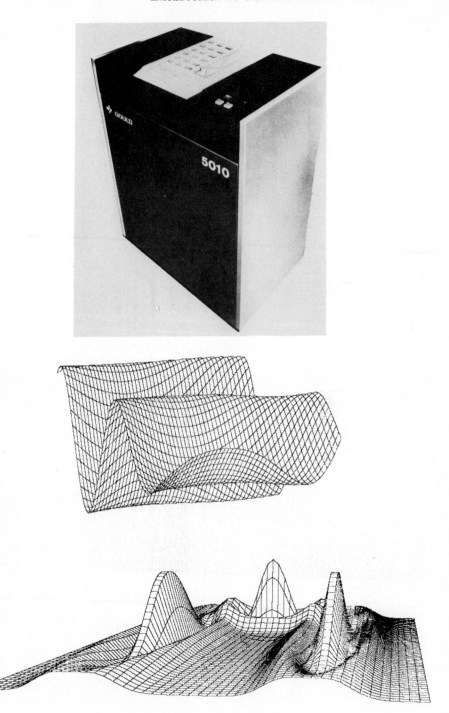

Figure 1-15   Electrostatic dot matrix
printer/plotter and typical output.

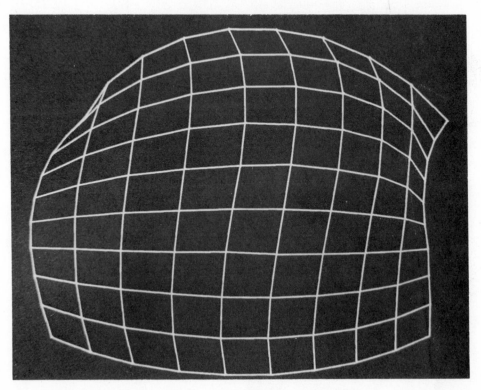

Figure 1-16   Storage tube CRT graphics device
and typical output.

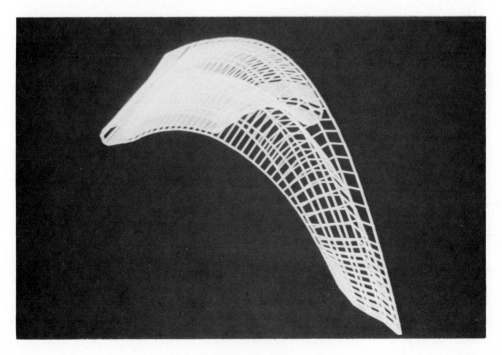

Figure 1-17   Refresh CRT graphics device
and typical output.

Figure 1-18   Typical output
from a digital incremental plotter.

An active graphics device allows the user to communicate with the computer graphically. Generally this implies that the user is supplying coordinate data information in some indirect manner, i.e., by means other than typing the appro-priate numbers. Since a picture, curve, or surface can be considered a matrix of coordinate data, the user is supplying true pictorial information. Usually an active graphics device has the ability to reposition the cursor and read its new position. Typical active graphics devices include simple cursor but-tons or thumb wheels (Fig. 1-16), digitizer or analog tablets (Fig. 1-9), light pens (Fig. 1-4), joy sticks (Fig. 1-6), trackball or mouse. Although digitizers may sometimes be used alone, these devices usually require some type of passive graphics device for support. This support graphics device is frequently based on a CRT.

Another method of classifying graphics devices is by whether they are point-plotting or line- (vector-) drawing. The fundamental difference here is whether a hardware vector generator is available. A hardware vector generator allows the drawing of lines with a minimum amount of data. This, of course, does not mean that a point-plotting device cannot be made to draw vectors by using software. A vector can, of course, be constructed as a series of points.

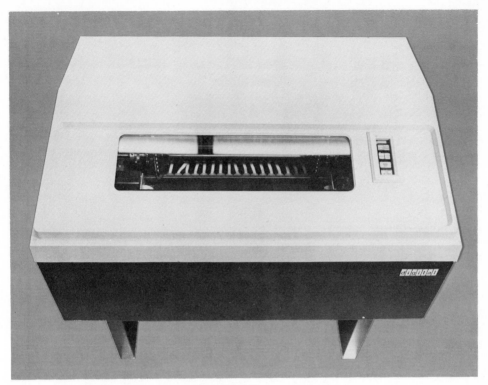

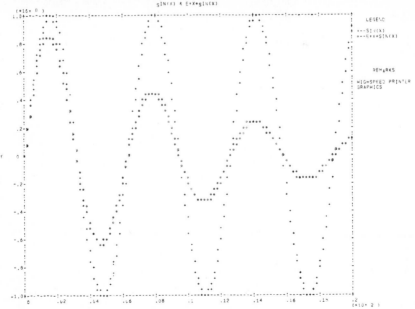

Figure 1-19   High-speed printer
and typical graphic output.

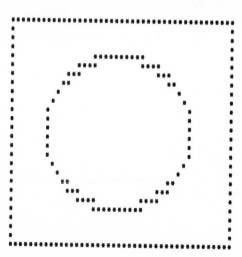

Figure 1-20   Teletype
and typical graphic output.

If points are plotted close enough together, they will appear to the eye to be
a solid line. All the storage tube CRT and most refresh CRT graphics devices
are line-drawing devices. All the pen plotters are line-drawing devices. Some
refresh CRT graphics devices, particularly raster scan (television-like) devices,
can be considered as point-plotting graphics devices. Teletypes, high-speed
line printers, and electrostatic dot matrix printers are classed as point-
plotting devices. The utility of a device can frequently be considered in terms
of its resolution; e.g., a teletype has a resolution of $\pm$ 1/20 inch horizontally
and $\pm$ 1/12 inch vertically, whereas an electrostatic dot matrix device may have
a resolution of $\pm$ 0.01 inch.

Still another method of classifying graphics devices requires determining
whether a device can accept true three-dimensional data or whether three-
dimensional data must first be converted to two-dimensional data by the application of some projective transformation and presented as two-dimensional data.
In essence this method requires determining whether a graphics device has two
or three registers to hold coordinate data. In the case of a three-dimensional
device the third or z coordinate is usually used to control the intensity of
a CRT beam. This feature is called intensity modulation or gray scaling. It
is used to give the illusion of depth to a picture.

Each of the classification methods will frequently place a particular
graphics device in a different category. However, each method does yield some
insight into the characteristics of the various graphics devices.

Appendices A and C contain the architecture of a software scheme based on
the concepts presented in this and in subsequent chapters. Of course, the
description of position vectors, lines, curves, and surfaces and the transformation of these geometric entities can be accomplished mathematically independent of any display technique or display software. The remainder of this book
is concerned with these mathematical, device-independent techniques.

References

1-1 Newman, W. M., and Sproull, R., Principles of Interactive Computer
     Graphics, McGraw-Hill Book Company, New York, 1973.
1-2 Bezier, P. E., "Example of an Existing Systems in the Motor Industry:
     The Unisurf System" Proc. Roy. Soc. (London), Vol A321, pp. 207-218,
     1971.

CHAPTER 2

POINTS AND LINES

2-1 Introduction

We begin our study of the fundamentals of the mathematics underlying computer graphics by considering the representation and transformation of points and lines. Points and the lines which join them are used to represent objects or to display information graphically on devices, such as discussed in Chapter 1. The ability to transform these points and lines is basic to computer graphics. When visualizing an object it may be desirable to scale, rotate, translate, distort, or develop a perspective view of the object. All of these transformations can be accomplished using the mathematical techniques discussed in this and the next chapter.

2-2 Representation Of Points

A point can be represented in two dimensions by its coordinates. These two values can be specified as the elements of a one-row, two-column matrix [x y]. In three dimensions a one by three matrix [x y z] is used. Alternately, a point can be represented by a two-row, one-column matrix $\begin{bmatrix} x \\ y \end{bmatrix}$ in two dimensions or by $\begin{bmatrix} x \\ y \\ z \end{bmatrix}$ in three dimensions. Row matrices like [x,y] or column matrices like $\begin{bmatrix} x \\ y \end{bmatrix}$ are frequently called vectors. A series of points, each of which is a position vector relative to a local coordinate system, may be stored in a computer as a matrix of numbers. The position of these points can be controlled by manipulating the matrix which defines the points. Lines can be drawn between the points using appropriate computer hardware or software to generate lines, curves, or pictures as output.

2-3 TRANSFORMATIONS AND MATRICES

The elements that make up a matrix can represent various quantities, such as a number store, a network, or the coefficients of a set of equations. The rules of matrix algebra define allowable operations on these matrices (cf Appendix B). Many physical problems lead to a matrix formulation. Here the problem may be formulated as: Given the matrices A and B find the solution matrix, i.e., AT = B. In this case the solution is $T = A^{-1}B$, where A^{-1} is the inverse of the square matrix A (see Ref. 2-1).

An alternate use of a matrix is to treat the T-matrix itself as an operator. Here matrix multiplication is used to perform a geometrical transformation on a set of points represented by the position vectors contained in matrix A. The matrices A and T are assumed known and it is required to determine the elements of the matrix B. This interpretation of matrix multiplication as a geometrical operator is the foundation of the mathematical transformations useful in computer graphics.

2-4 TRANSFORMATION OF POINTS

Consider the results of the matrix multiplication of a matrix [x y] containing the coordinates of a point P and a general 2 x 2 transformation matrix:

$$[x \ y] \begin{bmatrix} a & b \\ c & d \end{bmatrix} = [(ax + cy) \ (bx + dy)] = [x^* \ y^*] \tag{2-1}$$

This mathematical notation means that the initial coordinates x and y are transformed to x^* and y^*, where $x^* = (ax + cy)$ and $y^* = (bx + dy)$. We are interested in investigating the implications of considering x^* and y^* as the transformed coordinates. We begin by investigating several special cases.

Consider the case where a = d = 1 and c = b = 0. The transformation matrix then reduces to the identity matrix and

$$[x \ y] \begin{bmatrix} 1 & 0 \\ 0 & 1 \end{bmatrix} = [x \ y] = [x^* \ y^*] \tag{2-2}$$

and no change in the coordinates of the point P occurs.

Next consider d = 1, b = c = 0, i.e.,

$$[x \quad y] \begin{bmatrix} a & 0 \\ 0 & 1 \end{bmatrix} = [ax \quad y] = [x^* \quad y^*] \qquad (2\text{-}3)$$

This produces a scale change since $x^* = ax$. This transformation is shown in Fig. 2-1a. Hence this matrix multiplication has the effect of stretching the original coordinate in the x-direction.

Now consider $b = c = 0$, i.e.,

$$[x \quad y] \begin{bmatrix} a & 0 \\ 0 & d \end{bmatrix} = [ax \quad dy] = [x^* \quad y^*] \qquad (2\text{-}4)$$

This yields a stretching in both the x- and y-coordinates, as shown in Fig. 2-1b. If $a \neq d$, then the stretchings are not equal. If $a = d > 1$, then a pure enlargement or scaling of the coordinates of P occurs. If $0 < a = d < 1$, then a compression of the coordinates of P will occur.

If a and/or d are negative, then reflections occur. To see this, consider $b = c = 0$, $d = 1$ and $a = -1$. Then

$$[x \quad y] \begin{bmatrix} -1 & 0 \\ 0 & 1 \end{bmatrix} = [-x \quad y] = [x^* \quad y^*] \qquad (2\text{-}5)$$

and a reflection about the y-axis has occurred. The effect of this transformation is shown in Fig. 2-1c. If $b = c = 0$, $a = 1$, and $d = -1$, then a reflection about the x-axis occurs. If $b = c = 0$, $a = d < 0$, then a reflection about the origin will occur. This is shown in Fig. 2-1d, with $a = -1$, $d = -1$. Note that reflection, stretching, and scaling of the coordinates involve only the diagonal terms of the transformation matrix.

Now consider the case where $a = d = 1$, and $c = 0$. Thus

$$[x \quad y] \begin{bmatrix} 1 & b \\ 0 & 1 \end{bmatrix} = [x \quad (bx + y)] = [x^* \quad y^*] \qquad (2\text{-}6)$$

and the x-coordinate of the point P is unchanged, while y^* depends linearly on the original coordinates. This effect is called shear and is shown in Fig. 2-1e. Similarly when $a = d = 1$, $b = 0$, the transformation produces shear proportional to the y-coordinate, as shown in Fig. 2-1f. Thus, we see that the off-diagonal terms produce a shearing effect on the coordinates of the point P.

Before completing our discussion of the transformation of points, consider the effect of the general 2 x 2 transformation given by Eq. (2-1) when applied to the origin, i.e.,

$$[x \quad y] \begin{bmatrix} a & b \\ c & d \end{bmatrix} = [(ax + cy) \quad (bx + dy)] = (x^* \quad y^*) \qquad (2\text{-}1)$$

or for the origin,

$$[0 \quad 0] \begin{bmatrix} a & b \\ c & d \end{bmatrix} = [0 \quad 0] = [x^* \quad y^*]$$

Here we see that the origin is invariant under a general 2 x 2 transformation. This is a limitation which will be overcome by the use of homogeneous coordinates.

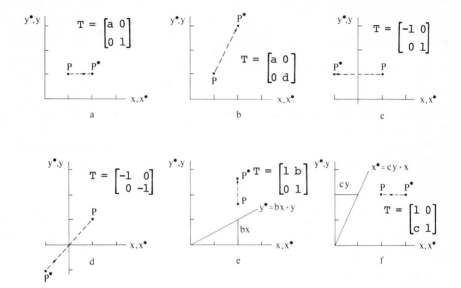

Figure 2-1 Transformation of points.

2-5 TRANSFORMATION OF STRAIGHT LINES

A straight line can be defined by two position vectors which specify the coordinates of its end points. The position and orientation of the line joining these two points can be changed by operating on these two position vectors. The actual operation of drawing a line between two points will depend on the output device used. Here we consider only the mathematical operations on the end position vectors.

A straight line between two points A and B in a two-dimensional plane is drawn in Fig. 2-2. The position vectors of points A and B are [0 1] and [2 3] respectively. Now consider the transformation matrix

$$T = \begin{bmatrix} 1 & 2 \\ 3 & 1 \end{bmatrix} \tag{2-7}$$

which we recognize from our previous discussion as producing a shearing effect. Using matrix multiplication on the position vectors for A and B produces the new transformed vectors A* and B* given by

$$AT = \begin{bmatrix} 0 & 1 \end{bmatrix} \begin{bmatrix} 1 & 2 \\ 3 & 1 \end{bmatrix} = \begin{bmatrix} 3 & 1 \end{bmatrix} = A^* \tag{2-8}$$

and

$$BT = [2 \quad 3] \begin{bmatrix} 1 & 2 \\ 3 & 1 \end{bmatrix} = [11 \quad 7] = B* \tag{2-9}$$

Thus, the resulting elements in A* are x* = 3 and y* = 1. Similarly, B* is a new point specified by x* = 11 and y* = 7. More compactly the line AB may be represented by the 2 x 2 matrix $L = \begin{bmatrix} 0 & 1 \\ 2 & 3 \end{bmatrix}$. Matrix multiplication then yields

$$LT = \begin{bmatrix} 0 & 1 \\ 2 & 3 \end{bmatrix} \begin{bmatrix} 1 & 2 \\ 3 & 1 \end{bmatrix} = \begin{bmatrix} 3 & 1 \\ 11 & 7 \end{bmatrix} = L* \tag{2-10}$$

where the components of L* represent the transformed position vectors A* and B*. The transformation of A to A* and B to B* is shown in Fig. 2-2. The initial axes are x,y and the transformed axes are x*, y*. This shearing effect has increased the length of the line and changed its orientation.

2-6 MIDPOINT TRANSFORMATION

Figure 2-2 shows that the 2 x 2 transformation matrix transforms the straight line y = x + 1, between points A and B, into another straight line y = (3/4)x - 5/4, between A* and B*. In fact a 2 x 2 matrix transforms any straight line into a second straight line. Points on the second line have a one to one correspondence with points on the first line. We have already shown this to be true for the end points of the line. To further confirm this we consider the transformation of the midpoint of the straight line between A and B. Letting $A = [x_1 \quad y_1]$, $B = [x_2 \quad y_2]$, and $T = \begin{bmatrix} a & b \\ c & d \end{bmatrix}$ and transforming both points simultaneously gives

$$\begin{bmatrix} x_1 & y_1 \\ x_2 & y_2 \end{bmatrix} \begin{bmatrix} a & b \\ c & d \end{bmatrix} = \begin{bmatrix} ax_1 + cy_1 & bx_1 + dy_1 \\ ax_2 + cy_2 & bx_2 + dy_2 \end{bmatrix} = \begin{bmatrix} A* \\ B* \end{bmatrix} \tag{2-11}$$

Hence, the transformed end points are

$$A* = [ax_1 + cy_1 \quad bx_1 + dy_1] = [x_1* \quad y_1*]$$
$$B* = [ax_2 + cy_2 \quad bx_2 + dy_2] = [x_2* \quad y_2*]$$

The midpoint of the initial line AB is

$$M_1 = \begin{bmatrix} \dfrac{x_1 + x_2}{2} & \dfrac{y_1 + y_2}{2} \end{bmatrix} \tag{2-12}$$

The transformation of this midpoint is

$$\begin{bmatrix} \dfrac{x_1 + x_2}{2} & \dfrac{y_1 + y_2}{2} \end{bmatrix} \begin{bmatrix} a & b \\ c & d \end{bmatrix} = \begin{bmatrix} \dfrac{ax_1 + ax_2 + cy_1 + cy_2}{2} \\[2ex] \dfrac{bx_1 + bx_2 + dy_1 + dy_2}{2} \end{bmatrix} \tag{2-13}$$

This transformation places the midpoint of AB on the midpoint of A*B* since the midpoint of A*B* is given by

$$x^* = \frac{ax_1 + cy_1 + ax_2 + cy_2}{2} = \frac{ax_1 + ax_2 + cy_1 + cy_2}{2} \qquad (2\text{-}14)$$

$$y^* = \frac{bx_1 + dy_1 + bx_2 + dy_2}{2} = \frac{bx_1 + bx_2 + dy_1 + dy_2}{2}$$

For the special case shown in Fig. 2-2, the midpoint of line AB is $M_1 =$ [1 2]. This transforms to

$$[1 \quad 2] \begin{bmatrix} 1 & 2 \\ 3 & 1 \end{bmatrix} = [7 \quad 4] \qquad (2\text{-}15)$$

which gives the midpoint on line A*B*. This process can be repeated for any subset of the initial line, and it is clear that all points on the initial line transform to points on the second line. Thus the transformation provides a one to one correspondence between points on the original line and points on the transformed line. For computer graphics applications, this means that any straight line can be transformed to any new position by simply transforming its end points and then redrawing the line between the transformed end points.

2-7 PARALLEL LINES

When a 2 x 2 matrix is used to transform a pair of parallel lines, the result is a second pair of parallel lines. To see this, consider a line between $A = [x_1 \ y_1]$ and $B = [x_2 \ y_2]$ and a line parallel to AB between E and F. To show that these lines and any transformation of them are parallel, we examine the slopes of AB, EF, A*B*, and E*F*. The slope of both AB and EF is

$$m_1 = \frac{y_2 - y_1}{x_2 - x_1} \qquad (2\text{-}16)$$

Transforming AB using a general 2 x 2 transformation yields the end points of A*B*:

$$\begin{bmatrix} x_1 & y_1 \\ x_2 & y_2 \end{bmatrix} \begin{bmatrix} a & b \\ c & d \end{bmatrix} = \begin{bmatrix} ax_1 + cy_1 & bx_1 + dy_1 \\ ax_2 + cy_2 & bx_2 + dy_2 \end{bmatrix} = \begin{bmatrix} x_1^* & y_1^* \\ x_2^* & y_2^* \end{bmatrix} = \begin{bmatrix} A^* \\ B^* \end{bmatrix} \qquad (2\text{-}17)$$

The slope of A*B* is then

$$m_2 = \frac{(bx_2 + dy_2) - (bx_1 + dy_1)}{(ax_2 + cy_2) - (ax_1 + cy_1)} = \frac{b(x_2 - x_1) + d(y_2 - y_1)}{a(x_2 - x_1) + c(y_2 - y_1)}$$

or

$$m_2 = \frac{b + d\left[\dfrac{y_2 - y_1}{x_2 - x_1}\right]}{a + c\left[\dfrac{y_2 - y_1}{x_2 - x_1}\right]} = \frac{b + dm_1}{a + cm_1} \qquad (2\text{-}18)$$

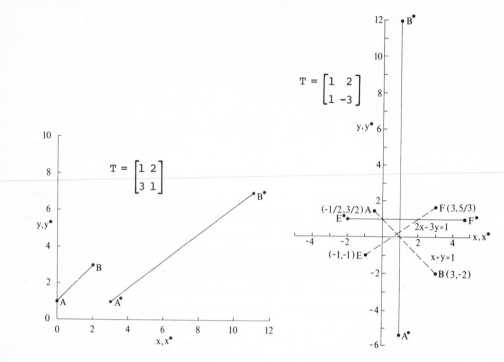

Figure 2-2 Transformation
of straight lines.

Figure 2-3 Transformation
of intersecting lines.

Since the slope m_2 is independent of x_1, x_2, y_1, and y_2, and since m_1, a, b, c, and d are the same for EF and AB, it follows that m_2 for both E*F* and A*B* are equal. Thus, parallel lines remain parallel after transformation. This means that parallelograms transform into other parallelograms as a result of operation by a 2 x 2 transformation matrix. These simple results begin to show the power of using matrix multiplication to produce graphical effects.

2-8 INTERSECTING LINES

Two dashed intersecting lines AB and EF are shown in Fig. 2-3. The point of intersection is at $x = 4/5$ and $y = 1/5$. We now multiply the matrices containing the end points of the two lines AB and EF by the transformation matrix $\begin{bmatrix} 1 & 2 \\ 1 & -3 \end{bmatrix}$. Thus,

$$\begin{bmatrix} -\dfrac{1}{2} & \dfrac{3}{2} \\ 3 & -2 \end{bmatrix} \begin{bmatrix} 1 & 2 \\ 1 & -3 \end{bmatrix} = \begin{bmatrix} 1 & -\dfrac{11}{2} \\ 1 & 12 \end{bmatrix}$$

$$\begin{bmatrix} -1 & -1 \\ 3 & \frac{5}{3} \end{bmatrix} \begin{bmatrix} 1 & 2 \\ 1 & -3 \end{bmatrix} = \begin{bmatrix} -2 & 1 \\ \frac{14}{3} & 1 \end{bmatrix}$$

This gives the solid lines A*B* and E*F* shown in Fig. 2-3. The transformed point of intersection is

$$[\tfrac{4}{5} \ \tfrac{1}{5}] \begin{bmatrix} 1 & 2 \\ 1 & -3 \end{bmatrix} = [1 \ \ 1]$$

That is, the point of intersection of the initial pair of lines transforms to the point of intersection of the transformed pair of lines. Close examination of the above transformation of intersecting straight lines will show that it has involved a rotation, a reflection, and a scaling of the original pair. However, the total effect of a 2 x 2 matrix transformation is easier to see, considering the effects of rotation, reflection, and scaling separately. In order to illustrate these individual effects, we shall consider a simple plane figure - namely, a triangle.

2-9 ROTATION

Consider the plane triangle ABC shown in Fig. 2-4a. This triangle is rotated through 90° about the origin in a counterclockwise sense by operating on each vertex with the transformation $\begin{bmatrix} 0 & 1 \\ -1 & 0 \end{bmatrix}$. If we use a 3 x 2 matrix containing the x- and y-coordinates of the vertices, then

$$\begin{bmatrix} 3 & -1 \\ 4 & 1 \\ 2 & 1 \end{bmatrix} \begin{bmatrix} 0 & 1 \\ -1 & 0 \end{bmatrix} = \begin{bmatrix} 1 & 3 \\ -1 & 4 \\ -1 & 2 \end{bmatrix} \tag{2-19}$$

This produces the triangle A*B*C*. A 180° rotation about the origin is obtained by using $\begin{bmatrix} -1 & 0 \\ 0 & -1 \end{bmatrix}$ and a 270° rotation about the origin by using $\begin{bmatrix} 0 & -1 \\ 1 & 0 \end{bmatrix}$.
Note that neither scaling nor reflection has occurred in these examples.

2-10 REFLECTION

Whereas a pure two-dimensional rotation in the xy-plane occurs about an axis normal to the xy-plane, a reflection is a 180° rotation about an axis in the xy-plane. Two reflections of the triangle DEF are shown in Fig. 2-4b. A reflection about the line y = x occurs by using $\begin{bmatrix} 0 & 1 \\ 1 & 0 \end{bmatrix}$.

The transformed, new vertices are given by

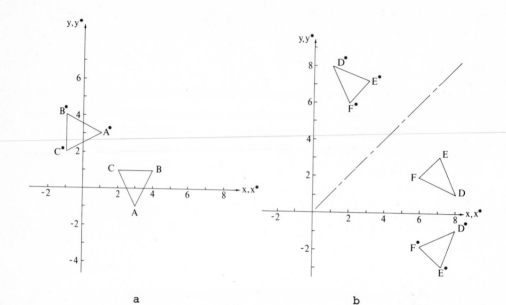

Figure 2-4 Rotation and reflection.

$$\begin{bmatrix} 8 & 1 \\ 7 & 3 \\ 6 & 2 \end{bmatrix} \begin{bmatrix} 0 & 1 \\ 1 & 0 \end{bmatrix} = \begin{bmatrix} 1 & 8 \\ 3 & 7 \\ 2 & 6 \end{bmatrix} \qquad\qquad (2\text{-}20)$$

A reflection about y = 0 is obtained from $\begin{bmatrix} 1 & 0 \\ 0 & -1 \end{bmatrix}$. In this case the new vertices are given by

$$\begin{bmatrix} 8 & 1 \\ 7 & 3 \\ 6 & 2 \end{bmatrix} \begin{bmatrix} 1 & 0 \\ 0 & -1 \end{bmatrix} = \begin{bmatrix} 8 & -1 \\ 7 & -3 \\ 6 & -2 \end{bmatrix}$$

2-11 SCALING

Recalling our discussion of the transformation of points, we can see that scaling is controlled by the magnitude of the two terms on the primary diagonal of the matrix. If the matrix $\begin{bmatrix} 2 & 0 \\ 0 & 2 \end{bmatrix}$ is used as an operator on the vertices of a triangle, a "2-times" enlargement occurs about the origin. If the magnitudes are unequal, a distortion occurs. These effects are shown in Fig. 2-5. Triangle ABC is transformed by $\begin{bmatrix} 2 & 0 \\ 0 & 2 \end{bmatrix}$; thus a scaling occurs, and triangle

DEF is transformed by $\begin{bmatrix} 3 & 0 \\ 0 & 2 \end{bmatrix}$ which yields

a distortion due to the unequal scale factors.

It is now clear how plane surfaces, defined by vertices joined by straight lines, can be manipulated in a variety of ways. By performing a matrix operation on the position vectors which define the vertices, the shape and position of the surface can be controlled. However, a desired orientation may require more than one transformation. Since matrix multiplication is noncommutative, the order of the transformations is important when performing combined operations.

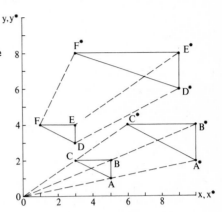

Figure 2-5 Uniform and nonuniform scaling or distortion.

2-12 COMBINED OPERATIONS

In order to illustrate the effect of noncommutative matrix multiplication, consider the operations of rotation and reflection on the vertices of a triangle [x y]. If a 90° rotation is followed by reflection about x = 0, these two consecutive transformations give

$$[x \quad y] \begin{bmatrix} 0 & 1 \\ -1 & 0 \end{bmatrix} = [-y \quad x]$$

and then

$$[-y \quad x] \begin{bmatrix} -1 & 0 \\ 0 & 1 \end{bmatrix} = [y \quad x]$$

On the other hand, if reflection is followed by rotation, a different result given by

$$[x \quad y] \begin{bmatrix} -1 & 0 \\ 0 & 1 \end{bmatrix} = [-x \quad y]$$

and

$$[-x \quad y] \begin{bmatrix} 0 & 1 \\ -1 & 0 \end{bmatrix} = [-y \quad -x]$$

is obtained.

So far we have concentrated on the behavior of points and lines to determine the effect of simple matrix transformations. However, the matrix is correctly considered to operate on *every* point in the plane. As has been shown,

the only point that remains invariant in a 2 x 2 matrix transformation is the
origin. All other points within the plane of the coordinate system are transformed. This transformation may be interpreted as a stretching of the initial
plane and coordinate system into a new shape. More formally, we say that the
transformation causes a mapping from one plane into a second plane. Examples
of this mapping are shown in the next section.

2-13 TRANSFORMATION OF A UNIT SQUARE

Consider a square-grid network consisting of unit squares in the xy-plane.
The four position vectors of a unit square with one corner at the origin of the
coordinate system are

$$\begin{bmatrix} 0 & 0 \\ 1 & 0 \\ 1 & 1 \\ 0 & 1 \end{bmatrix} \begin{matrix} \text{origin of the coordinates - A} \\ \text{unit point on the x-axis - B} \\ \text{outer corner - C} \\ \text{unit point on the y-axis - D} \end{matrix}$$

This unit square is shown in Fig. 2-6a. Application of a general 2 x 2 matrix
transformation $\begin{bmatrix} a & b \\ c & d \end{bmatrix}$ to the unit square yields

$$\begin{matrix} A \rightarrow \\ B \rightarrow \\ C \rightarrow \\ D \rightarrow \end{matrix} \begin{bmatrix} 0 & 0 \\ 1 & 0 \\ 1 & 1 \\ 0 & 1 \end{bmatrix} \begin{bmatrix} a & b \\ c & d \end{bmatrix} = \begin{bmatrix} 0 & 0 \\ a & b \\ a+c & b+d \\ c & d \end{bmatrix} \begin{matrix} \leftarrow A^* \\ \leftarrow B^* \\ \leftarrow C^* \\ \leftarrow D^* \end{matrix} \qquad (2\text{-}21)$$

The results of this transformation are shown in Fig. 2-6b. First notice from
Eq. (2-21) that the origin is not affected by the transformation, i.e., A = A*
= [0 0]. Further, notice that the coordinates of B* are equal to the first
row in the general transformation matrix, and the coordinates of D* are equal
to the second row in the general transformation matrix. Thus, once the coordinates of B* and D* (the transformed unit points [1 0] and [0 1] respectively)
are known, the general transformation matrix is determined. Since the sides
of the unit square are originally parallel and since we have previously shown
that parallel lines transform into parallel lines, the transformed figure is
a parallelogram.

The effect of the terms, a, b, c, and d in the 2 x 2 matrix can be identi-
fied separately. The terms b and c cause a shearing (cf Sec. 2-4) of the initial
square in the y- and x-directions respectively, as can be seen in Fig. 2-6.
The terms a and d act as scale factors as noted earlier. Thus, the general
2 x 2 matrix produces a combination of shearing and scaling.

It is also possible to easily determine the area of the parallelogram
A*B*C*D* shown in Fig. 2-6. The area within the parallelogram can be calculated

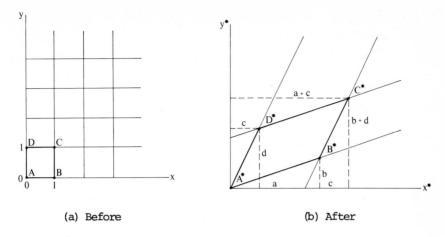

(a) Before   (b) After

Figure 2-6   General transformation of unit square.

as follows:
$$A_p = (a + c)(b + d) - \frac{1}{2}(ab) - \frac{1}{2}(cd) - \frac{c}{2}(b + b + d) - \frac{b}{2}(c + a + c)$$

which yields
$$A_p = ad - bc = \det \begin{bmatrix} a & b \\ c & d \end{bmatrix} \tag{2-22}$$

It can be shown that the area of any transformed parallelogram A_p is a function of the transformation matrix determinant and is related to the area of the initial square A_s by the simple relationship

$$A_p = A_s(ad - bc) \tag{2-23}$$

In fact, since the area of a general figure is the sum of unit squares, the area of any transformed figure A_t is related to the area of the initial figure A_i by

$$A_t = A_i(ad - bc) \tag{2-24}$$

This is a useful technique for determining the areas of arbitrary shapes.

2-14 ARBITRARY 2 x 2 ROTATION MATRIX

The general 2 x 2 matrix which results in pure rotation of a figure about

the origin can be obtained by considering the rotation of the unit square about
the origin. This is shown in Fig. 2-7
for positive rotation in the counterclockwise direction. Figure 2-7 shows that
point B, [1 0], is transformed to the
point B*, with x* = (1)cosθ and y* =
(1)sinθ and that point D, [0 1], is
transformed to D*, with x* = -(1)sinθ
and y* = (1)cosθ. Recalling our previous
observation that for an arbitrary 2 x 2
transformation matrix the coordinates of
B* must equal the first row in the transformation matrix and the coordinates of
D* form the second row, the general 2 x 2
rotation matrix is

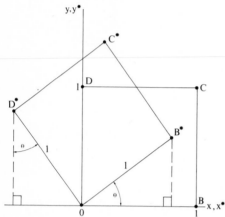

$$\begin{bmatrix} \cos\theta & \sin\theta \\ -\sin\theta & \cos\theta \end{bmatrix} \qquad (2\text{-}25)$$

For the special case of 90°, this reduces
to the result used earlier in Sec. 2-9,
i.e.,

$$\begin{bmatrix} 0 & 1 \\ -1 & 0 \end{bmatrix}$$

Figure 2-7 Rotation
of unit square.

In effect Eq. (2-25) is a combination of scaling and shearing which leaves the
final dimensions unchanged. Therefore, this transformation matrix produces a
pure rotation through an arbitrary angle θ.

2-15 Two-Dimensional Translations And Homogeneous Coordinates.

Up until the present time we have not discussed the translation of points
and lines or the figures or shapes resulting from combinations of points and
lines. Fundamentally this is because within the frame work of a general 2 x 2
matrix it is not possible to introduce the constants of translation. Following
Forrest (Ref. 2-2) we note that this difficulty can be overcome by introducing
a third component to the position vectors [x y] and [x* y*] making them
[x y 1] and [x* y* 1]. The transformation matrix then becomes a 3 x 2
matrix, say,

$$\begin{bmatrix} 1 & 0 \\ 0 & 1 \\ m & n \end{bmatrix}$$

This is necessary since the number of columns in the point matrix must equal the number of rows in the transformation matrix for the operation of matrix multiplication to be defined. Thus,

$$[x \quad y \quad 1] \begin{bmatrix} 1 & 0 \\ 0 & 1 \\ m & n \end{bmatrix} = [x + m \quad y + n] = [x^* \quad y^*] \qquad (2\text{-}26)$$

where we note that the constants m, n cause a translation of x* and y* relative to x and y. However, a 3 x 2 matrix is not square and thus does not have an inverse (cf Appendix B). This difficulty can be overcome by utilizing a full 3 x 3 matrix, say,

$$\begin{bmatrix} 1 & 0 & 0 \\ 0 & 1 & 0 \\ m & n & 1 \end{bmatrix}$$

as the transformation matrix. Notice that the third component of the position vectors is not affected by the addition of the third column to the transformation matrix. Using this matrix in Eq. (2-26) gives [x* y* 1] for the transformed vector.

The addition of the third element to the position vector and the third column to the transformation matrix allows us to perform a translation of the position vector. Alternately we may consider the third element as an additional coordinate of the position vector. For notational purposes we assume that when the position vector [x y 1] is operated on by a general 3 x 3 matrix it becomes the position vector [X Y H]. Previously the transformation was performed such that [X Y H] = [x* y* 1]. If we consider the transformation to be taking place in three-dimensional space, this confines our transformations to the plane H = 1. If, however, we assume that the third column of the general 3 x 3 transformation matrix T is

$$\begin{bmatrix} p \\ q \\ s \end{bmatrix} \quad \text{rather than} \quad \begin{bmatrix} 0 \\ 0 \\ 1 \end{bmatrix}$$

matrix multiplication yields [x y 1]T = [X Y H], where H ≠ 1.

The general plane in which the transformed position vector now lies is in three-dimensional space. However, at the present time we are not interested in what happens in three-dimensional space. Hence we obtain x* and y* by projecting from the general plane back onto the plane H = 1, using a pencil of rays through the origin. This effect is shown in Fig. 2-8. Using similar triangles we see that H/X = 1/x* and H/Y = 1/y*. With three components it follows that:

$$[x^* \quad y^* \quad 1] = [\tfrac{X}{H} \quad \tfrac{Y}{H} \quad 1] \qquad (2\text{-}27)$$

The three-dimensional vector representation of a two-dimensional position

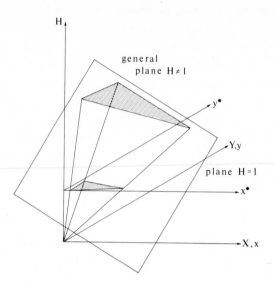

Figure 2-8 Geometric representation of
homogeneous coordinates.

vector, or in general the representation of an n-component vector by an n + 1
component vector, is called *homogeneous coordinate* representation. In homogeneous coordinate representation the transformation of n-dimensional vectors is
performed in (n + 1) dimensional space, and the transformed n-dimensional results
are obtained by projection back into the particular n-dimensional space of interest. Thus, in two dimensions the position vector [x y] is represented by
the three-component vector [hx hy h]. The extra component in the vector acts
like an additional coordinate. The ordinary or "physical" coordinates are related to the homogeneous coordinates by

$$x = \frac{hx}{h} \quad \text{and} \quad y = \frac{hy}{h} \tag{2-28}$$

There is no unique homogeneous coordinate representation of a point in
two-dimensional space. For example, the homogeneous coordinates [12 8 4],
[6 4 2], and [3 2 1] all represent the ordinary point [3 2]. For ease
of calculation we choose [x y 1] to represent a nontransformed point in two
dimensional homogeneous coordinates. Then the transformation*

$$[x^* \quad y^*] = [x \quad y] \begin{bmatrix} a & b \\ c & d \end{bmatrix}$$

*Note that here we have put the result of the transformation on the left-hand
side of the equation rather than on the right-hand side as was done previously;
i.e., we write matrix equations as B = AT rather than as AT = B. From hereon
we will adopt this convention for ease in translating results into computer
algorithms.

in regular coordinates is given by

$$[X \ Y \ H] = [x \ y \ 1] \begin{bmatrix} a & b & 0 \\ c & d & 0 \\ 0 & 0 & 1 \end{bmatrix}$$

in homogeneous coordinates. Carrying out the above two transformations shows that $X = x^*$, $Y = y^*$, and $H = 1$. That is, since the additional coordinate H is unity, the transformed homogeneous coordinates are the same as the transformed ordinary coordinates. In general, $H \neq 1$, and the transformed ordinary coordinates are obtained by normalizing the transformed homogeneous coordinates, e.g.,

$$x^* = \frac{X}{H} \quad \text{and} \quad y^* = \frac{Y}{H} \tag{2-29}$$

In a geometrical sense, all transformations of x and y fall within the plane H=1 after normalization of the transformed homogeneous coordinates.

The advantage of introducing homogeneous coordinates occurs in the general 3 x 3 transformation matrix

$$\begin{bmatrix} a & b & p \\ c & d & q \\ m & n & s \end{bmatrix}$$

where space is now available to include other transformations such as translation. The scaling and shearing effects of the matrix terms a, b, c, and d have been shown previously.

To show the effect of the third column in the 3 x 3 transformation matrix, consider the following operation:

$$[X \ Y \ H] = [x \ y \ 1] \begin{bmatrix} 1 & 0 & p \\ 0 & 1 & q \\ 0 & 0 & 1 \end{bmatrix} = [x \ y \ (px + qy + 1)] \tag{2-34}$$

Here $X = x$, $Y = y$, and $H = px + qy + 1$. The coordinate H which defines the plane containing the transformed points expressed in homogeneous coordinates now has the equation of a plane in three-dimensional space. This transformation is shown in Fig. 2-9, where the line AB in the two-dimensional xy-plane is projected to the line CD in the three-dimensional plane $pX + qY - H + 1 = 0$. In Fig. 2-9 the values $p = q = 1$ are used.

Normalizing to obtain the two transformed ordinary coordinates, we write

$$x^* = \frac{X}{H} = \frac{X}{pX + qY + 1}$$

$$y^* = \frac{Y}{H} = \frac{Y}{pX + qY + 1}$$

Letting $p = q = 1.0$ and using points A, [1 3] and B, [4 1] shown in Fig. 2-9 gives

$$x^* = \frac{1}{1 + 3 + 1} = \frac{1}{5} \quad \text{and} \quad y^* = \frac{3}{5}$$

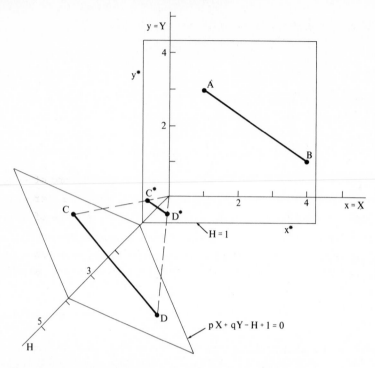

Figure 2-9 Transformation in homogeneous coordinates.

for the transformation and projection of A to C*, and

$$x^* = \frac{4}{1 + 4 + 1} = \frac{2}{3} \quad \text{and} \quad y^* = \frac{1}{6}$$

for the transformation and projection of B to D*. The homogeneous coordinates for C* and D* shown in Fig. 2-9 are [1/5 3/5 1] and [2/3 1/6 1] respectively. The effect of normalizing is to project the three-dimensional line CD back onto a two-dimensional line C*D* in the plane H = 1.0. As shown in Fig. 2-9, the center of projection is the origin.

The general 3 x 3 transformation matrix for two-dimensional homogeneous coordinates can be subdivided into four parts:

$$\begin{bmatrix} a & b & \vdots & p \\ c & d & \vdots & q \\ - & - & - & - \\ m & n & \vdots & s \end{bmatrix}$$

As we have seen a, b, c, and d produce scaling, shearing, and rotation; m and n produce translation; and p and q produce a projection. The fourth part, element s, produces overall scaling. To show this, consider the transformation

$$[X \quad Y \quad H] = [x \quad y \quad 1] \begin{bmatrix} 1 & 0 & 0 \\ 0 & 1 & 0 \\ 0 & 0 & s \end{bmatrix} = [x \quad y \quad s] \qquad (2\text{-}30)$$

Here, $X = x$, $Y = y$, and $H = s$. This gives

$$x* = \frac{x}{s} \quad \text{and} \quad y* = \frac{y}{s}$$

The effective transformation is $[x \; y \; 1] \rightarrow [x/s \; y/s \; 1]$, a uniform scaling of the position vector. If $s < 1$, then an enlargement occurs, and if $s > 1$, a reduction in scale occurs.

2-16 Points At Infinity

The use of homogeneous coordinates gives a convenient and efficient way of mapping a set of points from one coordinate system into a corresponding set in an alternate coordinate system. Usually the infinite range of one coordinate system will map into a finite range within the second coordinate system. Also, lines which are parallel in one system will usually not be parallel in the other. However, geometrical properties such as points of intersection can be evaluated in either coordinate system as shown below.

The two lines given by

$$x + y \;\; = 1$$
$$2x - 3y = 0$$

have a point of intersection at $x = 3/5$, $y = 2/5$. This solution can be obtained in terms of the homogeneous coordinates. By rewriting the equations as $x + y - 1 = 0$; $2x - 3y = 0$ it is possible to represent the two equations by the matrix equation

$$[x \; y \; 1] \begin{bmatrix} 1 & 2 \\ 1 & -3 \\ -1 & 0 \end{bmatrix} = [0 \; 0]$$

However, for a matrix to have an inverse it must be square. The following representation of the same set of equations can be used to meet this requirement;

$$[x \; y \; 1] \begin{bmatrix} 1 & 2 & 0 \\ 1 & -3 & 0 \\ -1 & 0 & 1 \end{bmatrix} = [0 \; 0 \; 1] \tag{2-31}$$

The inverse of this square matrix M is

$$M^{-1} = \begin{bmatrix} \frac{3}{5} & \frac{2}{5} & 0 \\ \frac{1}{5} & -\frac{1}{5} & 0 \\ \frac{3}{5} & \frac{2}{5} & 1 \end{bmatrix}$$

Multiplying both sides of Eq. (2-31) by M^{-1} and noting that $MM^{-1} = I$, the identity matrix yields

$$[x \ \ y \ \ 1] = \tfrac{1}{5} [0 \ \ 0 \ \ 1] \begin{bmatrix} 3 & 2 & 0 \\ 1 & -1 & 0 \\ 3 & 2 & 5 \end{bmatrix} = [\tfrac{3}{5} \ \ \tfrac{2}{5} \ \ 1]$$

Thus, $x = 3/5$ and $y = 2/5$ as required.

Consider two parallel lines defined by

$$x + y = 1$$
$$x + y = 0$$

Proceeding as above leads to the matrix equation

$$[x \ \ y \ \ 1] \begin{bmatrix} 1 & 1 & 0 \\ 1 & 1 & 0 \\ -1 & 0 & 1 \end{bmatrix} = [0 \ \ 0 \ \ 1]$$

However, even though a square matrix exists in this equation, it does not have an inverse, since two rows are identical. Another alternate equation is possible which does have an invertible matrix. This is given by (cf Ref. 2-3)

$$[x \ \ y \ \ 1] \begin{bmatrix} 1 & 1 & 1 \\ 1 & 1 & 0 \\ -1 & 0 & 0 \end{bmatrix} = [0 \ \ 0 \ \ x] \qquad (2\text{-}32)$$

The inverse of the 3 x 3 matrix in Eq. (2-32) is

$$M^{-1} = \begin{bmatrix} 0 & 0 & -1 \\ 0 & 1 & 1 \\ 1 & -1 & 0 \end{bmatrix}$$

Multiplying both sides of Eq. (2-32) by this inverse gives

$$[x \ \ y \ \ 1] = [0 \ \ 0 \ \ x] \begin{bmatrix} 0 & 1 & -1 \\ 0 & 1 & 1 \\ 1 & -1 & 0 \end{bmatrix} = [x \ \ -x \ \ 0] = x[1 \ \ -1 \ \ 0] \qquad (2\text{-}33)$$

The resulting homogeneous coordinates $[1 \ \ -1 \ \ 0]$ must represent the "point of intersection" for the two parallel lines, i.e., a point at infinity. In general, the two-dimensional homogeneous vector $[a \ \ b \ \ 0]$ represents the point at infinity on the line $ay - bx = 0$.

The fact that a vector with the homogeneous component H equal to zero does indeed represent a point at infinity can be illustrated by the limiting process given below. Consider the line $y^* = (3/4)x^*$ and the point $[X \ \ Y] = [4 \ \ 3]$. Recalling that a unique representation of a position vector does not exist in homogeneous coordinates, the point $[4 \ \ 3]$ can be represented in homogeneous coordinates in all the ways shown in Table 2-1. See Ref. 2-3. Note that in Table 2-1 as $H \to 0$, the ratio of y^*/x^* remains at 3/4 as is required by the governing equation. Further note that successive pairs of $[x^* \ \ y^*]$, all of which fall on the line $y^* = (3/4)x^*$, become closer to infinity. Thus, in the limit as $H \to 0$, the point at infinity $[x^* \ \ y^* \ \ 1] = [\infty \ \ \infty \ \ 1]$ is given by $[X \ \ Y \ \ H] =$

Table 2-1

Homogeneous Coordinates for the Point [4   3]

H	x*	y*	X	Y
1	4	3	4	3
1/2	8	6	4	3
1/3	12	9	4	3
1/4	16	12	4	3
.				
.				
.				
1/10	40	30	4	3
.				
.				
.				
1/100	400	300	4	3
.				
.				
.				

[4 3 0] in homogeneous coordinates. It follows that the position vector
[1 0 0] represents a point at infinity on the x*-axis and [0 1 0] represents
a point at infinity on the y*-axis. In this manner homogeneous coordinates
give a convenient representation of points at infinity in addition to the capability for generalized transformations.

2-17 TWO-DIMENSIONAL ROTATION ABOUT AN ARBITRARY AXIS

Previously we have considered rotations as occuring about the origin.
Homogeneous coordinates provide a mechanism for accomplishing rotations about
points other than the origin. In general a rotation about an arbitrary point
can be accomplished by first translating the center of rotation to the origin,
performing the required rotation, and then translating the result back to the
original center of rotation. Thus, rotation of the position vector [x y 1]
about the point m, n through an arbitrary angle can be accomplished by

$$[x \ y \ 1] \begin{bmatrix} 1 & 0 & 0 \\ 0 & 1 & 0 \\ -m & -n & 1 \end{bmatrix} \begin{bmatrix} \cos\theta & \sin\theta & 0 \\ -\sin\theta & \cos\theta & 0 \\ 0 & 0 & 1 \end{bmatrix} \begin{bmatrix} 1 & 0 & 0 \\ 0 & 1 & 0 \\ m & n & 1 \end{bmatrix} = [X \ Y \ H] \qquad (2\text{-}34)$$

By carrying out the two interior matrix products we can write

$$[X \ \ Y \ \ H] = [x \ \ y \ \ 1] \begin{bmatrix} \cos\theta & \sin\theta & 0 \\ -\sin\theta & \cos\theta & 0 \\ -m(\cos\theta - 1) + n(\sin\theta) & -m(\sin\theta) - n(\cos\theta - 1) & 1 \end{bmatrix} \quad (2\text{-}35)$$

For example, suppose the center of an object is at [4 3] and it is desired to rotate the object 90° counterclockwise about its own central axis. Operation by the matrix

$$\begin{bmatrix} 0 & 1 & 0 \\ -1 & 0 & 0 \\ 0 & 0 & 1 \end{bmatrix}$$

causes a rotation about the origin, not the object axis. As shown above, the necessary procedure is to first translate the object so that the desired center of rotation is at the origin by using the translation matrix

$$\begin{bmatrix} 1 & 0 & 0 \\ 0 & 1 & 0 \\ -4 & -3 & 1 \end{bmatrix}$$

then apply the rotation matrix, and finally translate the results of the rotation back to the original center by means of the reverse translation matrix. The entire operation

$$[X \ \ Y \ \ H] = [x \ \ y \ \ 1] \begin{bmatrix} 1 & 0 & 0 \\ 0 & 1 & 0 \\ -4 & -3 & 1 \end{bmatrix} \begin{bmatrix} 0 & 1 & 0 \\ -1 & 0 & 0 \\ 0 & 0 & 1 \end{bmatrix} \begin{bmatrix} 1 & 0 & 0 \\ 0 & 1 & 0 \\ 4 & 3 & 1 \end{bmatrix} \quad (2\text{-}36)$$

can be combined into one matrix operation by concatenating the transformation matrices, i.e.,

$$[X \ \ Y \ \ H] = [x \ \ y \ \ 1] \begin{bmatrix} 0 & 1 & 0 \\ -1 & 0 & 0 \\ 7 & -1 & 1 \end{bmatrix} \quad (2\text{-}37)$$

Then, $x^* = X/H$ and $y^* = Y/H$.

Two-dimensional rotations about each axis of an orthogonal axis system are represented in Fig. 2-10. A computer algorithm for performing a two-dimensional rotation about an arbitrary point is given in Appendix C, along with other algorithms for two-dimensional translation, scaling, and reflection.

REFERENCES

2-1 Fox, L. An Introduction to Numerical Linear Algebra, Oxford University Press, London, 1964.

2-2 Forrest, A. R., "Co-ordinates, Transformations, and Visualization Techniques," CAD Group Document No. 23, Cambridge University, June 1969.

2-3 Ahuja, D. C., and Coons, S. A., "Geometry for Construction and Display,"
     IBM Syst. J., vol. 7, nos. 3 and 4, pp. 188-205, 1968.

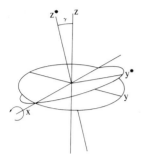

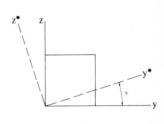

$$\begin{bmatrix} 1 & 0 & 0 \\ 0 & \cos\gamma & \sin\gamma \\ 0 & -\sin\gamma & \cos\gamma \end{bmatrix}$$

Rotation about x

a

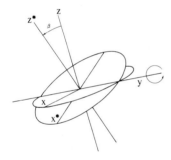

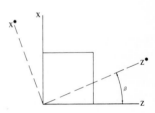

$$\begin{bmatrix} \cos\beta & 0 & -\sin\beta \\ 0 & 1 & 0 \\ \sin\beta & 0 & \cos\beta \end{bmatrix}$$

Rotation about y

b

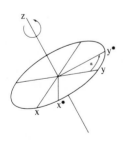

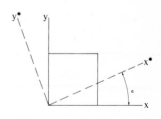

$$\begin{bmatrix} \cos\alpha & \sin\alpha & 0 \\ -\sin\alpha & \cos\alpha & 0 \\ 0 & 0 & 1 \end{bmatrix}$$

Rotation about z

c

Figure 2-10   Rotation.

CHAPTER 3

THREE DIMENSIONAL TRANSFORMATIONS AND PROJECTIONS

3-1 Introduction

The ability to represent or display a three-dimensional object is fundamental to the understanding of the shape of that object. Furthermore, the ability to rotate, translate, and project views of that object is also, in many cases, fundamental to the understanding of its shape. This is easily demonstrated by picking up a relatively complex unfamiliar object. Immediately one rotates it, holds it at arm's length, stands back from it, etc., in order to obtain an understanding of its shape. To do this with a computer we must extend our previous two-dimensional analyses to three dimensions. Based on our previous experience we immediately introduce homogeneous coordinates. Hence a point in three-dimensional space [x y z] is represented by a four-dimensional position vector [x y z 1] or [X Y Z H]. Again the transformation from homogeneous coordinates to ordinary coordinates is given by

$$[X \ Y \ Z \ H] = [x \ y \ z \ 1]T$$

and

$$[x^* \ y^* \ z^* \ 1] = [\frac{X}{H} \ \frac{Y}{H} \ \frac{Z}{H} \ 1] \qquad (3-1)$$

where T is some transformation matrix.

The generalized 4 x 4 transformation matrix for three-dimensional homogeneous coordinates is

$$T = \begin{bmatrix} a & b & c & p \\ d & e & f & q \\ h & i & j & r \\ \ell & m & n & s \end{bmatrix} \qquad (3\text{-}2)$$

The 4 x 4 transformation matrix in Eq. (3-2) can be partitioned into four separate sections:

$$\begin{bmatrix} 3 \times 3 & | & \begin{matrix} 3 \\ x \\ 1 \end{matrix} \\ \hline 1 \times 3 & | & 1 \times 1 \end{bmatrix}$$

The 3 x 3 matrix produces a linear transformation* in the form of scaling, shearing, and rotation. The 1 x 3 row matrix produces translation, and the 3 x 1 column matrix produces perspective transformation. The final single element produces overall scaling. The total transformation obtained by operating on a position vector with the 4 x 4 matrix and normalizing the transformed vector is called a bilinear transformation. This gives a combination of *shearing, local scaling, rotation, reflection, translation, perspective,* and *overall scaling.*

3-2 THREE-DIMENSIONAL SCALING

The diagonal terms of the general 4 x 4 transformation produce local and overall scaling. Consider

$$[x\ y\ z\ 1] \begin{bmatrix} a & 0 & 0 & 0 \\ 0 & e & 0 & 0 \\ 0 & 0 & j & 0 \\ 0 & 0 & 0 & 1 \end{bmatrix} = [ax\ ey\ jz\ 1] = [x^*\ y^*\ z^*\ 1] \qquad (3\text{-}3)$$

which shows the local scaling effect. Figure 3-1a shows a parallelepiped rescaled as a unit cube. Overall scaling is obtained by using the fourth diagonal element, i.e.,

$$[x\ y\ z\ 1] \begin{bmatrix} 1 & 0 & 0 & 0 \\ 0 & 1 & 0 & 0 \\ 0 & 0 & 1 & 0 \\ 0 & 0 & 0 & s \end{bmatrix} = [x\ y\ z\ s]$$

$$= [x^*\ y^*\ z^*\ 1] = [\frac{x}{s}\ \frac{y}{s}\ \frac{z}{s}\ 1]$$

---

*A linear transformation is one which transforms an initial linear combination of vectors into the same linear combination of transformed vectors.

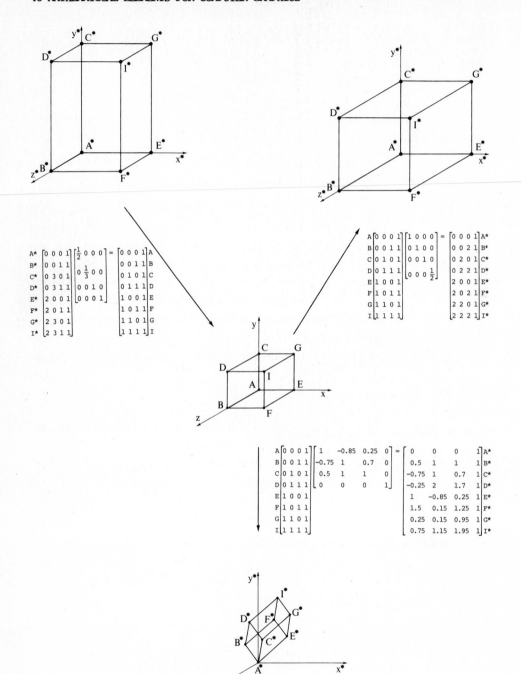

Figure 3-1 Three-dimensional scale transformations.

This effect is shown in Fig. 3-1b. Incidentally, the same effect can be obtained by means of equal local scalings. In this case the transformation matrix would be

$$\begin{bmatrix} \frac{1}{s} & 0 & 0 & 0 \\ 0 & \frac{1}{s} & 0 & 0 \\ 0 & 0 & \frac{1}{s} & 0 \\ 0 & 0 & 0 & 1 \end{bmatrix}$$

3-3 THREE-DIMENSIONAL SHEARING

The off-diagonal terms in the upper left 3 x 3 component matrix of the generalized 4 x 4 transformation matrix produce shear in three dimensions, e.g.,

$$[x\ y\ z\ 1] \begin{bmatrix} 1 & b & c & 0 \\ d & 1 & f & 0 \\ h & i & 1 & 0 \\ 0 & 0 & 0 & 1 \end{bmatrix} = [x + yd + hz \quad bx + y + iz \quad cx + fy + z \quad 1]$$

A simple three-dimensional shear on a unit cube is shown in Fig. 3-1c.

3-4 THREE-DIMENSIONAL ROTATIONS

In the previous sections we saw that a 3 x 3 component matrix produced a combination of scaling and shear. However, if the determinant (cf Appendix B) of the 3 x 3 component matrix is +1, then it produces a pure rotation about the origin. Before considering the general case of three-dimensional rotation about an arbitrary axis, we examine several special cases.

In a rotation about the x-axis, the x-dimensions do not change. Thus, the transformation matrix will have zeros in the first row and first column, except for unity on the main diagonal. The other terms are determined by considering the rotation of a unit cube in the same manner as discussed in Sec. 2-14. This leads to the transformation matrix for a rotation of angle θ about the x-axis given by

$$T = \begin{bmatrix} 1 & 0 & 0 & 0 \\ 0 & \cos\theta & \sin\theta & 0 \\ 0 & -\sin\theta & \cos\theta & 0 \\ 0 & 0 & 0 & 1 \end{bmatrix} \tag{3-6}$$

Rotation is assumed to be positive in a right-hand sense as one looks from the origin outward along the axis of rotation. Figure 3-2a shows a -90° rotation about the x-axis.

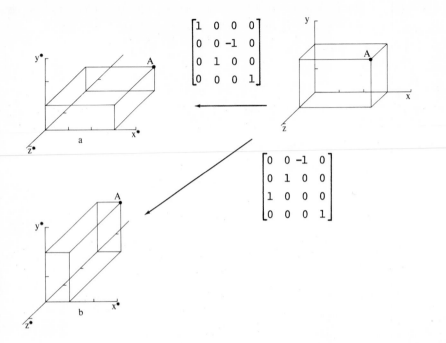

Figure 3-2 a   Three-dimensional rotations.

For a rotation of angle ϕ about the y-axis, zeros appear in the second row and second column of the transformation matrix, except for unity on the main diagonal. The complete matrix is

$$T = \begin{bmatrix} \cos\phi & 0 & -\sin\phi & 0 \\ 0 & 1 & 0 & 0 \\ \sin\phi & 0 & \cos\phi & 0 \\ 0 & 0 & 0 & 1 \end{bmatrix} \tag{3-7}$$

Figure 3-2b shows a 90° rotation about the y-axis.

In a similar manner, the transformation matrix for a rotation of angle ψ about the z-axis is

$$T = \begin{bmatrix} \cos\psi & \sin\psi & 0 & 0 \\ -\sin\psi & \cos\psi & 0 & 0 \\ 0 & 0 & 1 & 0 \\ 0 & 0 & 0 & 1 \end{bmatrix} \tag{3-8}$$

Examining the determinant of Eqs. (3-6) to (3-8) demonstrates that any rigid-body rotation matrix has a determinant value of +1.0.

Since rotations are caused by matrix multiplication, three-dimensional rotations are noncommutative; i.e., the order of multiplication will affect the final result. In order to show this, consider a rotation about the x-axis followed by an equal rotation about the y-axis. Using Eqs. (3-6) and (3-7) with $\theta = \phi$, we have

$$T = \begin{bmatrix} 1 & 0 & 0 & 0 \\ 0 & \cos\theta & \sin\theta & 0 \\ 0 & -\sin\theta & \cos\theta & 0 \\ 0 & 0 & 0 & 1 \end{bmatrix} \begin{bmatrix} \cos\phi & 0 & -\sin\phi & 0 \\ 0 & 1 & 0 & 0 \\ \sin\phi & 0 & \cos\phi & 0 \\ 0 & 0 & 0 & 1 \end{bmatrix} \qquad (3\text{-}9)$$

$$= \begin{bmatrix} \cos\theta & 0 & -\sin\theta & 0 \\ \sin^2\theta & \cos\theta & \cos\theta\sin\theta & 0 \\ \cos\theta\sin\theta & -\sin\theta & \cos^2\theta & 0 \\ 0 & 0 & 0 & 1 \end{bmatrix}$$

On the other hand, the reverse operation, i.e., a rotation about the y-axis followed by an equal rotation about the x-axis with $\theta = \phi$, yields

$$T = \begin{bmatrix} \cos\phi & 0 & -\sin\phi & 0 \\ 0 & 1 & 0 & 0 \\ \sin\phi & 0 & \cos\phi & 0 \\ 0 & 0 & 0 & 1 \end{bmatrix} \begin{bmatrix} 1 & 0 & 0 & 0 \\ 0 & \cos\theta & \sin\theta & 0 \\ 0 & -\sin\theta & \cos\theta & 0 \\ 0 & 0 & 0 & 1 \end{bmatrix} \qquad (3\text{-}10)$$

$$= \begin{bmatrix} \cos\theta & \sin^2\theta & -\cos\theta\sin\theta & 0 \\ 0 & \cos\theta & \sin\theta & 0 \\ \sin\theta & -\cos\theta\sin\theta & \cos^2\theta & 0 \\ 0 & 0 & 0 & 1 \end{bmatrix}$$

Comparison of the right-hand sides of Eqs. (3-9) and (3-10) shows that they are not the same. The fact that three-dimensional rotations are noncommutative must be kept in mind when more than one rotation is to be made.

The result of transformation of the upper left object in Figure 3-3 consisting of two 90° rotations using the matrix product given in Eqs. (3-9) is shown as the dashed figures. When the opposite order of rotation as specified by Eq. (3-10) is performed, the solid figures shown in Fig. 3-3 graphically demonstrate that different results are obtained by changing the order of rotation.

Frequently it is desirable to rotate an object about one of the cartesian coordinate axes. Algorithms given in Appendix C allow rotation about the x-, y-, and z-axes.

3-5 REFLECTION IN THREE DIMENSIONS

Some orientations of a three dimensional object require reflections. In three dimensions the simplest reflections occur through a plane. For a rigid-

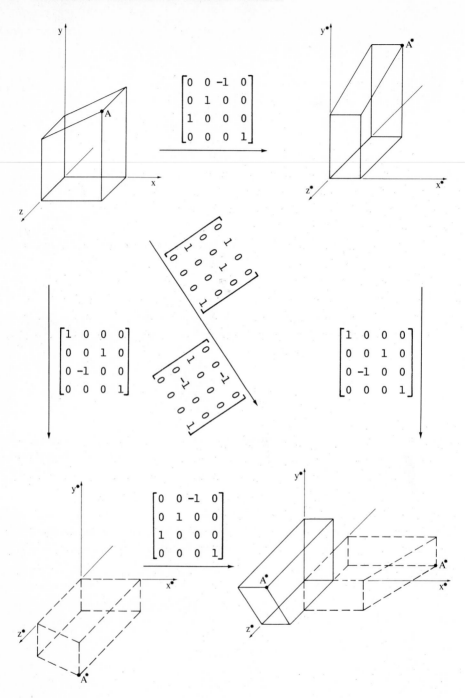

Figure 3-3   Three-dimensional rotations are noncommutative.

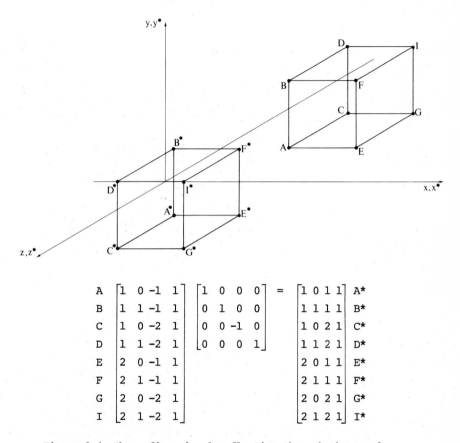

$$
\begin{array}{c}
A \\ B \\ C \\ D \\ E \\ F \\ G \\ I
\end{array}
\begin{bmatrix}
1 & 0 & -1 & 1 \\
1 & 1 & -1 & 1 \\
1 & 0 & -2 & 1 \\
1 & 1 & -2 & 1 \\
2 & 0 & -1 & 1 \\
2 & 1 & -1 & 1 \\
2 & 0 & -2 & 1 \\
2 & 1 & -2 & 1
\end{bmatrix}
\begin{bmatrix}
1 & 0 & 0 & 0 \\
0 & 1 & 0 & 0 \\
0 & 0 & -1 & 0 \\
0 & 0 & 0 & 1
\end{bmatrix}
=
\begin{bmatrix}
1 & 0 & 1 & 1 \\
1 & 1 & 1 & 1 \\
1 & 0 & 2 & 1 \\
1 & 1 & 2 & 1 \\
2 & 0 & 1 & 1 \\
2 & 1 & 1 & 1 \\
2 & 0 & 2 & 1 \\
2 & 1 & 2 & 1
\end{bmatrix}
\begin{array}{c}
A^* \\ B^* \\ C^* \\ D^* \\ E^* \\ F^* \\ G^* \\ I^*
\end{array}
$$

Figure 3-4 Three-dimensional reflection through the xy-plane.

body reflection the determinant of the reflection transformation will be -1.0.

In a reflection through the xy-plane, only the z-coordinate values of the object's position vectors will be changed. In fact they will be reversed in sign. Thus, the transformation matrix for a reflection through the xy-plane is

$$
T = \begin{bmatrix}
1 & 0 & 0 & 0 \\
0 & 1 & 0 & 0 \\
0 & 0 & -1 & 0 \\
0 & 0 & 0 & 1
\end{bmatrix}
\tag{3-11}
$$

The reflection of a unit cube through the xy-plane is shown in Figure 3-4. For
a reflection through the yz-plane,

$$T = \begin{bmatrix} -1 & 0 & 0 & 0 \\ 0 & 1 & 0 & 0 \\ 0 & 0 & 1 & 0 \\ 0 & 0 & 0 & 1 \end{bmatrix} \qquad (3-12)$$

and for a reflection through the xz-plane,

$$T = \begin{bmatrix} 1 & 0 & 0 & 0 \\ 0 & -1 & 0 & 0 \\ 0 & 0 & 1 & 0 \\ 0 & 0 & 0 & 1 \end{bmatrix} \qquad (3-13)$$

An algorithm which will perform three-dimensional reflections is given in
Appendix C. Reflections about other planes can be obtained by a combination of
rotation and reflection.

3-6 TRANSLATION IN THREE DIMENSIONS

Three-dimensional translation is obtained by writing

$$[X\ Y\ Z\ H] = [x\ y\ z\ 1] \begin{bmatrix} 1 & 0 & 0 & 0 \\ 0 & 1 & 0 & 0 \\ 0 & 0 & 1 & 0 \\ \ell & m & n & 1 \end{bmatrix} \qquad (3-14)$$

When expanded this yields

$$[X\ Y\ Z\ H] = [(x + \ell)\ (y + m)\ (z + n)\ 1] \qquad (3-15)$$

It follows that

$$x^* = \frac{X}{H} = x + \ell \qquad (3-16)$$

$$y^* = \frac{Y}{H} = y + m$$

$$z^* = \frac{Z}{H} = z + n$$

An algorithm for translations in three dimensions appears in Appendix C.

3-7 THREE-DIMENSIONAL ROTATIONS ABOUT AN ARBITRARY AXIS

The method of two-dimensional plane rotation about an arbitrary axis was
discussed in Sec. 2-17. The generalization of that problem is rotation about any
axis in three-dimensional space. Again, the procedure is to translate the object and the desired axis of rotation so that the rotation is made about an axis
passing through the origin of the coordinate system. The method involves a
three-dimensional translation, a rotation about the origin, and a translation
back to the initial position. If the axis about which rotation is desired

passes through the point A = [ℓ m n 1], then the form of the transformation matrix is

$$[X\ Y\ Z\ H] = [x\ y\ z\ 1] \begin{bmatrix} 1 & 0 & 0 & 0 \\ 0 & 1 & 0 & 0 \\ 0 & 0 & 1 & 0 \\ -\ell & -m & -n & 1 \end{bmatrix} \begin{bmatrix} & & & \\ & R & & \\ & & & \end{bmatrix} \begin{bmatrix} 1 & 0 & 0 & 0 \\ 0 & 1 & 0 & 0 \\ 0 & 0 & 1 & 0 \\ \ell & m & n & 1 \end{bmatrix} \qquad (3\text{-}17)$$

where the elements in the 4x4 rotation matrix R are in general given by

$$[R] = \begin{bmatrix} n_1^2 + (1 - n_1^2)\cos\theta & n_1 n_2 (1 - \cos\theta) + n_3 \sin\theta & n_1 n_3 (1 - \cos\theta) - n_2 \sin\theta & 0 \\ n_1 n_2 (1 - \cos\theta) - n_3 \sin\theta & n_2^2 + (1 - n_2^2)\cos\theta & n_2 n_3 (1 - \cos\theta) + n_1 \sin\theta & 0 \\ n_1 n_3 (1 - \cos\theta) + n_2 \sin\theta & n_2 n_3 (1 - \cos\theta) - n_1 \sin\theta & n_3^2 + (1 - n_3^2)\cos\theta & 0 \\ 0 & 0 & 0 & 1 \end{bmatrix} \qquad (3\text{-}18)$$

Since generalized three-dimensional rotation is a very important capability, a derivation for determining the elements of the rotation matrix R is given in the next section.

Equations (3-17) and (3-18) can be used as a basis for computer software algorithms. Such an algorithm is particularly useful for computer animations. This transformation, as well as others discussed in this chapter, can also be produced by use of hardware components in a display device.

An algorithm which will produce a three-dimensional rotation about an arbitrary axis in space based on Eq. (3-18) is given in Appendix C. The algorithms for rotation about the individual x-, y-, and z-axes previously discussed are special cases of the present algorithm.

3-8 ELEMENTS FOR THE GENERAL ROTATION MATRIX*

We begin by considering Fig. 3-5, which shows an arbitrary axis of rotation (ON) translated so that it passes through the origin. We then rotate a point on the translated object (such as point P) about the axis by an angle θ. This will move the point from P to P*. In Fig. 3-5, PQ = P*Q, and both of these lines are perpendicular to OQ. P*S is constructed to be perpendicular to PQ. To determine the elements in the matrix R, we must relate the transformed coordinates of P* to three variables: the coordinates of P, the rotation angle θ, and the direction of the axis of rotation as specified by the unit vector $\vec{n}$. This derivation is given below.

The direction of the axis of rotation is most easily expressed in terms of three direction cosines, $n_1 = \cos\alpha$, $n_2 = \cos\beta$ and $n_3 = \cos\gamma$. The angles α, β,

---

*This section may be ommitted without loss of continuity.

and γ are identified in Fig. 3-5. The direction cosines are the three components of the unit vector $\vec{n}$. For any general vector $\vec{Q} = q_1\vec{i} + q_2\vec{j} + q_3\vec{k}$, this unit vector is calculated by $\vec{n} = \vec{Q}/|\vec{Q}|$, where $|\vec{Q}|$ is the absolute value of the vector given by $|\vec{Q}| = \sqrt{q_1^2 + q_2^2 + q_3^2}$, and $\vec{i}$, $\vec{j}$, and $\vec{k}$ are unit vectors in the x-, y-, and z-directions respectively. It follows that

$$\cos\alpha = \frac{q_1}{\sqrt{q_1^2 + q_2^2 + q_3^2}} = n_1$$

$$\cos\beta = \frac{q_2}{\sqrt{q_1^2 + q_2^2 + q_3^2}} = n_2$$

$$\cos\gamma = \frac{q_3}{\sqrt{q_1^2 + q_2^2 + q_3^2}} = n_3$$

The unit vector is then given by

$$\vec{n} = n_1\vec{i} + n_2\vec{j} + n_3\vec{k}$$

In matrix form this is written as $\vec{n} = [n_1\ n_2\ n_3]$.

Two other results from vector calculus, the dot product and the cross

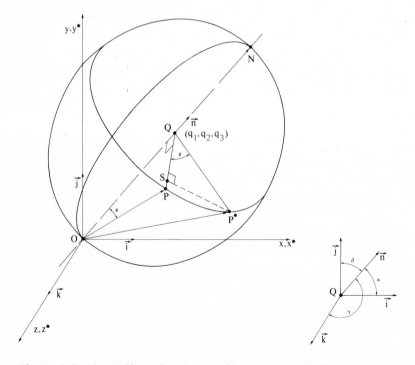

Figure 3-5 Three-dimensional rotation about an arbitrary axis.

product, are needed to relate P* to P. The vector dot product is given by

$$\vec{P} \cdot \vec{n} = |\vec{P}||\vec{n}|\cos\phi = |\vec{P}|\cos\phi$$

where ϕ is the angle between the two vectors, as shown in Fig. 3-5. Since $\vec{P} = [x\ y\ z]$ and $\vec{n} = [n_1\ n_2\ n_3]$, the dot product can also be expressed in matrix form as

$$\vec{P} \cdot \vec{n} = xn_1 + yn_2 + zn_3 = [x\ y\ z] \begin{bmatrix} n_1 \\ n_2 \\ n_3 \end{bmatrix}$$

The vector cross product is given by

$$\vec{n} \times \vec{P} = \det \begin{bmatrix} \vec{i} & \vec{j} & \vec{k} \\ n_1 & n_2 & n_3 \\ x & y & z \end{bmatrix} = \begin{vmatrix} n_2 & n_3 \\ y & z \end{vmatrix} - \begin{vmatrix} n_1 & n_3 \\ x & z \end{vmatrix} + \begin{vmatrix} n_1 & n_2 \\ x & y \end{vmatrix}$$

$$= \vec{i}(n_2 z - n_3 y) + \vec{j}(n_3 x - n_1 z) + \vec{k}(n_1 y - n_2 x)$$

In matrix form the cross product is

$$\vec{n} \times \vec{P} = [x\ y\ z] \begin{bmatrix} 0 & n_3 & -n_2 \\ -n_3 & 0 & n_1 \\ n_2 & -n_1 & 0 \end{bmatrix}$$

It is also true that

$$|\vec{n} \times \vec{P}| = |\vec{n}||\vec{P}|\sin\phi = |\vec{P}|\sin\phi$$

where ϕ is again the angle between the two vectors.

The following three vector equalities are obtained from Fig. 3-5:

$$\vec{Q} + \vec{QP^*} = \vec{P^*} \tag{3-19}$$

$$\vec{QP^*} = \vec{QS} + \vec{SP^*} \tag{3-20}$$

$$\vec{Q} + \vec{QP} = \vec{P} \tag{3-21}$$

From Eq. (3-21), $\vec{QP} = (\vec{P} - \vec{Q})$. Since the magnitudes of $\vec{QP}$ and $\vec{QP^*}$ are equal, the magnitude of vector $\vec{QS}$, which is in the direction of $\vec{QP}$, is given by $QS = |\vec{QP}|\cos\theta$. Thus $\vec{QS} = (\vec{P} - \vec{Q})\cos\theta$. Using this result and combining Eqs. (3-19) and (3-20) gives

$$\vec{P^*} = \vec{Q} + (\vec{P} - \vec{Q})\cos\theta + \vec{SP^*} \tag{3-21a}$$

The magnitude of $\vec{SP^*}$ is equal to

$$|\vec{SP^*}| = |\vec{QP}|\sin\theta = |\vec{P} - \vec{Q}|\sin\theta$$

The direction of $\vec{SP^*}$ is perpendicular to the plane PQN and is therefore parallel to the vector $\vec{n} \times \vec{P}$. The unit vector in this direction is

$$\vec{u} = \frac{\vec{n} \times \vec{P}}{|\vec{n} \times \vec{P}|} = \frac{\vec{n} \times \vec{P}}{|\vec{P}|\sin\phi}$$

It follows that

$$S\vec{P}* = \frac{\vec{n} \times \vec{P}}{|\vec{P}|\sin\phi} |\vec{P} - \vec{Q}|\sin\theta$$

but $|\vec{P}|\sin\phi = |Q\vec{P}| = |\vec{P} - \vec{Q}|$ and thus

$$S\vec{P}* = (\vec{n} \times \vec{P})\sin\theta$$

Equation (3-21a) can now be written

$$\vec{P}* = \vec{Q} + (\vec{P} - \vec{Q})\cos\theta + (\vec{n} \times \vec{P})\sin\theta \qquad (3-22)$$

Figure 3-5 shows that the vector $\vec{Q}$ is the projection of the vector $\vec{P}$ on the axis of rotation. The magnitude of $\vec{Q}$ is $\vec{P} \cdot \vec{n} = |\vec{P}|\cos\phi$, and the direction of $\vec{Q}$ is $\vec{n}$. Using the equality $\vec{Q} = (\vec{P} \cdot \vec{n})\vec{n}$, Eq. (3-22) becomes

$$\vec{P}* = (\vec{P} \cdot \vec{n})\vec{n}(1 - \cos\theta) + \vec{P}\cos\theta + (\vec{n} \times \vec{P})\sin\theta$$

As required, this equation gives the transformed point in terms of the initial point, the angle of rotation, and the direction of the axis of rotation. We now write this result in matrix form.

Using the matrix expression given earlier for the dot product $(\vec{P} \cdot \vec{n})$ and for the cross product $(\vec{n} \times \vec{P})$, the equation for $\vec{P}*$ becomes

$$\vec{P}* = [x\ y\ z]\begin{bmatrix} n_1 \\ n_2 \\ n_3 \end{bmatrix}[n_1\ n_2\ n_3](1 - \cos\theta) + [x\ y\ z]\cos\theta + [x\ y\ z]\begin{bmatrix} 0 & n_3 & -n_2 \\ -n_3 & 0 & n_1 \\ n_2 & -n_1 & 0 \end{bmatrix}\sin\theta \qquad (3-23)$$

This can be written in an equivalent form using homogeneous coordinates:

$$P* = [x\ y\ z\ 1]\left\{\begin{bmatrix} n_1^2 & n_1n_2 & n_1n_3 & 0 \\ n_1n_2 & n_2^2 & n_2n_3 & 0 \\ n_1n_3 & n_2n_3 & n_3^2 & 0 \\ 0 & 0 & 0 & 1 \end{bmatrix}(1 - \cos\theta) + \begin{bmatrix} 1 & 0 & 0 & 0 \\ 0 & 1 & 0 & 0 \\ 0 & 0 & 1 & 0 \\ 0 & 0 & 0 & 1 \end{bmatrix}\cos\theta + \begin{bmatrix} 0 & n_3 & -n_2 & 0 \\ -n_3 & 0 & n_1 & 0 \\ n_2 & -n_1 & 0 & 0 \\ 0 & 0 & 0 & 1 \end{bmatrix}\sin\theta\right\} \qquad (3-24)$$

The three terms within the braces give the required rotation matrix [R]. Finally, if desired they can be combined and written as

$$(3-18)$$

$$[R] = \begin{bmatrix} n_1^2 + (1 - n_1^2)\cos\theta & n_1n_2(1 - \cos\theta) + n_3\sin\theta & n_1n_3(1 - \cos\theta) - n_2\sin\theta & 0 \\ n_1n_2(1 - \cos\theta) - n_3\sin\theta & n_2^2 + (1 - n_2^2)\cos\theta & n_2n_3(1 - \cos\theta) + n_1\sin\theta & 0 \\ n_1n_3(1 - \cos\theta) + n_2\sin\theta & n_2n_3(1 - \cos\theta) - n_1\sin\theta & n_3^2 + (1 - n_3^2)\cos\theta & 0 \\ 0 & 0 & 0 & 1 \end{bmatrix}$$

It is seen that to produce a general rotation by use of Eq. (3-17), the $[x\ y\ z]$ coordinates of the point P, the direction cosines of the axis of rotation $[n_1\ n_2\ n_3]$, and the angle of rotation about the axis θ are needed to define [R]. As a specific example consider rotation about the z-axis. Then $n_1 = 0$, $n_2 = 0$, and $n_3 = 1.0$. For this special case the rotation matrix R becomes

$$R = \begin{bmatrix} \cos\theta & \sin\theta & 0 & 0 \\ -\sin\theta & \cos\theta & 0 & 0 \\ 0 & 0 & 1 & 0 \\ 0 & 0 & 0 & 1 \end{bmatrix}$$

grees with that given in Sec. 3-4 for rotation about the z-axis in

AND PERSPECTIVE GEOMETRY

idea of a vector to describe a point was initially conceived from geo-
concepts. Geometric theorems have been developed for both perspective
e geometry. The theorems of affine geometry are identical to those for
geometry. In affine geometry parallelism is an important concept, and
os between parallel lines is an integral part of the geometry. Since
in geometry has been taught in schools for many years, drawing and sketching techniques based upon this geometry have become standard methods for graphical communication.

An affine transformation is a combination of linear transformations followed
by translation. For an affine transformation, the last column in the general
4 x 4 transformation matrix must be $\begin{bmatrix} 0 \\ 0 \\ 0 \\ 1 \end{bmatrix}$. Otherwise, as shown in Sec. 3-11 below,
the transformed homogeneous coordinate H is not unity and there is not a one to
one correspondence between the affine transformation and the 4 x 4 matrix operator. Affine transformations form a useful subset of bilinear transformations,
since the product of two affine transformations is also affine. This allows one
to perform a general orientation of a set of points relative to an arbitrary
coordinate system while still maintaining a value of unity for the homogeneous
coordinate H.

Although perspective views are often used by artists and architects because
they yield more realistic pictures, they are seldom used in technical work because of the difficulty of construction. However, when homogeneous coordinates
are used to define an object within a computer, either affine or perspective
transformations can be obtained with equal ease. In perspective geometry no two
lines are parallel. In fact the perspective plane can be considered as a hemi-
spherical surface and the perspective transformation considered as a transformation from *one three space into another three space.*

When the elements in the last column of the general 4 x 4 transformation
matrix are not zero, a perspective transformation is formed. A perspective

transformation is frequently associated with a projection onto a plane, such as $z = C_1$, from a local center of projection. The combination of a perspective transformation with a projective transformation is called a perspective projection. A perspective projection represents a transformation from three space to two space. If the center of projection is located at infinity, then the perspective projection is called an axonometric projection. Otherwise, the form depends upon the location of the projection point.

3-10 AXONOMETRIC PROJECTIONS

An axonometric projection is produced by an affine transformation which has a zero value for its determinant. There are several different types of axonometric projections which find application in descriptive geometry and engineering drafting. To mathematically form an axonometric projection, the 4 x 4 transformation matrix is used to produce an affine transformation on a set of points. The points are then projected onto a plane from a center of projection at infinity. The common axonometric projections are classified in Table 3-1.

Table 3-1

Axonometric Projections

Projection	Description
Trimetric	The transformation matrix causes pure rotation. Thus, the coordinate axes remain orthogonal when projected
Dimetric	Two of the three axes are equally foreshortened when projected
Isometric	All three axes are equally foreshortened when projected

Axonometric projections were shown in Fig. 3-2 and 3-3. An axonometric projection from three-dimensional space onto a plane $z = n$ can be obtained by the following operation:

$$[X\ Y\ Z\ H] = [x\ y\ z\ 1] \begin{bmatrix} 1 & 0 & 0 & 0 \\ 0 & 1 & 0 & 0 \\ 0 & 0 & 0 & 0 \\ 0 & 0 & n & 1 \end{bmatrix} = [x\ y\ n\ 1] \qquad (3\text{-}25)$$

Then,

$$[x^*\ y^*\ z^*\ 1] = [x\ y\ n\ 1]$$

Notice that this transformation represents a translation in the z-direction by the amount n given by the transformation

$$T' = \begin{bmatrix} 1 & 0 & 0 & 0 \\ 0 & 1 & 0 & 0 \\ 0 & 0 & 1 & 0 \\ 0 & 0 & n & 1 \end{bmatrix}$$

followed by a projection from infinity onto the now z = 0 plane given by the transformation

$$T'' = \begin{bmatrix} 1 & 0 & 0 & 0 \\ 0 & 1 & 0 & 0 \\ 0 & 0 & 0 & 0 \\ 0 & 0 & 0 & 1 \end{bmatrix}$$

The concatenation of T' and T", i.e., T' T", will yield the transformation matrix given in Eq. (3-25). The effect of the translation is to move the z = 0 plane to some other position in the object. Projection onto the z = 0 plane then corresponds to projection onto the z = n plane.

Axonometric projection transformations onto the appropriate zero plane always contain a column of zeros, which corresponds to the plane of projection. Such projections are frequently called orthographic projections. They are commonly used in mechanical drawing. Examples of an axonometric projection onto the x = ℓ and y = m planes are given by

$$T' = \begin{bmatrix} 0 & 0 & 0 & 0 \\ 0 & 1 & 0 & 0 \\ 0 & 0 & 1 & 0 \\ \ell & 0 & 0 & 1 \end{bmatrix} \text{ and } T'' = \begin{bmatrix} 1 & 0 & 0 & 0 \\ 0 & 0 & 0 & 0 \\ 0 & 0 & 1 & 0 \\ 0 & m & 0 & 1 \end{bmatrix}$$

As noted in Table 3-1 the transformation matrix for a **trimetric** axonometric projection causes pure rotation. This type of transformation was studied in Sec. 3-4. Auxiliary views used in engineering drawings are trimetric projections. An example of a trimetric projection of the unit cube onto the z = 0 plane after a 90° rotation about the x-axis is shown in Fig. 3-6.

In order to develop the conditions for dimetric and isometric projections, recall that combined rotations followed by projection from infinity form the basis for generating all axonometric projections. In particular, we consider a rotation about the y-axis, followed by a rotation about the x-axis. From Eqs. (3-7) and (3-6) the matrix product which gives this is

$$[X\ Y\ Z\ H] = [x\ y\ z\ 1] \begin{bmatrix} \cos\phi & 0 & -\sin\phi & 0 \\ 0 & 1 & 0 & 0 \\ \sin\phi & 0 & \cos\phi & 0 \\ 0 & 0 & 0 & 1 \end{bmatrix} \begin{bmatrix} 1 & 0 & 0 & 0 \\ 0 & \cos\theta & \sin\theta & 0 \\ 0 & -\sin\theta & \cos\theta & 0 \\ 0 & 0 & 0 & 1 \end{bmatrix}$$

Concatenation yields

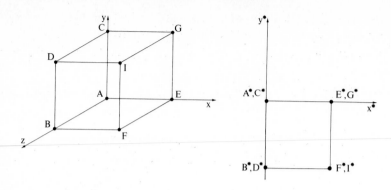

$$
\begin{array}{c}
A \\ B \\ C \\ D \\ E \\ F \\ G \\ I
\end{array}
\begin{bmatrix}
0 & 0 & 0 & 1 \\
0 & 0 & 1 & 1 \\
0 & 1 & 0 & 1 \\
0 & 1 & 1 & 1 \\
1 & 0 & 0 & 1 \\
1 & 0 & 1 & 1 \\
1 & 1 & 0 & 1 \\
1 & 1 & 1 & 1
\end{bmatrix}
\begin{bmatrix}
1 & 0 & 0 & 0 \\
0 & 0 & 0 & 0 \\
0 & -1 & 0 & 0 \\
0 & 0 & 0 & 1
\end{bmatrix}
=
\begin{bmatrix}
0 & 0 & 0 & 1 \\
0 & -1 & 0 & 1 \\
0 & 0 & 0 & 1 \\
0 & -1 & 0 & 1 \\
1 & 0 & 0 & 1 \\
1 & -1 & 0 & 1 \\
1 & 0 & 0 & 1 \\
1 & -1 & 0 & 1
\end{bmatrix}
\begin{array}{c}
A^* \\ B^* \\ C^* \\ D^* \\ E^* \\ F^* \\ G^* \\ I^*
\end{array}
$$

Figure 3-6   Axonometric Projections.

$$
[X\ Y\ Z\ H] = [x\ y\ z\ 1]
\begin{bmatrix}
\cos\phi & \sin\phi\sin\theta & -\sin\phi\cos\theta & 0 \\
0 & \cos\theta & \sin\theta & 0 \\
\sin\phi & -\cos\phi\sin\theta & \cos\phi\cos\theta & 0 \\
0 & 0 & 0 & 1
\end{bmatrix}
\qquad (3\text{-}26)
$$

By use of this transformation matrix, the unit vector on the x-axis, [1 0 0 1], transforms to

$$[X\ Y\ Z\ H] = [\cos\phi\ \sin\phi\sin\theta\ -\sin\phi\cos\theta\ 1]$$

and

$$x^* = \cos\phi, \quad y^* = \sin\phi\sin\theta, \quad z^* = -\sin\phi\cos\theta$$

In projecting onto the $z^* = 0$ plane, z^* is effectively neglected as previously shown by Eq. (3-25) with n = 0 and Eq. (3-28). As a result of this transformation, the initial x-axis unit vector now has a magnitude of

$$\sqrt{x^{*2} + y^{*2}} = \sqrt{\cos^2\phi + (\sin\phi\sin\theta)^2}$$

Similarly, the unit vector on the y-axis, [0 1 0 1], transforms to

$$[X\ Y\ Z\ H] = [0\ \cos\theta\ \sin\theta\ 1]$$

and

$$x^* = 0, \quad y^* = \cos\theta, \quad z^* = \sin\theta$$

The magnitude of the transformed y-axis unit vector is now

$$\sqrt{\cos^2\theta} = \cos\theta$$

To create a dimetric projection, the magnitude of the two transformed unit vectors is shortened by an equal amount. Equating the magnitude of the x- and y-axis vectors yields

$$\cos^2\phi + \sin^2\phi\sin^2\theta = \cos^2\theta$$

Using the identities $\cos^2\phi = 1 - \sin^2\phi$ and $\cos^2\theta = 1 - \sin^2\theta$, it follows that

$$\sin^2\phi = \frac{\sin^2\theta}{1 - \sin^2\theta} \qquad (3\text{-}27)$$

When the value of $\sin\theta$ is chosen, and ϕ is calculated by the use of Eq. (3-27), the matrix in Eq. (3-26) produces a dimetric projection.

We now consider a specific example for a dimetric projection. One method of choosing $\sin\theta$ is to shorten the z-axis by a fixed amount. Consider the unit vector on the z-axis, [0 0 1 1]. This transforms to

$$[X\ Y\ Z\ H] = [\sin\phi\ -\cos\phi\sin\theta\ \cos\phi\cos\theta\ 1]$$

and

$$x^* = \sin\phi, \quad y^* = -\cos\phi\sin\theta$$

Now we shorten the magnitude of this transformed unit vector to a value of 1/2 by setting

$$\sin^2\phi + \cos^2\phi\sin^2\theta = (\tfrac{1}{2})^2$$

or

$$\sin^2\phi + (1 - \sin^2\phi)\sin^2\theta = \tfrac{1}{4}$$

Introducing Eq. (3-27) leads to

$$8\sin^4\theta - 9\sin^2\theta + 1 = 0$$

This equation has roots of $\sin^2\theta = 1/8$ and $\sin^2\theta = 1.0$. When $\sin\theta = \sqrt{1/8}$ or $\theta = 20.705°$, then $\sin\phi = \sqrt{(1/8)/(1-1/8)}$ or $\phi = 22.208°$. The terms in the transformation matrix in Eq. (3-26) are thus determined.

Using the values for a dimetric projection, the transformation matrix (Eq. 3-26) is given by

$$[X\ Y\ Z\ H] = [x\ y\ z\ 1] \begin{bmatrix} 0.925820 & 0.133631 & -0.353553 & 0 \\ 0 & 0.935414 & 0.353553 & 0 \\ 0.377964 & -0.327321 & 0.866025 & 0 \\ 0 & 0 & 0 & 1 \end{bmatrix}$$

A dimetric projection is shown in Fig. 3-7.

Perhaps more common is the isometric projection. To form an isometric projection, all three transformed axes are equally shortened. This requires that both

$$\cos^2\phi + \sin^2\phi\sin^2\theta = \cos^2\theta$$

and

$$\sin^2\phi + \cos^2\phi\sin^2\theta = \cos^2\theta$$

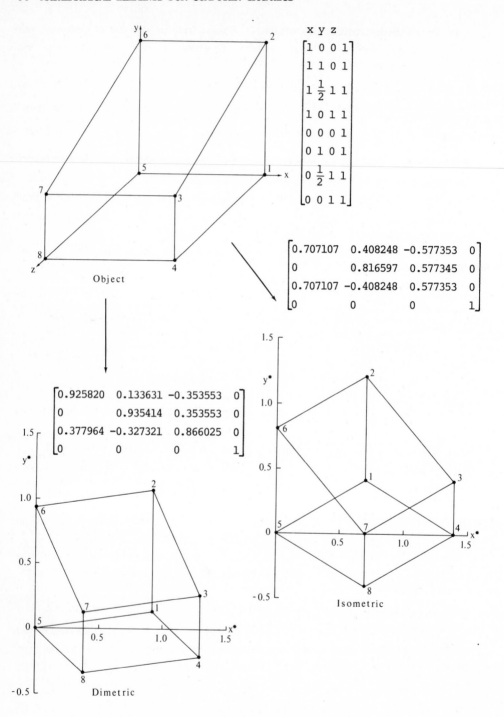

$$
\begin{array}{ccc}
x & y & z \\
\end{array}
$$

$$
\begin{bmatrix}
1 & 0 & 0 & 1 \\
1 & 1 & 0 & 1 \\
1 & \frac{1}{2} & 1 & 1 \\
1 & 0 & 1 & 1 \\
0 & 0 & 0 & 1 \\
0 & 1 & 0 & 1 \\
0 & \frac{1}{2} & 1 & 1 \\
0 & 0 & 1 & 1
\end{bmatrix}
$$

Object

$$
\begin{bmatrix}
0.707107 & 0.408248 & -0.577353 & 0 \\
0 & 0.816597 & 0.577345 & 0 \\
0.707107 & -0.408248 & 0.577353 & 0 \\
0 & 0 & 0 & 1
\end{bmatrix}
$$

$$
\begin{bmatrix}
0.925820 & 0.133631 & -0.353553 & 0 \\
0 & 0.935414 & 0.353553 & 0 \\
0.377964 & -0.327321 & 0.866025 & 0 \\
0 & 0 & 0 & 1
\end{bmatrix}
$$

Isometric

Dimetric

Figure 3-7 Axonometric projections.

The first condition again gives

$$\sin^2\phi = \frac{\sin^2\theta}{1 - \sin^2\theta}$$

The second condition gives

$$\sin^2\phi = \frac{1 - 2\sin^2\theta}{1 - \sin^2\theta}$$

It follows that $\sin^2\theta = 1/3$, or $\sin\theta = \sqrt{1/3}$ and $\theta = 35.26439°$. Then

$$\sin^2\phi = \frac{1/3}{1 - 1/3} = \frac{1}{2}$$

and

$$\cos^2\phi = 1 - \sin^2\phi = \frac{1}{2} \quad \text{or} \quad \phi = 45°$$

The angle which the projected x-axis makes with the horizontal is given by

$$\tan\alpha = \frac{\sin\phi\sin\theta}{\cos\phi}$$

For $\sin\theta = \sqrt{1/3}$, $\sin^2\phi = 1/2$, and $\cos^2\phi = 1/2$, this angle is

$$\alpha = \tan^{-1}\left(\frac{\sqrt{3}}{3}\right) = 30°$$

This result is well known to those who have produced an isometric projection on a drawing board. A plastic right triangle with included angles of 30° and 60° is a commonly used tool for this purpose.

Using the angular values for an isometric projection the transformation matrix in Eq. (3-26) becomes

$$[X \ Y \ Z \ H] = [x \ y \ z \ 1] \begin{bmatrix} 0.707107 & 0.408248 & -0.577353 & 0 \\ 0 & 0.816597 & 0.577345 & 0 \\ 0.707107 & -0.408248 & 0.577353 & 0 \\ 0 & 0 & 0 & 1 \end{bmatrix}$$

An example of an isometric projection is also shown in Fig. 3-7.

Oblique projections such as Cavalier and Cabinet do not preserve orthogonality of the coordinate system. The characteristics of these two are shown in Table 3-2. Since they are not frequently used in technical work they are not discussed further.

A simple orthographic projection onto a zero plane perpendicular to any of the three orthogonal axes results when the corresponding column in the 4 x 4 transformation matrix contains all zeros. For example, a projection onto the z = 0 plane will result when the following matrix is used.

$$T = \begin{bmatrix} 1 & 0 & 0 & 0 \\ 0 & 1 & 0 & 0 \\ 0 & 0 & 0 & 0 \\ 0 & 0 & 0 & 1 \end{bmatrix} \tag{3-28}$$

Table 3-2

Oblique Projections

Projection	Description
Cavalier	Two axes appear perpendicular and are not foreshortened; the third axis is inclined with respect to the horizontal and is not foreshortened
Cabinet	A special case of the Cavalier projection in which the third axis is foreshortened by a factor of 1/2

An algorithm for simple projections is given in Appendix C.

A trimetric projection can be obtained by using the three-dimensional rotation algorithms presented previously followed by the simple projection algorithm given above.

An algorithm which implements the specific dimetric and isometric transformation matrices discussed above [i.e., Eq. (3-26) with $\theta = 20.704811°$, $\phi = 22.20765°$ and $\theta = 35.26439°$, $\phi = 45°$ respectively] and assuming projection on the z = 0 plane is given in Appendix C.

3-11 PERSPECTIVE TRANSFORMATIONS

As previously mentioned, nonzero elements in the first three rows of the last column of the 4 x 4 transformation matrix yield a perspective transformation. A perspective projection is obtained by concatenation of a perspective transformation followed by a projection onto some two-dimensional "viewing" plane. A perspective projection onto the z = 0 plane is given by the transformation

$$[X \ Y \ Z \ H] = [x \ y \ z \ 1] \begin{bmatrix} 1 & 0 & 0 & 0 \\ 0 & 1 & 0 & 0 \\ 0 & 0 & 0 & r \\ 0 & 0 & 0 & 1 \end{bmatrix} = [x \ y \ 0 \ (rz + 1)] \qquad (3\text{-}29)$$

The ordinary transformed coordinates are then

$$x^* = \frac{X}{H} = \frac{x}{rz + 1} \qquad (3\text{-}30)$$

$$y^* = \frac{Y}{H} = \frac{y}{rz + 1}$$

$$z^* = \frac{Z}{H} = \frac{0}{rz + 1}$$

The geometrical effect of this transformation can be indicated with the aid

of Fig. 3-8. The nontransformed point
P is transformed to P* by the above
operation, with r = 1/k. In Fig. 3-8
the center of projection is located
at [0 0 -k] and the plane of projection is z = 0. Since the above operation produces no translation, the
origin is unchanged and the xy- and
x*y*-coordinates share the same
origin. By using the similar triangles shown in Fig. 3-8 it follows
that

$$\frac{x^*}{k} = \frac{x}{(z + k)}$$

or

$$x^* = \frac{x}{\frac{z}{k} + 1}$$

Considering the yz-plane in a similar
manner gives

$$y^* = \frac{y}{\frac{z}{k} + 1} \qquad (3\text{-}31)$$

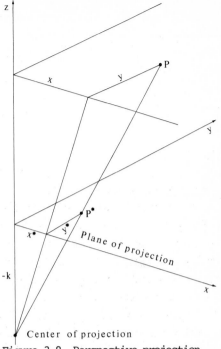

Figure 3-8 Perspective projection
of a point.

These are the transformed coordinates produced by the matrix operation with
r = 1/k. This operation produces a perspective projection on the z = 0 plane
from a center of projection located at z = -k. In a perspective transformation
the transformed space is not Euclidean, since orthogonality of the axes is not
preserved. When k approaches infinity, the axonometric transformation discussed
above is obtained.

Equations (3-30) and (3-31) show that when z = 0, then x* = x, and y* = y.
Due to this identity transformation, points in the viewing plane z = 0 are not
changed by a perspective projection. This is only true, however, when the homogeneous coordinate H is unity after the transformation has been applied to a
point [x y z 1]. Since affine transformations retain a value of unity for H,
a perspective transformation may be preceded by an arbitrary sequence of affine
transformations. Thus, to obtain perspective views from an arbitrary view point,
affine transformations are first used to establish a coordinate system with the
z-axis along the desired line of sight; then the perspective transformation is
applied and a projective transformation is used to project the total set of
points onto the viewing plane z = 0 of the current coordinate system. In prac-
tice, it is often necessary to apply further affine transformations to scale
and position the projected view (Ref. 3-3).

Above we have considered projection onto the z = 0 plane. However, this may not always be desirable. One reason is that projection onto the z = 0 plane loses the z-coordinated information which can be useful in controlling the brightness of displayed points on a plane (Ref. 3-4). To include the z-coordinate information the perspective transformation

$$[X \ Y \ Z \ H] = [x \ y \ z \ 1] \begin{bmatrix} 1 & 0 & 0 & 0 \\ 0 & 1 & 0 & 0 \\ 0 & 0 & 1 & r \\ 0 & 0 & 0 & 1 \end{bmatrix} = [x \ y \ z \ (rz + 1)] \qquad (3\text{-}32)$$

and

$$[x^* \ y^* \ z^* \ 1] = [\frac{x}{rz + 1} \ \frac{y}{rz + 1} \ \frac{z}{rz + 1} \ 1] \qquad (3\text{-}33)$$

may be used and the full three-dimensional results obtained.

Here we note that the origin of the coordinate system [0 0 0 1] is again unchanged. Notice that the point at infinity on the z-axis, [0 0 1 0], now transforms to the noninfinite point [X Y Z H] = [0 0 1 r] with the ordinary coordinates [x* y* z* 1] = [0 0 1/r 1], i.e., a finite point on the z*-axis. This means that the entire positive half of the domain (0 ≤ z ≤ ∞) is projected within a finite domain (0 ≤ z* ≤ 1/r). Further, lines which were originally parallel to the z-axis will now appear to pass throught the point [0 0 1/r 1]. This point is frequently called the vanishing point of the perspective transformation. When the results of the transformation are projected onto a plane, a perspective projection as mentioned above is obtained. Assuming that the z = 0 plane is the projection plane, the center of projection is located on the same axis as the vanishing point at an equal distance on the opposite side of the zero plane; i.e., if the vanishing point is located at z = 1/r on the z-axis, the center of projection is located at z = -1/r on the z-axis. This is shown in Fig. 3-9.

Similarly the perspective transformation

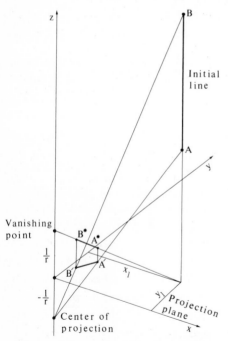

Figure 3-9   Projection of a line parallel to the z-axis.

$$[X \ Y \ Z \ H] = [x \ y \ z \ 1] \begin{bmatrix} 1 & 0 & 0 & 0 \\ 0 & 1 & 0 & q \\ 0 & 0 & 1 & 0 \\ 0 & 0 & 0 & 1 \end{bmatrix} = [x \ y \ z \ (qy + 1)] \qquad (3\text{-}34)$$

with ordinary coordinates

$$[x^* \ y^* \ z^* \ 1] = [\frac{x}{qy + 1} \ \frac{y}{qy + 1} \ \frac{z}{qy + 1} \ 1] \qquad (3\text{-}35)$$

will result in a vanishing point located on the y-axis at $[0 \ 1/q \ 0 \ 1]$, and the perspective transformation

$$[X \ Y \ Z \ H] = [x \ y \ z \ 1] \begin{bmatrix} 1 & 0 & 0 & p \\ 0 & 1 & 0 & 0 \\ 0 & 0 & 1 & 0 \\ 0 & 0 & 0 & 1 \end{bmatrix} \qquad (3\text{-}36)$$

$$= [x \ y \ z \ (px + 1)]$$

with ordinary coordinates

$$[x^* \ y^* \ z^* \ 1] = [\frac{x}{px + 1} \ \frac{y}{px + 1} \ \frac{z}{px + 1} \ 1] \qquad (3\text{-}37)$$

will result in a vanishing point located on the x-axis at $[1/p \ 0 \ 0 \ 1]$. The transformations given in Eqs. (3-32), (3-34), and (3-36) are called single-point or parallel perspective transformations. They result in views such as shown in Fig. 3-10a. Figure 3-10a shows a single-point perspective of a unit cube projected onto the z = 0 plane. The vanishing point is on the z-axis at z = -10. A more natural single-point perspective can be obtained by first centering the face BCGF with respect to the z-axis. That is, translate the eight corners of the unit cube by x = -0.5 and y = -0.5 before applying the perspective opera-tion. The resulting view is shown in Fig. 3-10b. This centered, single-point perspective is the type that artists often use. It can, however, give a dis-torted view of the depth of the object if the vanishing point is moved too far away from the center of the picture. This is what causes the "unnatural" view in Fig. 3-10a.

If two terms in the 4 x 1 column matrix are nonzero, then a two-point or angular perspective is obtained. The two-point perspective transformation

$$[X \ Y \ Z \ 1] = [x \ y \ z \ 1] \begin{bmatrix} 1 & 0 & 0 & p \\ 0 & 1 & 0 & q \\ 0 & 0 & 1 & 0 \\ 0 & 0 & 0 & 1 \end{bmatrix} = [x \ y \ z \ (px + qy + 1)] \qquad (3\text{-}38)$$

with ordinary coordinates,

$$[x^* \ y^* \ z^* \ 1] = [\frac{x}{px + qy + 1} \ \frac{y}{px + qy + 1} \ \frac{z}{px + qy + 1} \ 1] \qquad (3\text{-}39)$$

results in two vanishing points: one on the x-axis at $[1/p \ 0 \ 0 \ 1]$ and one on the y-axis at $[0 \ 1/q \ 0 \ 1]$. This is shown in Fig. 3-11a, where the results are

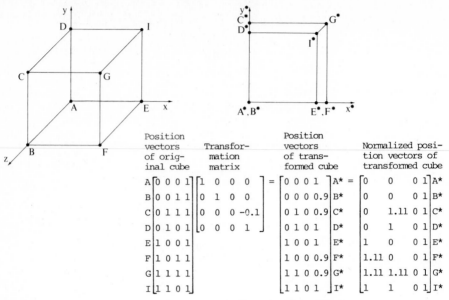

Position vectors of original cube · Transformation matrix · Position vectors of transformed cube · Normalized position vectors of transformed cube

$$
\begin{matrix}
A \\ B \\ C \\ D \\ E \\ F \\ G \\ I
\end{matrix}
\begin{bmatrix}
0 & 0 & 0 & 1 \\
0 & 0 & 1 & 1 \\
0 & 1 & 1 & 1 \\
0 & 1 & 0 & 1 \\
1 & 0 & 0 & 1 \\
1 & 0 & 1 & 1 \\
1 & 1 & 1 & 1 \\
1 & 1 & 0 & 1
\end{bmatrix}
\begin{bmatrix}
1 & 0 & 0 & 0 \\
0 & 1 & 0 & 0 \\
0 & 0 & 0 & -0.1 \\
0 & 0 & 0 & 1
\end{bmatrix}
=
\begin{bmatrix}
0 & 0 & 0 & 1 \\
0 & 0 & 0 & 0.9 \\
0 & 1 & 0 & 0.9 \\
0 & 1 & 0 & 1 \\
1 & 0 & 0 & 1 \\
1 & 0 & 0 & 0.9 \\
1 & 1 & 0 & 0.9 \\
1 & 1 & 0 & 1
\end{bmatrix}
\begin{matrix}
A^* \\ B^* \\ C^* \\ D^* \\ E^* \\ F^* \\ G^* \\ I^*
\end{matrix}
A^* =
\begin{bmatrix}
0 & 0 & 0 & 1 \\
0 & 0 & 0 & 1 \\
0 & 1.11 & 0 & 1 \\
0 & 1 & 0 & 1 \\
1 & 0 & 0 & 1 \\
1.11 & 0 & 0 & 1 \\
1.11 & 1.11 & 0 & 1 \\
1 & 1 & 0 & 1
\end{bmatrix}
\begin{matrix}
A^* \\ B^* \\ C^* \\ D^* \\ E^* \\ F^* \\ G^* \\ I^*
\end{matrix}
$$

a   Noncentered coordinates.

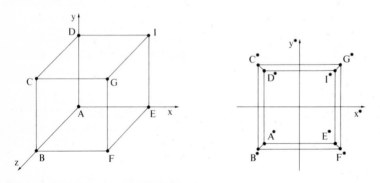

Position vectors of original cube · Translation matrix · Perspective & projection transformation matrix · Position vectors of transformed cube · Normalized position vectors

$$
\begin{matrix}
A \\ B \\ C \\ D \\ E \\ F \\ G \\ I
\end{matrix}
\begin{bmatrix}
0 & 0 & 0 & 1 \\
0 & 0 & 1 & 1 \\
0 & 1 & 1 & 1 \\
0 & 1 & 0 & 1 \\
1 & 0 & 0 & 1 \\
1 & 0 & 1 & 1 \\
1 & 1 & 1 & 1 \\
1 & 1 & 0 & 1
\end{bmatrix}
\begin{bmatrix}
1 & 0 & 0 & 0 \\
0 & 1 & 0 & 0 \\
0 & 0 & 1 & 0 \\
-0.5 & -0.5 & 0 & 1
\end{bmatrix}
\begin{bmatrix}
1 & 0 & 0 & 0 \\
0 & 1 & 0 & 0 \\
0 & 0 & 0 & -0.1 \\
0 & 0 & 0 & 1
\end{bmatrix}
=
\begin{bmatrix}
-0.5 & -0.5 & 0 & 1 \\
-0.5 & -0.5 & 0 & 0.9 \\
-0.5 & 0.5 & 0 & 0.9 \\
-0.5 & 0.5 & 0 & 1 \\
0.5 & -0.5 & 0 & 1 \\
0.5 & -0.5 & 0 & 0.9 \\
0.5 & 0.5 & 0 & 0.9 \\
0.5 & 0.5 & 0 & 1
\end{bmatrix}
\begin{matrix}
A^* \\ B^* \\ C^* \\ D^* \\ E^* \\ F^* \\ G^* \\ I^*
\end{matrix}
A^* =
\begin{bmatrix}
-0.5 & -0.5 & 0 & 1 \\
-0.556 & -0.556 & 0 & 1 \\
-0.556 & -0.556 & 0 & 1 \\
-0.5 & 0.5 & 0 & 1 \\
0.5 & -0.5 & 0 & 1 \\
0.556 & -0.556 & 0 & 1 \\
0.556 & 0.556 & 0 & 1 \\
0.5 & 0.5 & 0 & 1
\end{bmatrix}
\begin{matrix}
A^* \\ B^* \\ C^* \\ D^* \\ E^* \\ F^* \\ G^* \\ I^*
\end{matrix}
$$

b   Centered coordinates.

Figure 3-10 Single-point perspectives with vanishing point at z = -10.

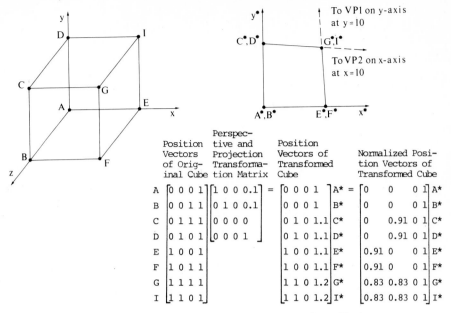

	Position Vectors of Original Cube	Perspective and Projection Transformation Matrix		Position Vectors of Transformed Cube		Normalized Position Vectors of Transformed Cube	
A	[0 0 0 1]	[1 0 0 0.1]	=	[0 0 0 1]	A* =	[0 0 0 1]	A*
B	[0 0 1 1]	[0 1 0 0.1]		[0 0 0 1]	B*	[0 0 0 1]	B*
C	[0 1 1 1]	[0 0 0 0]		[0 1 0 1.1]	C*	[0 0.91 0 1]	C*
D	[0 1 0 1]	[0 0 0 1]		[0 1 0 1.1]	D*	[0 0.91 0 1]	D*
E	[1 0 0 1]			[1 0 0 1.1]	E*	[0.91 0 0 1]	E*
F	[1 0 1 1]			[1 0 0 1.1]	F*	[0.91 0 0 1]	F*
G	[1 1 1 1]			[1 1 0 1.2]	G*	[0.83 0.83 0 1]	G*
I	[1 1 0 1]			[1 1 0 1.2]	I*	[0.83 0.83 0 1]	I*

a   Noncentered coordinates.

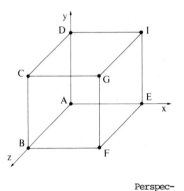

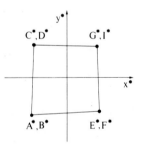

	Position Vectors of Original Cube	Transformation Matrix	Perspective and Projection Transformation Matrix		Position Vectors of Transformed Cube		Normalized Position Vectors of Transformed Cube	
A	[0 0 0 1]	[1 0 0 0]	[1 0 0 0.1]	=	[-0.5 -0.5 0 1]	A* =	[-0.5 -0.5 0 1]	A*
B	[0 0 1 1]	[0 1 0 0]	[0 1 0 0.1]		[-0.5 -0.5 0 1]	B*	[-0.5 -0.5 0 1]	B*
C	[0 1 1 1]	[0 0 1 0]	[0 0 0 0]		[-0.5 0.5 0 1.1]	C*	[-0.455 0.455 0 1]	C*
D	[0 1 0 1]	[-0.5 -0.5 0 1]	[0 0 0 1]		[-0.5 0.5 0 1.1]	D*	[-0.455 0.455 0 1]	D*
E	[1 0 0 1]				[0.5 -0.5 0 1.1]	E*	[0.455 -0.455 0 1]	E*
F	[1 0 1 1]				[0.5 -0.5 0 1.1]	F*	[0.455 -0.455 0 1]	F*
G	[1 1 1 1]				[0.5 0.5 0 1.2]	G*	[0.417 0.417 0 1]	G*
I	[1 1 0 1]				[0.5 0.5 0 1.2]	I*	[0.417 0.417 0 1]	I*

b   Centered coordinates.

Figure 3-11   Two-point perspectives.

projected onto the z = 0 plane. In Fig. 3-11a, the vanishing points are on the
x-axis at x = 10 and on the y-axis at y = 10. If we first center the z-axis
with respect to the front face as shown in Fig. 3-11b, a suitable two-point
perspective is still not obtained. This is due to the fact that the object
should first be rotated about the y-axis in order to attain an esthetically
pleasing two-point persepctive. This is discussed later.

If three terms in the 4 x 1 column matrix are nonzero, then a three-point
or oblique perspective is obtained. The three-point perspective transformation

$$[X\ Y\ Z\ H] = [x\ y\ z\ 1]\begin{bmatrix} 1 & 0 & 0 & p \\ 0 & 1 & 0 & q \\ 0 & 0 & 1 & r \\ 0 & 0 & 0 & 1 \end{bmatrix} = [x\ y\ z\ (px + qy + rz + 1] \qquad (3\text{-}40)$$

with ordinary coordinates

$$[x^*\ y^*\ z^*\ 1] = [\frac{x}{px + qy + rz + 1}\ \frac{y}{px + qy + rz + 1}\ \frac{z}{px + qy + rz + 1}\ 1] \qquad (3\text{-}41)$$

results in three vanishing points: one on the x-axis at [1/p 0 0 1], one on
the y-axis at [0 1/q 0 1], and one on the z-axis at [0 0 1/r 1]. A three-point
perspective view of a unit cube is shown in Fig. 3-12. The results are projected
onto the z = 0 plane. In Fig. 3-12 the three vanishing points are located on
the x-axis at x = 10, on the y-axis at y = 10, and on the z-axis at z = -10.

	Position Vectors of Original Cube	Transformation Matrix		Position Vectors of Transformed Cube		Normalized Position Vectors of Transformed Cube	
A	0 0 0 1	1 0 0 0.1	=	0 0 0 1	A* =	0 0 0 1	A*
B	0 0 1 1	0 1 0 0.1		0 0 0 0.9	B*	0 0 0 1	B*
C	0 1 1 1	0 0 0 -0.1		0 1 0 1	C*	0 1 0 1	C*
D	0 1 0 1	0 0 0 1		0 1 0 1.1	D*	0 0.91 0 1	D*
E	1 0 0 1			1 0 0 1.1	E*	0.91 0 0 1	E*
F	1 0 1 1			1 0 0 1	F*	1 0 0 1	F*
G	1 1 1 1			1 1 0 1.1	G*	0.91 0.91 0 1	G*
I	1 1 0 1			1 1 0 1.2	I*	0.83 0.83 0 1	I*

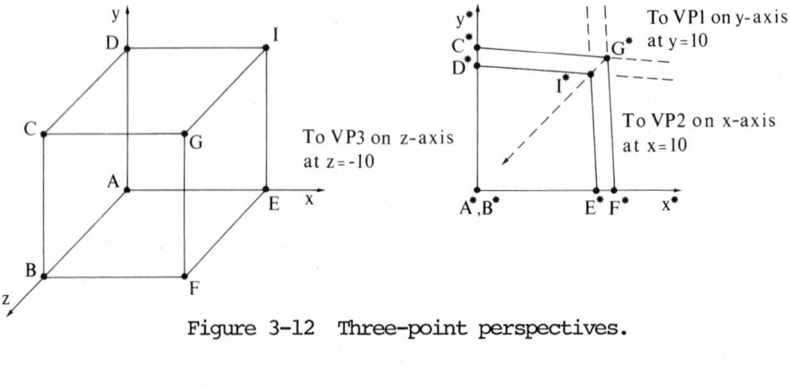

Figure 3-12 Three-point perspectives.

3-12 TECHNIQUES FOR GENERATING PERSPECTIVE VIEWS

When a perspective view of an object is created, the horizontal reference line is normally at eye level, as shown in Fig. 3-13. Vanishing points are then points on the horizon line (eye level) at which parallel lines converge. Figure 3-14a shows how the vanishing points are formed. In general, different sets of parallel lines will have different vanishing points. This is illustrated in Fig. 3-14b. Planes of an object which are tilted in relation to the ground plane have vanishing points which can fall above or below the horizon eye level. These are often called trace points and are shown in Fig. 3-14c.

When viewing a CRT display the position of the viewpoint or eye is normally fixed. Thus, rather than moving the viewpoint to obtain an acceptable perspective view, it is common to manipulate the position and orientation of the object displayed on the CRT. This will normally require one or more rotations and translations of the object.

As we have seen, if the viewing point is on a line normal to the center of a unit cube face, then a single-point perspective "looks right." In this view all receding planes converge to one vanishing point on the horizontal eye-level line, and all perpendiculars are drawn as true verticals. The front and back cube faces are parallel to the picture plan and do not converge.

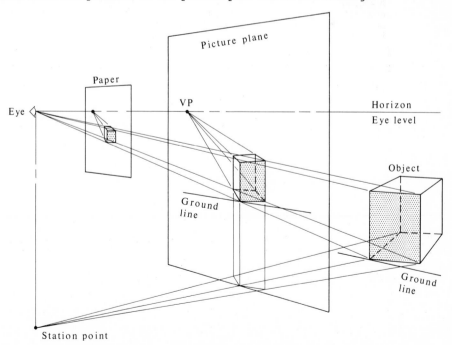

Figure 3-13 Perspective transformation to paper.

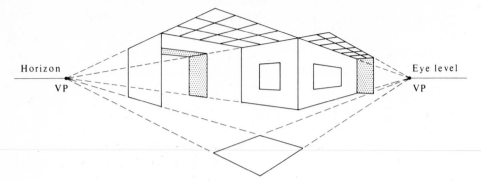

Figure 3-14a   Vanishing points for parallel lines.

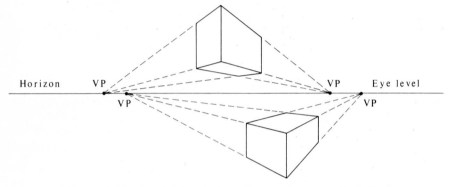

Figure 3-14b   Vanishing points for various parallel lines.

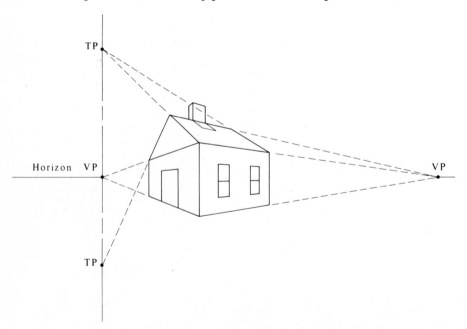

Figure 3-14c   Trace points and vanishing points.

We will now rotate the unit cube about the y-axis and translate it to the point [0 m n]. The resulting figure will then be viewed from a position k on the z-axis and finally projected onto the z = 0 plane. Using Eqs. (3-7), (3-11), and (3-29) with r = 1/k yields

$$
\begin{bmatrix} \cos\theta & 0 & -\sin\theta & 0 \\ 0 & 1 & 0 & 0 \\ \sin\theta & 0 & \cos\theta & 0 \\ 0 & m & n & 1 \end{bmatrix}
\begin{bmatrix} 1 & 0 & 0 & 0 \\ 0 & 1 & 0 & 0 \\ 0 & 0 & 0 & \frac{1}{k} \\ 0 & 0 & 0 & 1 \end{bmatrix}
=
\begin{bmatrix} \cos\theta & 0 & 0 & \frac{-\sin\theta}{k} \\ 0 & 1 & 0 & 0 \\ \sin\theta & 0 & 0 & \frac{\cos\theta}{k} \\ 0 & m & 0 & \frac{n}{k}+1 \end{bmatrix}
$$

Since projection onto the plane z = 0 was desired, the third column of this matrix is all zeros. Notice that two of the three terms in the fourth column which control perspective in the matrix are nonzero. Thus a two-point perspective view will result.

The eight vertices of the unit cube, expressed in homogeneous coordinates, can be represented as an 8 x 4 matrix. Multiplication of this matrix with the above transformation matrix produces the required transformation on each point. This is given by

$$
\begin{bmatrix} 0 & 0 & 0 & 1 \\ 0 & 0 & 1 & 1 \\ 0 & 1 & 1 & 1 \\ 0 & 1 & 0 & 1 \\ 1 & 0 & 0 & 1 \\ 1 & 0 & 1 & 1 \\ 1 & 1 & 1 & 1 \\ 1 & 1 & 0 & 1 \end{bmatrix}
\begin{bmatrix} \cos\theta & 0 & 0 & \frac{-\sin\theta}{k} \\ 0 & 1 & 0 & 0 \\ \sin\theta & 0 & 0 & \frac{\cos\theta}{k} \\ 0 & m & 0 & \frac{n}{k}+1 \end{bmatrix}
=
\begin{bmatrix}
0 & m & 0 & \frac{n}{k}+1 \\
\sin\theta & m & 0 & \frac{\cos\theta}{k}+\frac{n}{k}+1 \\
\sin\theta & 1+m & 0 & \frac{\cos\theta}{k}+\frac{n}{k}+1 \\
0 & 1+m & 0 & \frac{n}{k}+1 \\
\cos\theta & m & 0 & \frac{-\sin\theta}{k}+\frac{n}{k}+1 \\
\cos\theta+\sin\theta & m & 0 & \frac{-\sin\theta}{k}+\frac{\cos\theta}{k}+\frac{n}{k}+1 \\
\cos\theta+\sin\theta & 1+m & 0 & \frac{-\sin\theta}{k}+\frac{\cos\theta}{k}+\frac{n}{k}+1 \\
\cos\theta & 1+m & 0 & \frac{-\sin\theta}{k}+\frac{n}{k}+1
\end{bmatrix}
$$

For θ = 60°, m = 12, n = 1, and k = 1, this matrix of transformed, homogeneous coordinates is

$$
\begin{bmatrix}
0 & -2 & 0 & 2 \\
0.86 & -2 & 0 & 2.5 \\
0.86 & -1 & 0 & 2.5 \\
0 & -1 & 0 & 2 \\
0.5 & -2 & 0 & 1.14 \\
1.36 & -2 & 0 & 1.64 \\
1.36 & -1 & 0 & 1.64 \\
0.5 & -1 & 0 & 1.14
\end{bmatrix}
$$

Then, since

$$[x^* \ y^* \ 1] = [\tfrac{X}{H} \ \tfrac{Y}{H} \ 1]$$

the projected points x*, y* are given by

$$\begin{bmatrix} 0 & -1.0 \\ 0.344 & -0.8 \\ 0.344 & -0.4 \\ 0 & -0.5 \\ 0.44 & -1.75 \\ 0.83 & -1.22 \\ 0.83 & -0.61 \\ 0.44 & -0.88 \end{bmatrix}$$

The transformed cube is shown in Fig. 3-15.   Observe what has happened to
the parallel sides of the cube.   Lines which were initially parallel to the x-
and z-axes respectively now intersect at one of the two vanishing points.   The
intersections of the initial parallel lines occured at infinity.   They now occur
at finite values along the x*-axis.   Only lines initially parallel to the y-axis
remain parallel after the transformation.

Following similar logic, a three-point perspective can be created and
viewed from a position k on the z-axis by first performing rotations about two

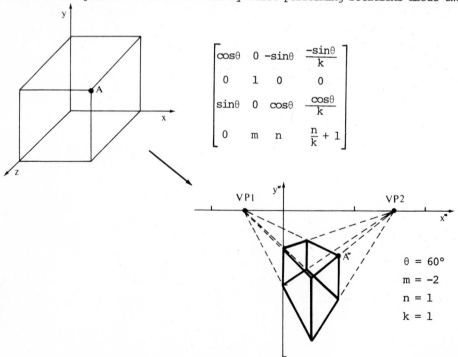

$$\begin{bmatrix} \cos\theta & 0 & -\sin\theta & \dfrac{-\sin\theta}{k} \\ 0 & 1 & 0 & 0 \\ \sin\theta & 0 & \cos\theta & \dfrac{\cos\theta}{k} \\ 0 & m & n & \dfrac{n}{k}+1 \end{bmatrix}$$

$\theta = 60°$

$m = -2$

$n = 1$

$k = 1$

Figure 3-15   Perspective transformation.

different axes. For example, one might rotate θ degrees about the y-axis and then ϕ degrees about the x-axis before applying the perspective transformation. A complete set of transformations on a unit cube to obtain a three-point perspective is then

$$
\begin{bmatrix} 1 & 0 & 0 & 0 \\ 0 & 1 & 0 & 0 \\ 0 & 0 & 1 & 0 \\ \ell & m & n & 1 \end{bmatrix}
\begin{bmatrix} \cos\theta & 0 & -\sin\theta & 0 \\ 0 & 1 & 0 & 0 \\ \sin\theta & 0 & \cos\theta & 0 \\ 0 & 0 & 0 & 1 \end{bmatrix}
\begin{bmatrix} 1 & 0 & 0 & 0 \\ 0 & \cos\phi & \sin\phi & 0 \\ 0 & -\sin\phi & \cos\phi & 0 \\ 0 & 0 & 0 & 1 \end{bmatrix}
\begin{bmatrix} 1 & 0 & 0 & 0 \\ 0 & 1 & 0 & 0 \\ 0 & 0 & 0 & \frac{1}{k} \\ 0 & 0 & 0 & 1 \end{bmatrix}
=
\begin{bmatrix} \cos\theta & \sin\theta\sin\phi & 0 & \frac{-1}{k}\sin\theta\cos\phi \\ 0 & \cos\phi & 0 & \frac{1}{k}\sin\phi \\ \sin\theta & -\cos\theta\sin\phi & 0 & \frac{1}{k}\cos\theta\cos\phi \\ \ell\cos\theta + n\sin\theta & m\cos\phi + (\ell\sin\theta - n\cos\theta)\sin\phi & 0 & (1 + \frac{m\sin\phi + \ell\sin\theta + n\cos\theta}{k}) \end{bmatrix}
$$

3-13 POINTS AT INFINITY

To show more clearly what has happened to points at infinity, consider the following example.

Example 3-1: PERSPECTIVE TRANSFORMATION

Three points are given by [1 0 0 0], [0 1 0 0], and [0 0 1 0]. These vectors represent points at infinity on the x-, y-, and z-axes respectively. Now, performing the two-point perspective transformation, given by,

$$
\begin{bmatrix} 1 & 0 & 0 & 0 \\ 0 & 1 & 0 & 0 \\ 0 & 0 & 1 & 0 \end{bmatrix}
\begin{bmatrix} 0.5 & 0 & 0 & -0.86 \\ 0 & 1 & 0 & 0 \\ 0.86 & 0 & 0 & 0.5 \\ 0 & -2 & 0 & 2 \end{bmatrix}
=
\begin{bmatrix} 0.5 & 0 & 0 & -0.86 \\ 0 & 1 & 0 & 0 \\ 0.86 & 0 & 0 & 0.5 \end{bmatrix}
$$

Thus, the point at $x = \infty$ transforms to $x^* = 0.5/-0.86 = -0.58$ and $y^* = 0$. This is the vanishing point VP1 in Fig. 3-15. The point at $y = \infty$ transforms to $y^* = \infty$, and the point $z = \infty$ transforms to $x^* = 0.86/0.5 = 1.7$ and $y^* = 0$. This is the vanishing point VP2 in Fig. 3-15. The result is that points at infinity in one coordinate system have been transformed to finite points in a second system by use of homogeneous coordinates.

To further clarify this important characteristic of homogeneous coordinates, we again consider the transformation of a line parallel to the z-axis onto the x*z*-plane. The line AB is shown in Fig. 3-9. Applying a perspective transformation matrix to a general point on the line gives

$$[X\ Y\ Z\ H] = [x\ y\ z\ 1]\begin{bmatrix}1 & 0 & 0 & 0\\ 0 & 1 & 0 & 0\\ 0 & 0 & 1 & \frac{1}{k}\\ 0 & 0 & 0 & 1\end{bmatrix} = [x\ y\ z\ (\frac{z}{k}+1)]$$

$$[x^*\ y^*\ z^*\ 1] = \begin{bmatrix}\dfrac{x}{(\frac{z}{k}+1)} & \dfrac{y}{(\frac{z}{k}+1)} & \dfrac{z}{(\frac{z}{k}+1)} & 1\end{bmatrix}$$

This operation (with $k = 1/4$) transforms the initial line AB to the line A*B* shown in Fig. 3-9. A*B* lies on a line which passes through a vanishing point at $[0\ 0\ k]$. When the z-coordinate is neglected, the line A*B* is projected onto the plane $z^* = 0$, as shown by line A'B'. The net result is a projection from the line AB onto the plane $z^* = 0$, from a center of projection at $[0\ 0\ -k]$. Notice the symmetry of the vanishing point and the center of projection.

An algorithm which will generate a general perspective view is given in Appendix C.

3-14 RECONSTRUCTION OF THREE-DIMENSIONAL INFORMATION

The reconstruction of a three-dimensional object or position in space is a common problem. It occurs continuously in utilizing mechanical drawings which are orthographic projections. The method of reconstructing a three-dimensional object or position from two or more views (orthographic projections) given on a mechanical drawing is well known. However, the technique of reconstructing a three-dimensional position vector from two perspective projections, for example, two photographs is not as well known. Of course if the method is valid for perspective projections, then it is also valid for the simpler orthographic projections, and in fact for all the projections mentioned above. Further, as we will show below, if certain other information is available, then no direct knowledge is required about the transformation.

Recall that the general perspective transformation can be represented as a general 4 x 4 matrix. Thus

$$[x\ y\ z\ 1]T' = [X\ Y\ Z\ H] \tag{3-42}$$

where

$$T' = \begin{bmatrix}T'_{11} & T'_{12} & T'_{13} & T'_{14}\\ T'_{21} & T'_{22} & T'_{23} & T'_{24}\\ T'_{31} & T'_{32} & T'_{33} & T'_{34}\\ T'_{41} & T'_{42} & T'_{43} & T'_{44}\end{bmatrix}$$

The results can be projected onto a two-dimensional plane, say, $z = 0$ by using

Eq. (3-28), i.e.,

$$T'' = \begin{bmatrix} 1 & 0 & 0 & 0 \\ 0 & 1 & 0 & 0 \\ 0 & 0 & 0 & 0 \\ 0 & 0 & 0 & 1 \end{bmatrix} \tag{3-28}$$

Concatenation of the two matrices yields

$$T = T''T' = \begin{bmatrix} T_{11} & T_{12} & 0 & T_{14} \\ T_{21} & T_{22} & 0 & T_{24} \\ T_{31} & T_{32} & 0 & T_{34} \\ T_{41} & T_{42} & 0 & T_{44} \end{bmatrix} \tag{3-43}$$

It is useful to write the transformation, say,

$$[x \ y \ z \ 1] \begin{bmatrix} T_{11} & T_{12} & 0 & T_{14} \\ T_{21} & T_{22} & 0 & T_{24} \\ T_{31} & T_{32} & 0 & T_{34} \\ T_{41} & T_{42} & 0 & T_{44} \end{bmatrix} = [X \ Y \ 0 \ H] \tag{3-44}$$

$$= H[x^* \ y^* \ 0 \ 1] \tag{3-45}$$

Note that x^* and y^* are the coordinates in the perspective projection onto the $z = 0$ plane. The same procedure could be accomplished using projections onto the $x = 0$ or $y = 0$ planes.

Writing out Eq. (3-45) yields

$$T_{11}x + T_{21}y + T_{31}z + T_{41} = Hx^* \tag{3-46a}$$

$$T_{12}x + T_{22}y + T_{32}z + T_{42} = Hy^* \tag{3-46b}$$

$$T_{14}x + T_{24}y + T_{34}z + T_{44} = H \tag{3-46c}$$

Using H from Eq. (3-46c) and substituting yields

$$(T_{11} - T_{14}x^*)x + (T_{21} - T_{24}x^*)y + (T_{31} - T_{34}x^*)z + (T_{41} - T_{44}x^*) = 0 \tag{3-47a}$$

$$(T_{12} - T_{14}y^*)x + (T_{22} - T_{24}y^*)y + (T_{32} - T_{34}y^*)z + (T_{42} - T_{44}y^*) = 0 \tag{3-47b}$$

As suggested by Sutherland (Ref. 3-9) this pair of equations can be considered in three different ways. First assume T and x, y, z are known. Then there are two equations in the two unknowns x^* and y^*. Thus, they may be used to solve directly for the coordinates of the perspective projection. This is the approach taken in all the previous discussions in this chapter.

Alternately T, x^*, y^* can be assumed known. In this case we have two equations in the three unknown space coordinates x, y, z. The system of equations cannot be solved. However, if two perspective projections say two photographics are available, then Eq. (3-47) may be written for both projections.

This yields

$$(T_{11}^1 - T_{14}^1 x^{*1})x + (T_{21}^1 - T_{24}^1 x^{*1})y + (T_{31}^1 - T_{34}^1 x^{*1})z + (T_{41}^1 - T_{44}^1 x^{*1}) = 0$$

$$(T_{12}^1 - T_{14}^1 y^{*1})x + (T_{22}^1 - T_{24}^1 y^{*1})y + (T_{32}^1 - T_{34}^1 y^{*1})z + (T_{42}^1 - T_{44}^1 y^{*1}) = 0$$

$$(T_{11}^2 - T_{14}^2 x^{*2})x + (T_{21}^2 - T_{24}^2 x^{*2})y + (T_{31}^2 - T_{34}^2 x^{*2})z + (T_{41}^2 - T_{44}^2 x^{*2}) = 0$$

$$(T_{12}^2 - T_{14}^2 y^{*2})x + (T_{22}^2 - T_{24}^2 y^{*2})y + (T_{32}^2 - T_{34}^2 y^{*2})z + (T_{42}^2 - T_{44}^2 y^{*2}) = 0$$

where the superscripts 1 and 2 indicate the first and second perspective projection views. Note that the transformations T^1 and T^2 need not be the same. These equations may be rewritten in matrix form as

$$[A][X] = [B] \tag{3-48}$$

where

$$[A] = \begin{bmatrix} T_{11}^1 - T_{14}^1 x^{*1} & T_{21}^1 - T_{24}^1 x^{*1} & T_{31}^1 - T_{34}^1 x^{*1} \\ T_{12}^1 - T_{14}^1 x^{*1} & T_{22}^1 - T_{24}^1 y^{*1} & T_{32}^1 - T_{34}^1 y^{*1} \\ T_{11}^2 - T_{14}^2 x^{*2} & T_{21}^2 - T_{24}^2 x^{*2} & T_{31}^2 - T_{34}^2 x^{*2} \\ T_{12}^2 - T_{14}^2 y^{*2} & T_{22}^2 - T_{24}^2 y^{*2} & T_{32}^2 - T_{34}^2 y^{*2} \end{bmatrix}$$

$$[X]^T = [x\ y\ z\ ]$$

$$[B]^T = [T_{44}^1 x^{*1} - T_{41}^1 \quad T_{44}^1 y^{*1} - T_{42}^1 \quad T_{44}^2 x^{*2} - T_{41}^2 \quad T_{44}^2 y^{*2} - T_{42}^2]$$

Equation (3-48) represents four equations in the three unknown space coordinates x,y,z. The problem is over specified and thus can be solved only in some mean or best fit sense.* This is an extremely powerful technique for obtaining three-dimensional positional data.

Example 3-2:   THREE-DIMENSIONAL RECONSTRUCTION

Assume that the measured position of a point in one perspective projection is [0.3763 -0.8258 0 1] and in a second perspective projection is [0.6548 0 0.2886 1]. The first perspective projection transformation is known to be the result of a 30° rotation about the y-axis followed by a 60° rotation

---

*A mean squares fit can be computed by solving the equation

$$[A]^T[A][X] = [A]^T[B]$$

where $[A]^T[A]$ is square and of the correct dimension for [B]. In particular $[X] = [[A]^T[A]]^{-1}[A]^T[B]$. Note that if no solution results, then the imposed conditions are redundant and no unique solution which gives a "least" error condition exists.

about the x-axis plus a translation of 2 units in the negative y-direction. The point of projection is at $z = 1$, and the result is projected onto the $z = 0$ plane.

The second perspective projection is the result of a 30° rotation about the x- and y-axes. The point of projection is at $y = 1$, and the result is projected onto the $y = 0$ plane. T^1 and T^2 are thus

$$T^1 = \begin{bmatrix} 0.5 & 0 & 0 & -0.867 \\ 0 & 1 & 0 & 0 \\ 0.867 & 0 & 0 & 0.5 \\ 0 & -2 & 0 & 2 \end{bmatrix} \text{ and } T^2 = \begin{bmatrix} 0.867 & 0 & -0.5 & 0 \\ 0.25 & 0 & 0.433 & 0.867 \\ 0.433 & 0 & 0.75 & -0.5 \\ 0 & 0 & 0 & 1 \end{bmatrix}$$

The A-matrix is then

$$[A] = \begin{bmatrix} 0.826252 & 0 & 0.67885 \\ -0.715969 & 1 & 0.4129 \\ 0.867 & -0.317712 & 0.7604 \\ -0.5 & 0.182784 & -0.8943 \end{bmatrix}$$

and

$$[B]^T = [0.7526 \ 0.3484 \ 0.6548 \ 0.2886]$$

solution yields $X = [0.5 \ 0.5 \ 0.5]$, i.e., the center of a unit cube.

An algorithm which utilizes this technique is given in Appendix C.

As a third way of considering Eq. (3-47) we note that if the location of several points which appear in the perspective projection are known in object space and in the perspective projection, then it is possible to determine the transformation elements, i.e., the T_{ij}'s. These transformation elements can subsequently be used to determine the location of unknown points using the technique described above. To see this we again examine Eq. (3-46), which may be rewritten as

$$T_{11}x + T_{21}y + T_{31}z + T_{41} - T_{14}xx^* - T_{24}yx^* - T_{34}zx^* - T_{44}x^* = 0 \qquad (3\text{-}49a)$$

$$T_{12}x + T_{22}y + T_{32}z + T_{42} - T_{14}xy^* - T_{24}yy^* - T_{34}zy^* + T_{44}y^* = 0 \qquad (3\text{-}49b)$$

Assuming that x^* and y^* as well as x, y, z are known, the Eqs. (3-49a,b) represent two equations in the 12 unknown transformation elements T_{ij}. Applying these equations to six noncoplanar known locations in object space and in the perspective projection yields a system of 12 equations in 12 unknowns. These equations can be solved for the T_{ij}'s. Thus we have determined the transformation. Notice that in this case no prior knowledge of the transformation is required. If, for example, the perspectice projections are photographs, neither the location nor the orientation of the camera is required.

In matrix form the system of 12 equations can be written as

$$\begin{bmatrix}
x_1 & 0 & -x_1x_1^* & y_1 & 0 & -y_1x_1^* & z_1 & 0 & -z_1x_1^* & 1 & 0 & x_1^* \\
0 & x_1 & -x_1y_1^* & 0 & y_1 & -y_1y_1^* & 0 & z_1 & -z_1y_1^* & 0 & 1 & y_1^* \\
x_2 & 0 & -x_2x_2^* & y_2 & 0 & -y_2x_2^* & z_2 & 0 & -z_2x_2^* & 1 & 0 & x_2^* \\
0 & x_2 & -x_2y_2^* & 0 & y_2 & -y_2y_2^* & 0 & z_2 & -z_2y_2^* & 0 & 1 & y_2^* \\
x_3 & 0 & -x_3x_3^* & y_3 & 0 & -y_3x_3^* & z_3 & 0 & -z_3x_3^* & 1 & 0 & x_3^* \\
0 & x_3 & -x_3y_3^* & 0 & y_3 & -y_3y_3^* & 0 & z_3 & -z_3y_3^* & 0 & 1 & y_3^* \\
x_4 & 0 & -x_4x_4^* & y_4 & 0 & -y_4x_4^* & z_4 & 0 & -z_4x_4^* & 1 & 0 & x_4^* \\
0 & x_4 & -x_4y_4^* & 0 & y_4 & -y_4y_4^* & 0 & z_4 & -z_4y_4^* & 0 & 1 & y_4^* \\
x_5 & 0 & -x_5x_5^* & y_5 & 0 & -y_5x_5^* & z_5 & 0 & -z_5x_5^* & 1 & 0 & x_5^* \\
0 & x_5 & -x_5y_5^* & 0 & y_5 & -y_5y_5^* & 0 & z_5 & -z_5y_5^* & 0 & 1 & y_5^* \\
x_6 & 0 & -x_6x_6^* & y_6 & 0 & -y_6x_6^* & z_6 & 0 & -z_6x_6^* & 1 & 0 & x_6^* \\
0 & x_6 & -x_6y_6^* & 0 & y_6 & -y_6y_6^* & 0 & z_6 & -z_6y_6^* & 0 & 1 & y_6^*
\end{bmatrix}
\begin{bmatrix}
T_{11} \\ T_{12} \\ T_{14} \\ T_{21} \\ T_{22} \\ T_{24} \\ T_{31} \\ T_{32} \\ T_{34} \\ T_{41} \\ T_{42} \\ T_{44}
\end{bmatrix} = 0 \qquad (3\text{-}50)$$

where the subscripts correspond to points with known locations. Equations (3-50) can be written in more compact form as

$$[A'] \, [T] = 0$$

Since Eqs. (3-50) are homogeneous, they will contain an arbitrary scale factor. Hence T_{44} may, for example, be defined as unity and the resulting transformation normalized. This reduces the requirement to 11 equations or 5 1/2 points. If the transformation is normalized, then the last column in $[A']$ is moved to the right-hand side and the nonhomogeneous matrix equation is solved.

Example 3-3:   ELEMENTS FOR RECONSTRUCTION

As a specific example, consider the unit cube with the six known corner points in the physical plane given by

$$[P] = \begin{bmatrix}
0 & 0 & 0 \\
0 & 0 & 1 \\
0 & 1 & 1 \\
0 & 1 & 0 \\
1 & 0 & 0 \\
1 & 0 & 1
\end{bmatrix}$$

the corresponding points in the transformed view are given by

$$[P*] = \begin{bmatrix} 0 & -1 \\ 0.344 & -0.8 \\ 0.344 & -0.4 \\ 0 & -0.5 \\ 0.44 & -1.75 \\ 0.83 & -1.22 \end{bmatrix}$$

Equation (3-48) then becomes

$$\begin{bmatrix} 0 & 0 & 0 & 0 & 0 & 0 & 0 & 0 & 0 & 1 & 0 & 0 \\ 0 & 0 & 0 & 0 & 0 & 0 & 0 & 0 & 0 & 0 & 1 & -1 \\ 0 & 0 & 0 & 0 & 0 & 0 & 1 & 0 & -0.344 & 1 & 0 & 0.344 \\ 0 & 0 & 0 & 0 & 0 & 0 & 0 & 1 & 0.8 & 0 & 1 & -0.8 \\ 0 & 0 & 0 & 1 & 0 & -0.344 & 1 & 0 & -0.344 & 1 & 0 & 0.344 \\ 0 & 0 & 0 & 0 & 1 & 0.4 & 0 & 1 & 0.4 & 0 & 1 & -0.4 \\ 0 & 0 & 0 & 1 & 0 & 0 & 0 & 0 & 0 & 1 & 0 & 0 \\ 0 & 0 & 0 & 0 & 1 & 0.5 & 0 & 0 & 0 & 0 & 1 & -0.5 \\ 1 & 0 & -0.44 & 0 & 0 & 0 & 0 & 0 & 0 & 1 & 0 & 0.44 \\ 0 & 1 & 1.75 & 0 & 0 & 0 & 0 & 0 & 0 & 0 & 1 & -1.75 \\ 1 & 0 & -0.83 & 0 & 0 & 0 & 1 & 0 & -0.83 & 1 & 0 & 0.83 \\ 0 & 1 & 1.22 & 0 & 0 & 0 & 0 & 1 & 1.22 & 0 & 1 & -1.22 \end{bmatrix} \begin{bmatrix} T_{11} \\ T_{12} \\ T_{14} \\ T_{21} \\ T_{22} \\ T_{24} \\ T_{31} \\ T_{32} \\ T_{34} \\ T_{41} \\ T_{42} \\ T_{44} \end{bmatrix} = 0$$

Solution yields

$$[T] = \begin{bmatrix} 0.25 \\ 0 \\ -0.43 \\ 0 \\ 0.5 \\ 0 \\ 0.43 \\ 0 \\ 0.25 \\ 0 \\ -1 \\ 1 \end{bmatrix}$$

An algorithm which utilizes this technique is given in Appendix C.

3-15 STEREOGRAPHIC PROJECTION

Once an object has been transformed to a desired position, many techniques can be used to actually display the object. Techniques such as shading, coloring, etc., are frequently device-dependent and are beyond the scope of this book. Others, such as hidden-line removal and clipping can be accomplished in either software or hardware. Another useful display technique is the use of stereo pairs to create the illusion of depth. Often stereographic projection can be used for this purpose rather than hidden-line removal. Graphical output of engineering structures such as bridges and towers lend themselves nicely to stereographic projection. Also, the representation of three-dimensional arrangements such as piping systems, architectural designs, medical x-ray studies, the chemical structure of organic molecules, and solid crystal configurations can be improved by the use of stereographic projection.

In a stereographic projection, a separate perspective view must be created for each eye. Then a stereo viewer such as shown in Fig. 3-16 can be used to view the apparent single three-dimensional object. If desired, a stereo viewer can be designed and attached directly to the computer controlled output device.

For a human with average eyesight, the strongest stereo effect occurs at a distance of about 50 cm in front of the eyes. Thus, for an eye separation of

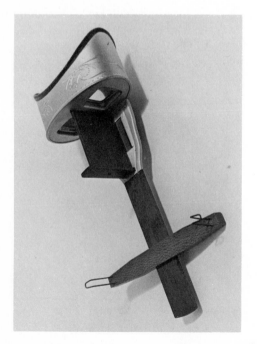

Figure 3-16 Stereo viewer.

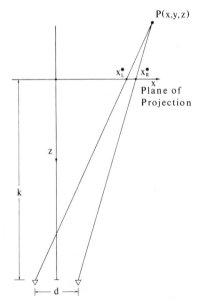

Figure 3-17 Stereographic perspectives.

5.0 cm, the stereo angle is $\varepsilon = \tan^{-1}(5/50) = 5.71°$. For a stereo viewer we let d be the scaled separation distance between the eyes (cf Fig. 3-17). If the viewer has a focal length of k units, then the value of d is fixed by the requirement $\tan^{-1}(d/k) = 5.71°$. Thus, $d = k/10$ is required to maintain the correct stereo angle ε. To obtain this scaled eye-separation distance from a single view of the object, a $+d/2 = +k/20$ horizontal translation is performed before creating the left-eye perpsective view and a $-d/2 = -k/20$ horizontal translation is performed before creating the right-eye perspective view.

Before generating a stereographic projection it is convenient to center the object with respect to the z-axis and then rotate it about the y-axis in preparation for a two-point perspective, or about y and x in preparation for a three-point perspective. One final precaution is advisable. Rotation may cause some of the points to be behind the point of observation, $z = k$. These over the shoulder points cause a distortion of perspective views. To prevent this a final translation in the negative z-direction can be made to ensure that all points on the object lie on or behind the x*y*-plane, e.g., $-z* \le 0$. These preliminary operations result in new position vectors which describe the trans-formed initial object.

To create a stereo pair, the matrix containing the new position vectors is transformed by use of the two matrices

$$
\overset{\text{Left eye}}{\begin{bmatrix} 1 & 0 & 0 & 0 \\ 0 & 1 & 0 & 0 \\ 0 & 0 & 0 & -\dfrac{1}{k} \\ \dfrac{k}{20} & 0 & 0 & 1 \end{bmatrix}}
\qquad
\overset{\text{Right eye}}{\begin{bmatrix} 1 & 0 & 0 & 0 \\ 0 & 1 & 0 & 0 \\ 0 & 0 & 0 & -\dfrac{1}{k} \\ -\dfrac{k}{20} & 0 & 0 & 0 \end{bmatrix}}
$$

This creates two separate perspective views, one for the left eye and one for the right eye. At this intermediate step the left-eye view is to the right of the origin, and the right-eye view is to the left, as shown in Fig. 3-18.

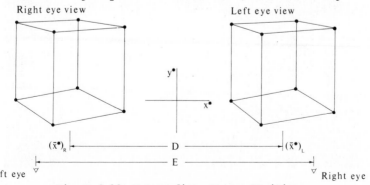

Figure 3-18 Intermediate Stereo Position.

The last operation is to separate the two perspective views by the proper distance along the x-axis in order to place each view directly in front of the proper eye. As shown in Fig. 3-18, $(\bar{x}^*)_R$ is the average value between the largest and smallest value of x^*_R and $(\bar{x}^*)_L$ is the average value between the largest and smallest value of x^*_L. We let $D = (\bar{x}^*)_L - (\bar{x}^*)_R$. The value of D must be calculated by searching the normalized x^*-values of each perspective view.

A final horizontal translation in the x-direction of $L = D + (E - D)/2$ for the right-eye view and $-L$ for the left-eye view places the stereo pair in proper position. The value of E is the actual eye separation distance for the human observer, *measured in the scale of the output device.* For example, if the final points for the right-eye view fall between $2 \leq x^*_R \leq 4$, and the final points for the left-eye view fall between $-4 \leq x^*_L \leq -2$, then one might choose to plot these two views on a standard sheet of paper, using a 10-unit scale between $-5 \leq x^* \leq 5$. Then, the actual 5-cm distance between human eyes measured relative to this scale would be about $E = 2.5$. One or two iterations may be useful to determine the best value of E to use.

An algorithm to generate a stereo pair for an object which has been positioned and rotated to form the desired view and perspective is given in Appendix C. It uses the left and right stereo matrix pair presented above to

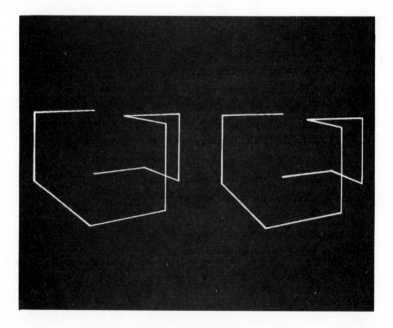

Figure 3-19 Simple stereo view.

create the two perspectives and a final translation matrix to generate the required eye separation distance.

An example of a stereo view of a simple three-dimensional wire frame generated using the STEREO subprogram of Appendix C is shown in Fig. 3-19. The position vectors describing the wire frame are

$$\begin{bmatrix} 0 & 0 & 0 \\ 1 & 0 & 0 \\ 1 & 0 & 1 \\ 1 & 1 & 1 \\ 0 & 1 & 1 \\ 0 & 1 & 2 \\ 0 & 0 & 2 \\ -1 & 0 & 2 \\ -1 & 0 & 0 \\ -1 & 1 & 0 \\ 0 & 1 & 0 \end{bmatrix}$$

Prior to calling the STEREO subprogram, this data was first translated by using subprogram 3DTRANS (Appendix C, Sec. C-10), with $\ell = -0.5$, $m = -1.5$, and $n = -0.5$. Then a 20° rotation about the y-axis was performed in preparation for a two-point perspective. The subprogram 3DYROT (Appendix C, Sec. C-7) was used for this operation. At this point a computer search showed that the maximum z-value was 1.9226. Then 3DTRANS was used again with $\ell = 0$, $m = 0$ and $n = -1.9226$ to place the object behind the x*y*-plane. At this point STEREO (Appendix C, Sec. C-17) was called, using $k = 4$ and $E = 2$. This resulted in the stereo pair shown in Fig. 3-19. However, a final overall scaling was applied to produce Fig. 3-19 in order to fit the output to a particular storage tube CRT.

References

3-1 Roberts, L.G., "Homogeneous Matrix Representation and Manipulation of N-Dimensional Constructs," Document MS 1405, Lincoln Laboratory, M.I.T., Cambridge, Massachusetts, May 1965.

3-2 Ahuja, D. V., and Coons, S. A., "Geometry for Construction and Display," IBM Syst. J., vol. 7, nos. 3 and 4, pp. 188-205, 1968.

3-3 Woodsford, P. A., "The Design and Implementation of the GINO 3D Graphics Software Package," Software-Pract. Exper., vol. 1, 1971.

3-4 Woodsford, P. A., "GINO-Design and Implementation," CAD Group Doc. 27, UML, Cambridge University, 1969.

3-5   Coons, S.A., "Transformation and Matrices," unpublished notes, University of Michigan Short Course in Computer Aided Design, 1971.

3-6   Forrest, A. R., "Co-ordinates, Transformations, and Visualization Techniques," CAD Group Doc. 23, Cambridge University, June 1969.

3-7   Forrest, A. R., "Computational Geometry," Proc. Roy. Soc. (London), vol. A321, pp. 187-195, 1971.

3-8   Kubert, B., Szabo, J., and Giulieri, S., "The Perspective Representation of Functions of Two Variables," J. Assoc. Comput. Mach., vol. 15, 2, pp. 193-204, April 1968.

3-9   Sutherland, I. E., "Three Dimensional Data Input by Tablet," Proc. IEEE, vol. 62, 2, pp. 453-461, April 1974.

CHAPTER 4

PLANE CURVES

4-1 Introduction

Today a multitude of techniques are available for manually drawing and designing curves. The instrument used can be chosen from a wide variety of pencils, pens, brushes, knives, etc. A compass, straight edge, French curve, ships curves, splines, templates, and many other mechanical devices, as well as models, color charts, and perspective grids, may be used to assist in the construction of a curve. A great many different techniques and tools for curve generation and display will also be needed when using computer graphics. Some of the ideas that have proven useful for generating plane, two-dimensional curves are discussed in this chapter.

The previous two chapters have treated the transformation of points. A curve may be presented by a collection of points, provided they are closely spaced as the radius of curvature decreases. However, there are several reasons why a mathematical representation of a curve has an advantage over its representation by a grid of points. Some of these are

1. A mathematical representation is precise, and the properties of the curve such as slope and radius of curvature can be easily calculated.

2. A mathematical representation can be compactly stored in a computer.

3. Drawings of an object represented mathematically in a computer can

be easily produced.

4. When curves are analytically defined over the region of interest, no interpolation scheme is needed to compute intermediate points.

5. The use of points to represent curves has proven difficult when it is desirable to continually alter the shape of the curves to meet certain design criteria. A mathematical representation of the curves has proven much more useful for this purpose.

We now consider various techniques for mathematically representing two-dimensional curves.

4-2 NONPARAMETRIC CURVES

Either a parametric or a nonparametric form can be used to represent a curve mathematically. A nonparametric expression can be explicit or implicit in form. For a plane curve, the explicit, nonparametric expression takes the form

$$y = f(x) \qquad (4-1)$$

In this form there is only one y-value for each x-value. For this reason the explicit form cannot represent closed or multiple-valued curves. This limitation can be overcome by using an implicit expression of the form

$$f(x,y) = 0 \qquad (4-2)$$

However, a point on an implicit curve segment must be calculated by finding the correct root of an algebraic equation. The determination of roots of implicit curves sometimes requires lengthy calculations.

Both explicit and implicit nonparametric curves are axis-dependent. Thus, the choice of the coordinate system can affect the ease of using the curves and calculating their properties. In spite of these limitations, nonparametric curves have been used with success (cf Refs. 4-1 and 4-2). Simple second-and third-degree equations provide a wide variety of curve forms.

From a mathematical point of view, the problem of defining a curve from a known set of data points is one of interpolation. The curve can be made to pass through all known points by use of polynomial interpolation. This requires determining the coefficients in the mathematical equation for a polynomial of some degree. The actual shape between the data points depends upon the order of the polynomial and the mathematical boundary conditions which are applied.

On the other hand, if the data points are only approximations to some unknown "true" values, then a curve is required which indicates the correct trend of the data. In general this curve may pass through only a few data points and, in fact, may not pass through any of the data points. This requirement exists when a curve is needed to fit (interpolate) data obtained from experimental measurements or other observed data. This curve fit gives estimated values over the range of observation.

When the data points inherently contain uncertainties, the method of least squares approximation is a commonly used curve fitting (or curve fairing) technique. This technique produces a curve fit of prescribed form $y = f(x)$ which minimizes the sum of squared y-deviations between the observed and estimated values. The prescribed form is usually based on a knowledge of the physical phenomenon which produced the data.

Commonly prescribed explicit, nonparametric forms used in the least squares technique are power functions, exponential functions, and polynomials. A power function might be prescribed as $y = ax^b$ and an exponential form as $y = ae^{bx}$, where a and b are constants. A general polynomial has the form $y = c_1 + c_2x + c_3x^2 + \ldots + c_{m+1}x^m$. Regardless of the prescribed curve form, the least squares technique requires solving a set of simultaneous, linear algebraic equations in order to determine the unknown constants in the prescribed equation.

Most computer facilities have library programs for least square curve fitting. Reference 4-3 contains a well documented BASIC algorithm which implements this technique. For the remainder of this chapter we consider plane curves which pass through the specified data points.

A general second-degree, implicit equation is written as

$$ax^2 + 2bxy + cy^2 + 2dx + 2ey + f = 0 \qquad (4\text{-}3)$$

If the curve is defined relative to a local coordinate system and passes through the origin, then $f = 0$. By defining the constant coefficients a, b, c, d, e, and f, several types of plane curves can be produced. Boundary conditions are used to establish a particular curve through specific points, as shown below.

If we now choose $c = 1.0$ in the general equation, then to define a curve segment between two points, five independent conditions must be specified to determine the values of the remaining five coefficients. One choice is to specify the position of the two end points, the slope of the curve segment at each end point, and an intermediate point through which the curve must pass.

If, instead, we specify $b = 0$ and $c = 1.0$, then the analytical description of the resulting curve is fixed by specifying only four additional conditions, such as the two end points and the two end slopes. An even simpler curve can be defined by first setting $a = 1.0$, $b = 0$, and $c = 1.0$. Then the form of the curve is given by

$$x^2 + y^2 + 2dx + 2ey + f = 0 \qquad (4\text{-}4)$$

The three conditions required to fix d, e, and f can be the two end points and either the slope at the beginning or the slope at the end of the curve segment.

Another choice is to specify the two end points and a third internal point through which the curve must pass.

A straight line is obtained by setting a = b = c = 0. Then the equation is

$$dx + ey + f = 0 \tag{4-5}$$

or

$$y = -\left(\frac{d}{e}\right)x - \frac{f}{e} = mx + b \tag{4-6}$$

where m is the slope of the straight line. The values of m and b are fixed by specifying the two end points of the line.

To create an inflection point in the curve segment, it is necessary to use a higher order curve such as a cubic. This curve form can be expressed by

$$a + bx + cx^2 + dx^3 - y = 0 \tag{4-7}$$

Specifying the two end points and the slopes at these two points fixes the values of the four coefficients.

A difficulty arises when using axis-dependent nonparametric curves if the end point of a curve has a vertical slope relative to the chosen coordinate system. This infinite slope cannot be used as a numerical boundary condition. It is necessary to change the coordinate system or approximate an infinite slope with a large positive or negative value. Further, when points on an axis-dependent nonparametric curve are calculated with equal increments in x, the position of the points will not be distributed evenly along the length of the curve. This can affect the quality and accuracy of the graphical output. These difficulties lead to an interest in parametric curves for computer graphics.

4-3 PARAMETRIC CURVES

In parametric form each coordinate of a point on a curve is represented as a function of one or more parameters. For a curve of one parameter, the position vector for a point on a curve is fixed by one value of the parameter. If the parameter is t and the curve is two-dimensional, one writes

$$\begin{aligned} x &= f(t) \\ y &= g(t) \end{aligned} \tag{4-8}$$

The position vector for a point on the curve is then a single row matrix given by

$$P(t) = [f(t)\ g(t)] \tag{4-9}$$

If required, the nonparametric form can be obtained from the parametric form by eliminating the parameter from Eq. (4-8) to obtain one equation in terms of x and y.

In addition to simple curves, the parametric form is suitable for

representing closed curves and curves
with multiple values at a given value of
an independent variable. The tangent
vector at a point on a parametric curve
is given by

$$P'(t) = [x' \ y'] = [f'(t) \ g'(t)] \quad (4\text{-}10)$$

where the ' denotes differentiation with
respect to the parameter. The slope of
the curve, dy/dx, is written as

$$\frac{dy}{dx} = \frac{dy/dt}{dx/dt} = \frac{g'(t)}{f'(t)} \quad (4\text{-}11)$$

When the term $f'(t) = 0$ in Eq. (4-11),
the slope dy/dx is infinite. Since an
infinite slope occurs when one component
of the tangent vector is equal to zero,
it does not introduce computational
difficulties.

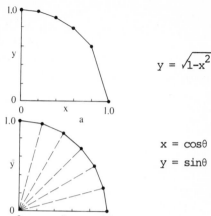

$$y = \sqrt{1-x^2}$$

$$x = \cos\theta$$
$$y = \sin\theta$$

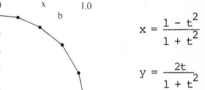

$$x = \frac{1 - t^2}{1 + t^2}$$

$$y = \frac{2t}{1 + t^2}$$

Since a point on a parametric curve
is specified by a single value of the
parameter, the parametric form is axis-
independent. The curve length is fixed by the range of the parameter. It is
often convenient to normalize the parameter so that the parametric curve falls
between $0 \le t \le 1.0$. Due to its axis-independent nature, a parametric curve is
easily transformed into a curve of the same shape but with various orientations.
This is accomplished by using the matrix multiplication techniques discussed in
the previous chapters to perform rotation, translation, scaling, and perspective
projection.

Figure 4-1 Circle representations

A comparison of the parametric and nonparametric form of a circular arc is
shown in Fig. 4-1. This figure was used by Woodsford (Ref. 4-4) to show that
a choice of parametric functions can be used to improve the distribution of
computed points on a curve and thus give a better graphical representation. The
quadrant of the circle shown in Fig. 4-1a is represented by the nonparametric
form $y = \sqrt{1 - x^2}$. Equal increments of x were used to obtain the points on the
arc. This form is inconvenient to compute because a square root algorithm is
necessary. It also produces poor results since the arc lengths are unequal.
Figure 4-1b is obtained from the basic parametric form given by

$$P(t) = [\cos\theta \ \sin\theta] \quad (4\text{-}12)$$

This produces good output since the arc lengths are equal, but the calculation
is inefficient because trigonometric functions require several operations to
compute. Figure 4-1c is an alternate parametric representation given by

$$P(t) = \left[\frac{(1 - t^2)}{(1 + t^2)} \quad \frac{2t}{(1 + t^2)}\right] \qquad (4\text{-}13)$$

Where $t = \tan\theta/2$. This choice requires very little computation time, but it is a compromise since the arc lengths are not exactly equal.

Now, consider the problem of determining the value of y when the value of x is known. As an example assume that $x = 0.5$ and that it is required to determine y on a unit circle. For the explicit representation this is straightforward:

$$y = \sqrt{1 - x^2} = \sqrt{0.75} = 0.866$$

For the parametric representation it is first necessary to solve for the parameter t in terms of x and then use this value to obtain y. Specifically for the parametric representation of Eq. (4-12) we have

$$x = \cos\theta$$
$$y = \sin\theta$$

Thus,

$$\theta = \cos^{-1}x = \cos^{-1}(0.5) = 60°$$
$$y = \sin(60°) = 0.866$$

Alternately, for Eq. (4-13)

$$x = \frac{1 - t^2}{1 + t^2} \qquad (4\text{-}14a)$$

$$y = \frac{2t}{1 + t^2} \qquad (4\text{-}14b)$$

Solving the first of these equations for t yields

$$t = \left(\frac{1 - x}{1 + x}\right)^{1/2} = \frac{1}{\sqrt{3}} = 0.57735$$

and thus

$$y = \frac{2/\sqrt{3}}{4/3} = \frac{\sqrt{3}}{2} = 0.866$$

For more complicated parametric representations an iterative search technique may be more convenient to find the unknown values of an explicit variable.

4-4 NONPARAMETRIC REPRESENTATION OF CONIC SECTIONS

Conic sections form useful planar curves for many applications. We now summarize some useful relationships from analytic geometry. Figure 4-2 illustrates how the intersection of a plane and right circular cone defines the various conic sections, i.e., the circle, parabola, ellipse and hyperbola. The general definition of a conic section can be given as:

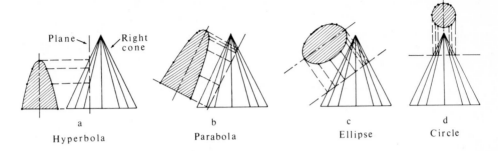

Figure 4-2   Conic Sections

A conic section is a curve described by a point which moves such that its distance from a fixed point (called the focus) divided by its distance from a fixed line (called the directrix) is a constant ε (called the eccentricity).

All the conic sections can be described by the general implicit second-degree curve

$$ax^2 + bxy + cy^2 + dx + ey + f = 0$$

The cross product term bxy in this equation controls the orientation of the resulting conic with respect to some reference axis system. If the reference axis system is selected such that one of the axes is an axis of symmetry of the curve, then b = 0. Since we can always rotate the curve such that the axis of symmetry is one of the axes of the reference system, we need only consider the equation

$$a'x'^2 + c'y'^2 + d'x' + e'y' + f' = 0 \qquad (4\text{-}15)$$

where

$$a' = a\cos^2\alpha + b\cos\alpha\sin\alpha + c\sin^2\alpha$$

$$c' = a\sin^2\alpha - b\sin\alpha\cos\alpha + c\cos^2\alpha$$

$$d' = d\cos\alpha + e\sin\alpha$$

$$e' = -d\sin\alpha + e\cos\alpha$$

$$f' = f$$

and

$$\cot(2\alpha) = \frac{a - c}{b} \qquad (4\text{-}16)$$

Alternately if the curve exists such that one of the reference axes is an axis of symmetry, then it can be rotated through any angle α to a new orientation. If the coefficients a', c', d', e', and f' are known for the original axis of symmetry orientation, then the coefficients a, b, c, d, e, and f of

Eq. (4-14) in the new orientation are

$$a = a'\cos^2\alpha + c'\sin^2\alpha$$
$$b = 2(c' - a')\cos\alpha\sin\alpha$$
$$c = a'\sin^2\alpha + c'\cos^2\alpha \qquad (4\text{-}17)$$
$$d = d'\cos\alpha + e'\sin\alpha$$
$$e = e'\cos\alpha - d'\sin\alpha$$
$$f = f'$$

Equation (4-14) can then be used to generate the required curve.

The character of the conic described by Eq. (4-14) is an ellipse, a parabola, or a hyperbola, depending on the value of the discriminate $b^2 - 4ac$ (cf Ref. 4-5). Namely, the curve is

a parabola if $b^2 - 4ac = 0$

an ellipse or a circle if $b^2 - 4ac < 0$

a hyperbola if $b^2 - 4ac > 0$

Considering Eq. (4-15), a circle occurs if a' = c'. The equation of the circle with center at h, k and radius r is given by

$$(x' - h)^2 + (y' - k)^2 = r^2 \qquad (4\text{-}18)$$

where

$$h = \frac{-d'}{2a'}$$

$$k = \frac{-e'}{2a'}$$

and

$$r = \left(\frac{d'^2 + e'^2 - 4a'f'}{4a'^2}\right)^{1/2} \qquad r \geq 0$$

If r = 0, the circle degenerates to a point.

A parabola occurs if a' ≠ 0 and c' = 0. Written in the common form the equation of the parabola is

$$(x' - h)^2 = 4p(y' - k) \qquad (4\text{-}19)$$

where

$$h = -\frac{d'}{2}$$

$$p = \frac{e'}{4}$$

$$k = \frac{2f' - d'^2}{2e'} \qquad e' \neq 0$$

Equation (4-19) represents a parabola whose axis of symmetry is y'. If the roles of x' and y' are interchanged, the x'-axis will be the axis of symmetry. If p > 0, the parabola will open up or to the right; if p < 0, it will open down or to the left.

An ellipse occurs when neither a' nor c' in Eq. (4-15) is zero and both a' and c' have the same sign, i.e., when a'c' > 0. The equation of the ellipse with center at (h,k) is then

$$\frac{(x' - h)^2}{\alpha^2} - \frac{(y' - k)^2}{\beta^2} = 1 \quad \alpha > \beta \tag{4-20}$$

where

$$h = \frac{-d'}{2a'}$$

$$k = \frac{-e'}{2c'}$$

$$\alpha^2 = \frac{g}{a'}$$

$$\beta^2 = \frac{g}{c'}$$

and

$$g = -f' + \frac{d'^2}{4a'} + \frac{e'^2}{4c'} \quad g \geq 0$$

When g = 0, a point results. The eccentricity of the ellipse ε is

$$\varepsilon = \frac{\sqrt{\alpha^2 - \beta^2}}{\alpha} < 1$$

A hyperbola is generated by Eq. (4-15) when neither a' nor c' is zero and both have opposite signs, i.e., when a'c' < 0. The equation of the hyperbola with center at (h,k) is then

$$\frac{(x' - h)^2}{\alpha^2} - \frac{(y' - k)^2}{\beta^2} = 1 \tag{4-21a}$$

or

$$\frac{(y' - k)^2}{\alpha^2} - \frac{(x' - h)^2}{\beta^2} = 1 \tag{4-21b}$$

where

$$h = - \frac{d'}{2a'}$$

$$k = - \frac{e'}{2c'}$$

$$\alpha^2 = \frac{g}{a'}$$

$$\beta^2 = \frac{g}{c'}$$

and

$$g = -f' + \frac{d'^2}{4a'} + \frac{e'^2}{4c'} \qquad g \geq 0$$

If g = 0, the hyperbola degenerates into a pair of intersecting straight lines. Note that in the case of a hyperbola the direction of opening is determined by the signs of a' and c' in constrast to an ellipse, where the orientation is controlled by the relative sizes of a' and c'. The eccentricity of the hyperbola is given by

$$\varepsilon = \frac{\sqrt{\alpha^2 + \beta^2}}{\alpha} > 1$$

4-5 Nonparametric Circular Arcs

Many of the early techniques for curve definition were based on the use of nonparametric conic sections. As long as relatively short curve segments were defined, coordinates could be chosen which produced reasonably smooth curves, even through the point distribution was not uniform. The shape of ships and airplanes were adequately defined in this manner. One advantage of this approach was the relative ease in calculating the intersection of two curves, each defined by nonparametric, algebraic equations.

Example 4-1: CIRCULAR ARC THROUGH THREE POINTS

Consider the determination of a circle through three points given by [1 1], [2 2], and [3 2] respectively (see also Sec. 4-11). To generate a circle through these points, let a' = c' = 1 and write Eq. (4-15) as

$$x^2 + y^2 + dx + ey + f = 0$$

where we have dropped the primes for convenience. Evaluating this equation at the three points yields

$$2 + d + e + f = 0$$
$$8 + 2d + 2e + f = 0$$
$$13 + 3d + 2e + f = 0$$

Solving these three equations for the three unknowns gives d = -5, e = -1, and f = 4. Thus, the equation for the circular arc through the three given points is

$$x^2 + y^2 - 5x - y + 4 = 0; \quad 1 \leq x \leq 3$$

The center of the circular arc is located at x = h = -d/2a = 5/2 and y = k = e/2a = 1/2. Using Eq. (4-18) the radius is r = $\sqrt{10}/2$ = 1.5811. Differentiation yields

$$2xdx + 2ydy - 5dx - dy = 0$$

---

or

$$\frac{dy}{dx} = \frac{5 - 2x}{(2y - 1)}$$

It follows that $dy/dx = 0$ when $x = 5/2$ and $dy/dx = \infty$ when $y = 1/2$. However, note that this infinite slope does not occur within the arc segment between [1 1] and [3 2].

When one creates curves for use in computer graphics, consideration must be given to how the user will define the curve. For example, it may be necessary to create a circular arc with a specified radius between two end points, rather than passing through three specified points as in the previous example.

Example 4-2: CIRCULAR ARC WITH FIXED RADIUS

Let the two end points be [1 1] and [3 2] as before. In addition we require a radius of $r = 5$. From Eq. (4-15) we obtain the three equations which result from these three conditions:

$$2 + d + e + f = 0$$
$$13 + 3d + 2e + f = 0$$

and

$$25 = \frac{d^2 + e^2 - 4af}{4a^2}$$

The solution to the above equations is more difficult due to the nonlinear terms in the third equation. An iterative technique must be used. By trial and error, it can be shown that an approximate solution to the above set of equations is

$$d = -8.4$$
$$e = 5.7$$

and

$$f = 0.7$$

for $a = c = 1.0$

Thus, the center of the circular arc which meets the imposed conditions occurs at $x = 4.2$ and $y = -2.85$. The arc no longer passes through the intermediate point [2 2].

On the other hand, it may be necessary to control the slope of the circular arc at the initial and/or final points. This can be done by choosing an alternate set of conditions.

Example 4-3:   CIRCULAR ARC WITH A FIXED TURN ANGLE

If an initial slope of +1 is required at [1 1] and a final slope of zero is necessary, then the final point on the circular arc cannot be independently specified.   For this case, we require

$$\text{at } x = 1, \; y = 1$$

$$\text{at } x = 1, \; \left.\frac{dy}{dx}\right|_{y = 1} = 1$$

$$\text{at } x = 3, \; \frac{dy}{dx} = 0$$

These three conditions lead to

$$2 + d + e + f = 0$$
$$4 + d + e = 0$$
$$6 + d = 0$$

which has the solution d = -6, e = 2, f = 2.   The equation for the circular arc is thus

$$x^2 + y^2 - 6x + 2y + 2 = 0; \quad 1 \le x \le 3$$

Notice that x = 3, y = $(-2 \pm \sqrt{32})/2$ = 1.828; i.e., the final point is [3 1.828].

If the final point on a circular arc must be specified, then only one end slope can be specified in addition to two end points.   For example, to produce a fillet between two straight lines, one might specify the initial point, the final point, and the final slope.

Example 4-4:   CIRCULAR ARC WITH GIVEN END SLOPE

Given the end points [1 1] and [3 2] with dy/dx = 0 at x = 3 yields

$$2 + d + e + f = 0$$
$$13 + 3d + 2e + f = 0$$
$$6 + d = 0$$

Then d = -6, e = 1, and f = 3, with h = 3, k = 1/2, and r = 5/2.   This solution produces a slope of 4/3 at the initial point.   This may be unacceptable and an iterative solution may be required to find a final point which allows an acceptable initial slope.   An alternate approach is to require the user to specify the radius which will produce acceptable slopes at the two end points and to proceed as in Example 4-2.

These examples illustrate the problems encountered when trying to provide a computer software (or hardware) interface between the user and the graphical output. The creation of the desired curve may be straightforward, or it may require iterative techniques, depending on the known or desired characteristics of the curve. Even when the required equation for the curve is known, calculations which produce well-distributed points along the curve may be expensive in terms of computer time. Further, when nonparametric curves are created, care must be taken to find the real roots rather than imaginary ones, and independent variable step sizes between consecutive data points may require changes based upon the local curvature and coordinate system.

Consider again the problem of passing a circular arc through three points. If the points are far removed from the origin of the coordinate system, large values of the coefficients can occur. To avoid this, translate the origin of the original coordinate system to the first point and define a new coordinate system x'y' as shown in Fig. 4-3. The coordinates of the three points, relative to this transformed system, are then

$$P_0 = [0 \ 0]$$

$$P_1 = [(x_1 - x_0) \ (y_1 - y_0)] = [x_1' \ y_1']$$

$$P_2 = [(x_2 - x_0) \ (y_2 - y_0)] = [x_2' \ y_2']$$

Since $x_0' = y_0' = 0$ due to the location of the transformed coordinate system, $f' = 0$. The other two equations, obtained by evaluating the general equation at P_1 and P_2, are

$$x_1'^2 + y_1'^2 + d'x_1' + e'y_1' = 0$$

$$x_2'^2 + y_2'^2 + d'x_2' + e'y_2' = 0$$

Solving for d' and e' yields

$$d' = \frac{y_2'(x_1'^2 + y_1'^2) - y_1'(x_2'^2 + y_2'^2)}{(x_2'y_1' - x_1'y_2')}$$

$$e' = \frac{x_2'(x_1'^2 + y_1'^2) - x_1'(x_2'^2 + y_2'^2)}{(x_1'y_2' - y_1'x_2')}$$

It follows that the center of the circular arc, relative to the x'y'-coordinate system, is

$$x_c' = -\frac{d'}{2a'} = \frac{y_2'(x_1'^2 + y_1'^2) - y_1'(x'^2 + y_2'^2)}{2(x_1'y_2' - x_2'y_1')}$$

$$y_c' = -\frac{e'}{2a'} = \frac{x_1'(x_2'^2 + y_2'^2) - x_2'(x_1'^2 + y_1'^2)}{2(x_1'y_2' - x_2'y_1')}$$

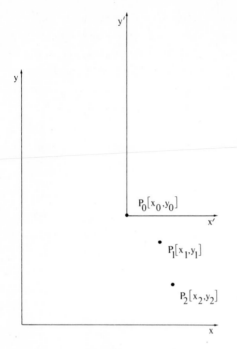

Figure 4-3 Translated coordinate
system for a circle

The center coordinates relative to the
original coordinate system are simply

$$x_c = x'_c + x_0$$

$$y_c = y'_c + y_0$$

When points of intersection, offsets
for cutter tools, enclosed areas or
volumes, or other such geometric information is needed, the required calculations may be simplified by expressing the
equations in explicit form. The explicit
form of the circular arc is given as
either $y = f(x)$ or $x = g(y)$. In terms
of the coefficients of the general second-
order polynomial equation, the first form
is

$$y' = -\frac{e' \pm \sqrt{e'^2 - 4(x'^2 + d'x')}}{2}$$

and the second form is

$$x' = -\frac{d' \pm \sqrt{d'^2 - 4(y'^2 + e'y')}}{2}$$

In these forms calculations such as an area given by $\int y'dx'$ or intersections
of the circle with the line $y' = mx' + b$ can be made using mathematical techniques.

As an example of the generation of a nonparametric conic section, an algorithm for generating a complete circle nonparametrically is given in Appendix
C. The basic concept behind the algorithm is that near the x-axis equal
increments in Δy are used. Thus, between $y = 0$ and $y = \pm r\sqrt{2}$ equal increments
Δx are used, and between $x = \pm r\sqrt{2}$ and $x = 0$ equal increments in Δy are used.
This algorithm allows only multiples of eight points. Further, to avoid problems
with the square root of negative numbers, the absolute value of the square root
argument is used. The algorithm is complicated and inefficient. An example
of a full circle generated with this algorithm is shown in Fig. 4-4. It generates reasonable circular segments in the middle third of each quadrant, but
very crude segments elsewhere. More points can be used to improve the result.
If a smooth graphical output is the prime consideration, the parametric representation subsequently discussed in Sec. 4-7 is recommended.

4-6 PARAMETRIC REPRESENTATION OF CONIC SECTIONS

A parametric representation of conic sections is of interest because it produces axis-independent curves. These can have advantages over nonparametric curves for some applications. However, neither type of curve representation is a panacea, since both have advantages and disadvantages and both find useful applications in computer graphics.

The conic sections can be simply represented in parametric form. The origin-centered circle can be parametrically represented as

$$x = r\cos\theta \qquad (4\text{-}22)$$
$$y = r\sin\theta \qquad (4\text{-}23)$$

where r is the radius of the circle and θ is the parameter. In Sec. 4-3 we remarked that although equal increments of θ would produce good output on a display device, the calculation was inefficient because the trigonometric functions must be repeatedly calculated. Following Ref. 4-6 we shall show below that a more efficient algorithm is possible.

4-7 PARAMETRIC REPRESENTATION OF A CIRCLE

The circle can be efficiently represented parametrically by eliminating the necessity for calculating the trigonometric functions at each step. This can be accomplished by using the double-angle formulas:

$$\cos(\theta + d\theta) = \cos\theta\cos d\theta - \sin\theta\sin d\theta$$
$$\sin(\theta + d\theta) = \cos\theta\sin d\theta + \cos d\theta\sin\theta$$

Noting that the circle will be completely swept out for a range of θ from 0 to 2π and assuming that a fixed number of points will be used, then $d\theta$ will be a constant. The Cartesian coordinates of any point on an origin-centered circle are then given by

$$x_{n+1} = r\cos(\theta + d\theta) \qquad (4\text{-}24)$$
$$y_{n+1} = r\sin(\theta + d\theta) \qquad (4\text{-}25)$$

Using the double-angle formulas allows Eqs. (4-24) and (4-25) to be rewritten as

$$x_{n+1} = x_n\cos d\theta - y_n\sin d\theta \qquad (4\text{-}26)$$
$$y_{n+1} = x_n\sin d\theta + y_n\cos d\theta \qquad (4\text{-}27)$$

If the circle is located at h, k relative to the origin of the coordinate system, then we have

$$x_{n+1} = h + (x_n - h)\cos d\theta - (y_n - k)\sin d\theta \qquad (4\text{-}28)$$
$$y_{n+1} = k + (x_n - h)\sin d\theta + (y_n - k)\cos d\theta \qquad (4\text{-}29)$$

A BASIC subroutine incorporating this algorithm is given in Appendix C.

Since $d\theta$ is constant, the values $\sin d\theta$ and $\cos d\theta$ need to be calculated only once. This produces an efficient algorithm. The results of using this algorithm are shown in Fig. 4-5. Notice the equal spacing of the points.

4-8 PARAMETRIC REPRESENTATION OF AN ELLIPSE

From the results for the circle we note that a fixed number of points provided a good representation of the circle when connected by short straight vectors.
With a circle, the distribution of that fixed number of points is obvious -
equal-angle increments. However, for an ellipse, if equal angle increments
are used to calculate the display points, an unacceptable result will be obtained.
This is particularly true for ellipses with high eccentricities ($\varepsilon \simeq 1$), as shown
in Fig. 4-6. Here we see that the ends are not adequately represented. This is
because near the ends of the ellipse the curvature is too large to be represented
by a few points.

An alternate method might be to use equal perimeter lengths. For a sufficient number of lengths this would give a better representation. However, the
ellipse would be overspecified along the sides, where the curvature is small,
with a resultant waste of computer time. Further, as pointed out in Ref. 4-5,
determination of the equal perimeter lengths involves calculation of an elliptic
integral, a time-consuming task. One would like to take small increments in

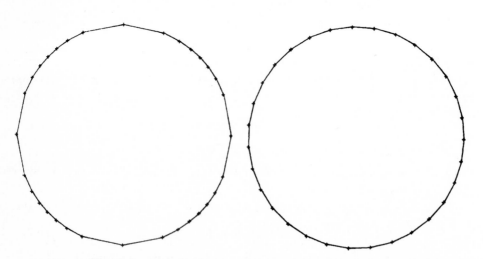

Figure 4-4 Crude nonparametric
representation of a circle.

Figure 4-5 Parametric Representation
of a Circle.

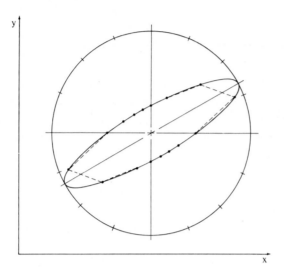

Figure 4-6 Equal-angle representation of a high-eccentricity ellipse.
perimeter length near the ends, where the curvature is large, and larger perimeter increments along the side, where the curvature is small.

To overcome the problems of point distribution, consider the parametric
representation of an origin-centered ellipse of semimajor axis a and semiminor
axis b. Then

$$x = a\cos\theta \qquad (4-30)$$
$$y = b\sin\theta \qquad (4-31)$$

where θ is again the parameter. Varying θ between 0 and 2π sweeps out the entire
ellipse. A specified fixed number of points can be used to represent the ellipse
by taking fixed increments in the parameter θ, say, increments of $2\pi/(n - 1)$,
where n is the number of points.

Examining the derivatives

$$dx = -a\sin\theta d\theta \qquad (4-32)$$
$$dy = b\cos\theta d\theta \qquad (4-33)$$

shows that the desired perimeter increments are automatically obtained. When
θ is near 0 or π, i.e., near the ends, we have $|dx| \doteq 0$ and $|dy| \doteq bd\theta$, and when
θ is near $\pi/2$ or $3\pi/2$, i.e. along the sides, $|dx| \doteq ad\theta$ and $|dy| \doteq 0$. Thus,
near the ends we have more points and along the sides fewer points. In fact
the ratio of the perimeter increment size at the ends to that along the sides
is approximately b/a. Further, note that in the case of a circle where b = a

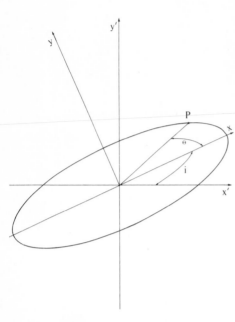

Figure 4-7 Ellipse

the optimum representation also results, i.e., equal perimeter or equal angle increments.

Since equal increments in the parameter θ, i.e., a fixed number of points, is to be used, an efficient algorithm can be developed by again using the double-angle formulas (Ref. 4-6). Here the ellipse is assumed to be inclined at an angle i to the horizontal, as shown in Fig. 4-7. Hence

$$x' = x\cos i - y\sin i \qquad (4\text{-}34)$$
$$y' = x\sin i + y\cos i \qquad (4\text{-}35)$$

or

$$x' = a\cos\theta\cos i - b\sin\theta\sin i \qquad (4\text{-}36)$$
$$y' = a\cos\theta\sin i + b\sin\theta\cos i \qquad (4\text{-}37)$$

Introducing the coordinates of the center of the ellipse yields

$$x'_{n+1} = x_c + x'_n\cos i - y'_n\sin i \qquad (4\text{-}38)$$
$$y'_{n+1} = y_c + x'_n\sin i + y'_n\cos i \qquad (4\text{-}39)$$

For the recursion formulas, note that the ellipse algorithm in Appendix C uses a somewhat different technique than used previously in the circle algorithm. In this case a temporary variable T1 is used in the inner loop.

Smith (Ref. 4-6) has shown that this algorithm can be made still more efficient such that only four additions and four multiplications are required within the inner loop. Smith has also shown that this technique yields the inscribed polygon with maximum area. Thus, the additions and multiplications give an efficient representation of the ellipse, such as the example shown in Fig. 4-8.

4-9 PARAMETRIC REPRESENTATION OF A PARABOLA

Consider an origin-centered parabola opening to the right, i.e., with the axis of symmetry the positive x-axis, as shown in Fig. 4-9. In rectangular coordinates such a parabola is represented in nonparametric form by

$$y^2 = 4ax \qquad (4\text{-}40)$$

A parametric representation of Eq. (4-40) is

$$x = \tan^2\theta \qquad (4\text{-}41)$$
$$y = \pm 2\sqrt{a}\tan\theta \qquad (4\text{-}42)$$

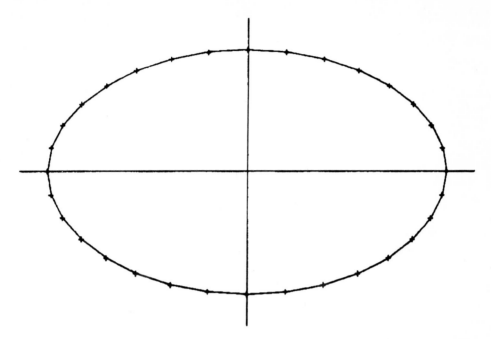

Figure 4-8 Parametric representation of an ellipse.

where $0 \leq \theta \leq \pi/2$. Although this provides an adequate representation of a parabola, Smith (Ref. 4-6) points out that it does not yield a figure with maximum
inscribed area and thus is not the most efficient representation. An alternate
parametric representation which does yield maximum inscribed area is

$$x = a\theta^2 \tag{4-43}$$

$$y = 2a\theta \tag{4-44}$$

where $0 \leq \theta \leq \infty$ sweeps out the entire parabola. The parabola, however, unlike
the ellipse, is not a closed curve. Thus, the amount of the parabola to be
displayed must be limited by choosing a maximum value for $\theta = \theta_{max}$. This can be
done in a variety of ways; e.g., the range of the x-coordinate could be limited.
If this is done then

$$\theta_{max} = \frac{\sqrt{x_{max}}}{a} \tag{4-45}$$

If the range of the y-coordinate is limited, then

$$\theta_{max} = \frac{y_{max}}{2a} \tag{4-46}$$

Once θ_{max} is established, an algorithm to calculate N representative points for
the parabola in the first quadrant can be developed. Once the parabola is obtained in the first quadrant, the rest of the parabola which appears in the fourth

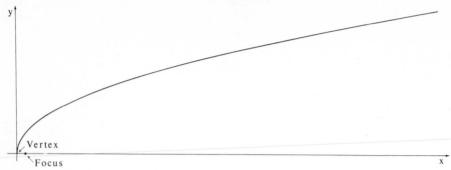

Figure 4-9 Parabola.

quadrant can be obtained by reflection about the x-axis (cf Sec. 2-10). An
appropriate algorithm to obtain the required points in the first quadrant is
given in Appendix C. In the algorithm a fixed number of points is specified
and a constant increment in θ is used. Parabolas with displaced centers or at
other orientations can be obtained using rotation and translation.

For $\theta_{n+1} = \theta_n + d\theta$, Eqs. (4-43) and (4-44) become

$$x_{n+1} = a\theta_n^2 + 2a\theta_n d\theta + a(d\theta)^2$$

$$y_{n+1} = 2a\theta_n + 2ad\theta$$

which may be written as

$$x_{n+1} = x_n + y_n d\theta + a(d\theta)^2 \qquad (4-47)$$

$$y_{n+1} = y_n + 2ad\theta \qquad (4-48)$$

Figure 4-10 shows an example of a parabola generated using these recursion
relationships.

For specific purposes other parametric representations can be more useful.
This generally depends on the information specified by the user. For example, if
a parabolic arc is to be drawn between two points, and control of the end slopes
is necessary, then the following form is suggested:

$$x(t) = (Q_x - 2R_x + P_x)t^2 + 2(R_x - P_x)t + P_x$$

$$y(t) = (Q_y - 2R_y + P_y)t^2 + 2(R_y - P_y)t + P_y \qquad 0 \le t \le 1.0$$

Here the parameter is t, and the two end points of the parabola are $P = [P_x\ P_y]$
and $Q = [Q_x\ Q_y]$. The point $R = [R_x\ R_y]$ is the point of intersection of the two
end tangents. We call this method the vertex definition of a parabola, since
use of three vertices P, Q, R defines the parabola as shown in Fig. 4-11. A
more general method of defining a curve by use of vertices of an open polygon
was developed by Bezier and is discussed in the next chapter.

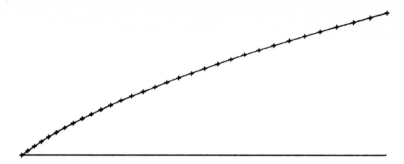

Figure 4-10   Parabola generated by the PARABOLA algorithm.

4-10 PARAMETRIC REPRESENTATION OF A HYPERBOLA

As was the case for the parabola, we assume that we want to generate a hyperbola which is origin-centered, with the axis of symmetry being the positive x-axis. The rectangular nonparametric coordinate representation of this hyperbola is

$$\frac{x^2}{a^2} - \frac{y^2}{b^2} = 1$$

which implies that the vertex is at a and the asymptotic slopes are ±b/a.   A parametric representation is given by

$$x = \pm a\sec\theta \qquad (4\text{-}49)$$

$$y = \pm b\tan\theta \qquad (4\text{-}50)$$

where $0 \le \theta \le \pi/2$ yields the desired hyperbola. Smith (Ref. 4-6) points out that with this parametric representation the inscribed polygon is not of maximum area. However, it is of nearly maximum area, and the double-angle formulas can be used to yield an efficient algorithm. To see this recall that

$$\sec(\theta + d\theta) = \frac{1}{\cos(\theta + d\theta)}$$

$$= \frac{1}{\cos\theta\cos d\theta - \sin\theta\sin d\theta}$$

and

$$\tan(\theta + d\theta) = \frac{\tan\theta + \tan d\theta}{1 - \tan\theta\tan d\theta}$$

Thus we may write

$$x_{n+1} = \pm a\sec(\theta + d\theta) = \pm \frac{ab/\cos\theta}{b\cos d\theta - b\tan\theta\sin d\theta}$$

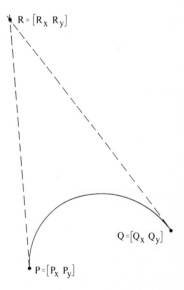

Figure 4-11   Vertex definition of a parametric parabola.

$$x_{n+1} = \pm \frac{bx_n}{b\cos d\theta - y_n \sin d\theta}$$

and

$$y_{n+1} = \pm b\tan(\theta + d\theta) = \pm \frac{b\tan\theta + b\tan d\theta}{1 - \tan\theta\tan d\theta}$$

$$y_{n+1} = \pm \frac{b(y_n + b\tan d\theta)}{b - y_n \tan d\theta}$$

(4-52)

The algorithm HYPERB1 in Appendix C uses these relationships.

An alternate parametric representation of a hyperbola which yields the polygon with maximum inscribed area is

$$x = a\cosh\theta \qquad (4\text{-}53)$$

$$y = b\sinh\theta \qquad (4\text{-}54)$$

The hyperbolic functions are defined as $\cosh\theta = (e^\theta + e^{-\theta})/2$ and $\sinh\theta = (e^\theta - e^{-\theta})/2$. As θ varies from 0 to ∞ the hyperbola is traced out. The double-angle formulas for cosh and sinh are

$$\cosh(\theta + d\theta) = \cosh\theta\cosh d\theta + \sinh\theta\sinh d\theta$$

$$\sinh(\theta + d\theta) = \sinh\theta\cosh d\theta + \cosh\theta\sinh d\theta$$

These allow writing Eqs. (4-53) and (4-54) as

$$x_{n+1} = a(\cosh\theta\cosh d\theta + \sinh\theta\sinh d\theta)$$

and

$$y_{n+1} = b(\sinh\theta\cosh d\theta + \cosh\theta\sinh d\theta)$$

or

$$x_{n+1} = x_n\cosh d\theta + \frac{a}{b} y_n\sinh d\theta \qquad (4\text{-}55)$$

$$y_{n+1} = \frac{b}{a} x_n\sinh d\theta + y_n\cosh d\theta \qquad (4\text{-}56)$$

As was the case for the parabola, the maximum value of $\theta = \theta_{max}$ must be set in order to limit the extent of the hyperbola. If we consider the branch of the hyperbola in the first and fourth quadrants and wish to plot the portion of the hyperbola for $a \le x \le a + c$, then

$$\theta_{max} = \cosh^{-1}\left(\frac{a + c}{a}\right) \qquad (4\text{-}57)$$

Similarly other limits can be determined. The algorithm HYPERB2 given in Appendix C uses Eqs. (4-55) and (4-56). Since most computer systems do not have hyperbolic functions, the exponential relations have been used, i.e.,

$$\cosh d\theta = \frac{e^{d\theta} + e^{-d\theta}}{2}$$

$$\sinh d\theta = \frac{e^{d\theta} - e^{-d\theta}}{2}$$

and the inverse hyperbolic cosine has been written as

$$\cosh^{-1}x = \frac{\log(1 + x) - \log(x - 1)}{2}$$

An example of a hyperbola using this technique is shown in Fig. 4-12.

4-11 A PROCEDURE FOR THE USE OF CONIC SECTIONS

In Sec. 4-5 the nonparametric representation of a circle through three points was considered. An essentially brute force approach was adopted. Here we consider the same problem; i.e., determine the location of the center and the radius of a circle which will pass through three specific points. However, here we divorce the problem of drawing the appropriate circle from determining what it is.

Consider three arbitrary points P_1, P_2, P_3 in the x,y,-coordinate system, as shown in Fig. 4-13. The general, nonparametric equation for the circle through these points is

$$(x - h)^2 + (y - k)^2 = r^2 \qquad (4-58)$$

Since P_1, P_2, P_3 may be anywhere in the xy-plane, direct substitution into Eq. (4-58) may yield extremely large numbers. This would make solution of the resulting equations difficult. We therefore translate the origin of the coordinate system to the first point P_1. As we shall see, this will also make the

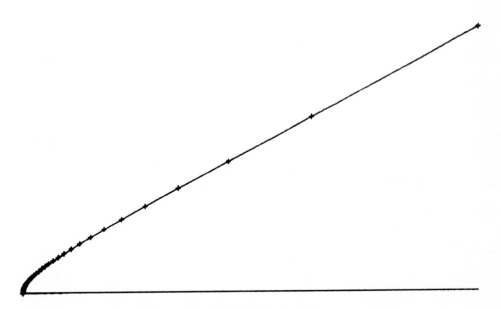

Figure 4-12 Parametric representation of a hyperbola

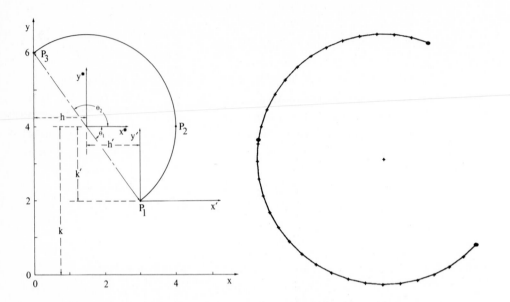

Figure 4-13 Circular arc
through three points (geometry).

Figure 4-14 Circular arc
through three points (parametric).

solution more convenient, Letting

$$x' = x - m \quad \text{and} \quad y' = y - n$$

where m and n are the translation factors (cf Sec. 2-27), we have $m = x_1$, $n = y_1$.
Equation (4-58) may then be written in the x'y'-coordinate system as

$$(x' - h')^2 + (y' - k')^2 = r^2 \qquad (4\text{-}59)$$

where

$$h' = h - m \quad \text{and} \quad k' = k - n$$

Direct substitution of the coordinates of P_1, P_2, P_3 in the x'y'-coordinate
system yields

$$h'^2 + k'^2 - r^2 = 0 \quad \text{for } P_1$$

$$x_i'^2 - 2x_i'h' + h'^2 + y_i'^2 - 2y_i'k' + k'^2 - r^2 = 0; \quad i = 2, 3 \text{ for } P_2, P_3$$

These equations represent three equations in the three unknowns h', k', and r
and thus may be solved. However, the system of equations is nonlinear and requires an iterative solution, which is undesirable. Notice, however, that because
the origin is at the first point, the first equation can always be subtracted
from the second and third equations such that the nonlinear terms are eliminated.
The resulting equations are

$$2x_i'h' + 2y_i'k' = x_i'^2 + y_i'^2 \quad i = 2,3 \qquad (4\text{-}60)$$

These are two linear equations in the two unknowns h' and k' which can be solved directly. The radius r can then be determined from the first equation $r^2 = h'^2 + k'^2$. The location of the center of the circle and its radius are now known.

To draw the arc of the circle, we first translate directly to the center of the circle, i.e., to h', k' or h, k, as shown in Fig. 4-13. With

$$\theta_1 = \tan^{-1}\frac{y_1{}^*}{x_1{}^*} \quad \text{and} \quad \theta_2 = \tan^{-1}\frac{y_3{}^*}{x_3{}^*} \qquad (4\text{-}61)$$

known, a standard origin-centered algorithm, either parametric or nonparametric, can be used to generate the points which describe the circular arc from P_1 to P_3 through P_2.

Examples 4-5: CIRCULAR ARC PROCEDURE

Consider the three points given by $P_1(3,2)$, $P_2(4,4)$, and $P_3(0,6)$. Translating to P_1 yields $P_1'(0,0)$, $P_2'(1,2)$, and $P_3'(-3,4)$. Equations (4-60) are then

$$2h' + 4k' = 5$$
$$-6h' + 8k' = 25$$

Solution yields $k' = 2$, $h' = -3/2$, and $r = 5/2$. Translation to the center yields $P_1{}^*(3/2, -2)$, $P_2{}^*(5/2,0)$, and $P_3{}^*(-3/2,2)$. Thus, Eqs. (4-61) give

$$\theta_1 = \tan^{-1}(-2/(3/2)) = \tan^{-1}(-4/3) = -53.13°$$

$$\theta_2 = \tan^{-1}(2/(-3/2)) = \tan^{-1}(-4/3) = 126.87°$$

This provides the angular input for the arc drawing subroutine.

A parametric form is chosen to improve the point distribution along the arc. Figure 4-14 shows the resulting parametric representation. The algorithm used to generate this curve is called 3PCIRARC and is given in Appendix C. The parametric circular arc subroutine was discussed in Sec. 4-7.

4-12 CIRCULAR ARC INTERPOLATION

The smoothness or fairness of a curve is generally a qualitative judgment based on what is pleasing to the human eye. Nevertheless, it is possible to select a quantitative measure of smoothness and generate curves according to this criterion. One such criterion used successfully by Mehlum (Ref. 4-8) is to minimize the integral along the arc length of the square of the curvature. Curvature can be expressed as

$$K = \frac{y''}{(1 + y'^2)^{3/2}}$$

(4-62)

where the primes indicate differentiation with respect to x. Thus, the problem is to minimize I, where I is given by

$$I = \int K^2 ds$$

(4-63)

The problem of minimizing the value of I by use of variational calculus was solved by Mehlum (Ref. 4-8). An important result of this solution, expressed as a theorem, is stated as follows:

When a piecewise curve is drawn which minimizes the integral along the arc length of the square of the curvature, then the curve segments lie in a direction along which the curvature varies linearly between the end points of each segment.

Assume that such a curve is to be drawn between two specified end points and several intermediate data points. The curvature profile between these points might look like that shown in Fig. 4-15a. However, as pointed out by Mehlum,

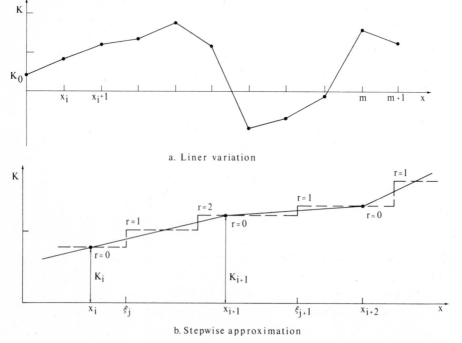

a. Liner variation

b. Stepwise approximation

Figure 4-15 Curvature profiles

the actual direction of the linear curvature variation is difficult to determine. It requires the solution to elliptic integrals whose integration constants are dependent in a complicated way on the specified boundary conditions. Mehlum suggested that an approximation to the piecewise linear curvature be made by replacing the linear variation with a series of discontinuous steps, each with constant curvature, as indicated in Fig. 4-15b. The curvature profile is then piecewise constant over the curve length. Since a constant curvature describes a circular arc, the piecewise curve is represented by a series of circular arcs with various centers and radii of curvature. A large number of steps, i.e., circular arcs, will produce a closer fit to the ideal curvature. The required number of circular arcs depends upon the separation distance between the data points, the change in curvature over the curve segment, and the required accuracy of the graphical output. Details of this technique for generating smooth curves by circular arc interpolation are given in the cited reference. The output of the iteration process gives the value of radius and center point for each circular arc, as well as the specified x-values where the curvature changes. Then subroutines for generating parametric circular arcs can be used to produce the actual piecewise curve.

REFERENCES

4-1 DATASAAB, "Formela General Description," Reg. No. 917-E, SAAB AKTIEBOLAG, 58188, Linkoping, Sweden, 1965.

4-2 "Computer Graphics Arrangement Program, COGAP Systems Manual," NAVSHIPS 0900-037-9030, CASDAC 233083/MFTS, Naval Ship Engineering Center, Washington D.C., Nov. 1972.

4-3 Gottfried, B. S., Programming with Basic, Schaum's Outline Series, McGraw-Hill Book Company, New York, 1975.

4-4 Woodsford, P. A., "Mathematical Methods in Computer Graphics - A Survey," Gesellschaft für Informatike, vol. 5, Symposium on Computer Graphics, Berlin, Oct. 1971.

4-5 Thomas, G. B., Sr., Calculus and Analytical Geometry, Addison-Wesley Publishing Company, Cambridge, Mass., 1954.

4-6 Smith, L. B., "Drawing ellipses, hyperbolas or parabolas with a fixed number of points and maximum inscribed area," Comput. J., vol. 14, p. 81, 1!

4-7 Cohen, D., "Linear Difference Curves," in Advanced Computer Graphics, Plenum Press, New York, 1971.

4-8 Mehlum, E., "Curve and Surface Fitting based on Variational Criteriae for Smoothness," Central Institute for Industrial Research (CIIR), Oslo, Norway Dec. 1969.

CHAPTER 5

SPACE CURVES

5-1 Introduction

Most objects encountered in the real world are three-dimensional in nature.
However, most drawing techniques are two-dimensional, the results being produced
on a plane surface such as a drawing board. This frequently results in the
representation of three-dimensional objects by means of two-dimensional views
or sectional drawings. The use of a digital computer to generate curves adds
a new dimension to drawing techniques. Three-dimensional space curves can be
defined, generated, stored, manipulated, and produced as output. Space curves
can be displayed on a two-dimensional plane by use of axonometric and perspective projections, as discussed in Chapter 3, or three-dimensional models can
be produced directly by using a numerically controlled cutting tool. The
present chapter extends the previous discussions for curve description to three-
dimensional space curves.

5-2 Representation of Space Curves

As was the case for plane curves, space curves may be represented either
nonparametrically or parametrically. Three-dimensional space curves expressed

in nonparametric form are given explicitly by a set of equations of the form

$$x = x \qquad (5-1)$$
$$y = f(x)$$
$$z = g(x)$$

Alternately a space curve may be expressed in a nonparametric, implicit form. In this case the space curve is represented mathematically by the intersection of the two surfaces given by

$$f(x,y,z) = 0 \qquad (5-2)$$
$$g(x,y,z) = 0$$

As an example, consider the two second-degree surfaces given by

$$f(x,y,z) = y - z^2 = 0 \qquad (5-3)$$
$$g(x,y,z) = zx - y^2 = 0$$

For $z \neq 0$, x and y can be expressed in terms of z to obtain the explicit form of the curve defined by the intersecting surfaces

$$x = \frac{y^2}{z} = z^3 \qquad (5-4)$$
$$y = z^2$$

Notice that the intersection of two second-degree surfaces leads to a third-degree space curve. This technique of solving for z from the implicit surface functions is valid provided that

$$\det \begin{vmatrix} \dfrac{\partial f}{\partial x} & \dfrac{\partial f}{\partial y} \\[2mm] \dfrac{\partial g}{\partial x} & \dfrac{\partial g}{\partial y} \end{vmatrix} \neq 0$$

at a point (x,y,z) which satisfies the two surface equations. A similar argument applies when solving for $x = f(y)$, $z = g(y)$ or $y = f(x)$, $z = g(x)$.

In general, a parametric space curve is expressed as

$$x = x(t) \qquad (5-5)$$
$$y = y(t)$$
$$z = z(t)$$

where the parameter t varies over a given range $t_1 \leq t \leq t_2$. Reconsidering Eq. (5-1) we see that x itself can be considered a parameter, $x = t$, and the same curve is then expressed in parametric form by

$$x = t \qquad (5-6)$$
$$y = f(t)$$
$$z = g(t)$$

Further, if we reconsider the nonparametric implicit representation given in Eq. (5-4) we see that we can let $z = t$, and the parametric equations for that curve are

$$x = t^3$$
$$y = t^2 \qquad\qquad (5\text{-}7)$$
$$z = t$$

Some useful parametric space curves have known analytic solutions. For example, a parametric space curve that is shaped like the seam on a tennis or baseball is expressed by the following equations:

$$x = \lambda[a\cos(\theta + \tfrac{\pi}{4}) - b\cos 3(\theta + \tfrac{\pi}{4})] \qquad\qquad (5\text{-}8)$$

$$y = \mu[a\sin(\theta + \tfrac{\pi}{4}) + b\sin 3(\theta + \tfrac{\pi}{4})]$$

$$z = c\sin(2\theta)$$

where

$$\lambda = 1 + d\sin(2\theta) = 1 + d(\tfrac{z}{c})$$

$$\mu = 1 - d\sin(2\theta) = 1 - d(\tfrac{z}{c})$$

and the parameter $\theta = 2\pi t$, where $0 \leq t \leq 1.0$. If $d = 0$ and $c^2 = 4ab$, then the space curve lies on a sphere of radius $a + b$. If $a = 1.0$, $b = 0.5$, $c = \sqrt{2}$, and $d = 0$, then the curve lies on a sphere of radius 1.5.

Another example of a parametric space curve is the circular helix. The parametric equations are given by

$$x = a\cos t \qquad\qquad (5\text{-}9)$$
$$y = a\sin t$$
$$z = bt$$

for a and $b \neq 0$ and $-\infty < t < \infty$. This curve lies on the surface of a right cir-cular cylinder of radius $|a|$. The effect of the equation $z = bt$ is to move the points of the curve uniformly in the z-direction. After each 2π interval in the parameter t, the variables x and y return to their initial values, but z increases or decreases by $2\pi|b|$, depending upon the sign of b. This change in z is called the pitch of the helix.

When an analytical description for a curve is not known, an interpolation scheme may be used to fit a curve through a given set of data points. This involves specifying boundary conditions for the space curve in order to deter-mine the coefficients for a given polynomial curve form and establishing a smoothness criterion.

Many considerations enter into the decision of how to represent a space curve. The form of computer input desired, the type of manipulations required, the available interface between user and computer, and the display device used for graphical output can all introduce considerations and limitations. When the input is a series of points which lie on the desired curve, spline segments are often used to form a smooth curve through the points. These are discussed in the next section.

5-3 CUBIC SPLINES

The mathematical spline derives from its physical counterpart - the lofts-man's spline. A physical spline is a long narrow strip of wood or plastic used by a loftsman to fair in curves between specified data points. The splines are shaped by lead weights called "ducks." By varying the number and position of the lead weights the spline can be made to pass through the specified data points such that the resulting curve appears smooth or "fair."

If the physical spline is considered to be a thin elastic beam, then Eulers equation (cf Ref. 5-1) yields

$$M(x) = \frac{EI}{R(x)}$$

where $M(x)$ is the bending moment, E is Young's modulus, I is the moment of inertia, and $R(x)$ is the radius of curvature. For small deflections the radius of curvature $R(x)$ may be replaced by $1/y''$, where the prime denotes differentiation with respect to x. Thus, we have

$$y''(x) = \frac{M(x)}{EI}$$

Assuming that the ducks act as simple supports, then $M(x)$ is a linear function between the supports. Letting $M(x) = A + Bx$ and integrating the above equation twice shows that the physical spline is described by cubic polynomials between supports.

In general the mathematical spline is a piecewise polynomial of degree K with continuity of derivatives of order K - 1 at the common joints between segments. Thus, the cubic spline has second-order continuity at the joints. Piecewise splines of low degree polynomials are usually more useful for forming a curve through a series of points. The use of low-degree polynomials reduces the computational requirements and reduces numerical instabilities that arise with higher order curves. These instabilities can cause an undesirable wiggle when several points must be joined in a common curve. However, since low-degree polynomials cannot span an arbitrary series of points, adjacent polynomial segments are needed. Based on these considerations and the analogy with the physical spline, a common technique is to use a series of cubic splines with each segment spanning only two points. Further, the cubic spline is advantageous since it is the lowest degree space curve which allows a point of inflection and has the ability to twist through space.

The equation for a single parametric cubic spline segment, in terms of a parameter t, is given by

$$P(t) = \sum_{i=1}^{4} B_i t^{i-1}; \quad t_1 \leq t \leq t_2 \tag{5-10}$$

where $P(t) = [x(t) \; y(t) \; z(t)]$. $P(t)$ can be considered the position vector of any point on the spline. It has three components $x(t)$, $y(t)$, and $z(t)$ which may be considered the cartesian coordinates of the position vector. The coefficients B_i are determined by specifying four boundary conditions for the spline segment.

In expanded form Eq. (5-10) may be written as

$$P(t) = B_1 + B_2 t + B_3 t^2 + B_4 t^3 \tag{5-11}$$

Let a given pair of points through which a curve segment passes be the vectors P_1, P_2 (see Fig. 5-1a). Corresponding tangent vectors at these given points are indicated by P_1', P_2', the derivatives with respect to the parameter t. Within the cubic segment the parameter t varies between two end-point values t_1 and t_2. To simplify the calculations, we can assign $t_1 = 0$.

The required boundary conditions for each cubic segment consist of the two end points and the tangent vector at each end point. For the single segment between P_1 and P_2, these conditions are given by

$$P(0) = P_1 \tag{5-12}$$

$$P(t_2) = P_2$$

$$\left. \frac{dP}{dt} \right|_{t=0} = P_1'$$

$$\left. \frac{dP}{dt} \right|_{t=t_2} = P_2'$$

Four relationships follow from Eqs. (5-11) and (5-12):

$$P(0) = B_1 = P_1 \tag{5-13}$$

$$\left. \frac{dP}{dt} \right|_{t=0} = \left. \sum_{i=1}^{4} (i-1) t^{i-2} B_i \right|_{t=0} = B_2 = P_1' \tag{5-14}$$

$$P(t_2) = \left. \sum_{i=1}^{4} B_i t^{i-1} \right|_{t=t_2} = B_1 + B_2 t_2 + B_3 t_2^2 + B_4 t_2^3 \tag{5-15}$$

$$\left. \frac{dP}{dt} \right|_{t=t_2} = \left. \sum_{i=1}^{4} (i-1) t^{i-2} B_i \right|_{t=t_2} = B_2 + 2B_3 t_2 + 3B_4 t_2^2 \tag{5-16}$$

Solving for B_3 and B_4 yields

$$B_3 = \frac{3(P_2 - P_1)}{t_2^2} - \frac{2P_1'}{t_2} - \frac{P_2'}{t_2} \tag{5-17}$$

and

$$B_4 = \frac{2(P_1 - P_2)}{t_2^3} + \frac{P_1'}{t_2^2} + \frac{P_2'}{t_2^2} \qquad (5\text{-}18)$$

along with $B_1 = P_1$ and $B_2 = P'_1$. These values of B_1, B_2, B_3, and B_4 fix the curve for the cubic segment. The shape of the cubic spline segment depends on the end-point position and tangent vectors. Further, notice that the value of the parameter $t = t_2$ at the end of the segment occurs in the results. Since each of the end-point vectors and end tangent vectors has three components, the parametric equation for a cubic space curve depends upon 12 vector components and the parameter value t_2 at the end of the segment.

Substituting Eqs. (5-13), (5-14), (5-17), and (5-18) into Eq. (5-11) yields the equation for a cubic spline segment:

$$P(t) = P_1 + P'_1 t + [\frac{3(P_2 - P_1)}{t_2^2} - \frac{2P'_1}{t_2} - \frac{P'_2}{t_2}]t^2 + [\frac{2(P_1 - P_2)}{t_2^3} + \frac{P'_1}{t_2^2} + \frac{P'_2}{t_2^2}]t^3 \qquad (5\text{-}19)$$

Equation (5-19) is for one cubic spline segment. It can be generalized for any two adjacent cubic segments $P_K(t)$ and $P_{K+1}(t)$, $1 \le K \le n - 2$, where n is the number of data points through which the curve must pass (see Fig. 5-1b). The generalized equations are of the form

$$P_K(t) = P_K + P'_K t + \left[\frac{3(P_{K+1} - P_K)}{t_2^2} - \frac{2P'_K}{t_2} - \frac{P'_{K+1}}{t_2}\right]t^2 + \left[\frac{2(P_K - P_{K+1})}{t_2^3} + \frac{P'_K}{t_2^2} + \frac{P'_{K+1}}{t_2^2}\right]t^3 \qquad (5\text{-}20)$$

and

$$P_{K+1}(t) = P_{K+1} + P'_{K+1} t + \left[\frac{3(P_{K+2} - P_{K+1})}{t_3^2} - \frac{2P'_{K+1}}{t_3} - \frac{P'_{K+2}}{t_3}\right]t^2 + \left[\frac{2(P_{K+1} - P_{K+2})}{t_3^3} + \frac{P'_{K+1}}{t_3^2} + \frac{P'_{K+2}}{t_3^2}\right]t^3 \qquad (5\text{-}21)$$

Here we assume that the parameter variation is $0 \le t \le t_2$ for the first segment and $0 \le t \le t_3$ for the second segment, etc.

For example, if only three position vectors (data points) are specified, the known conditions for the entire curve between P_1 and P_3 are the position vectors P_1, P_2, and P_3 and the tangent vectors at the ends of the curve, i.e., P'_1 and P'_3. To ensure second-order continuity for a cubic spline, we impose the condition for constant curvature at the internal joint between the two spans. This implies that the second derivative, i.e., $P''(t)$, be continuous across the joint.

From Eq. (5-10) we have

$$P''(t) = \sum_{i=1}^{4} (i - 1)(i - 2) B_i t^{i-3}; \quad t_1 \le t \le t_2 \qquad (5\text{-}22)$$

At the end of the first cubic spline segment, where $t = t_2$,

$$P'' = 6B_4 t_2 + 2B_3$$

and at the beginning of the second spline segment, where $t=0$,

$$P'' = 2B_3$$

Equating these two results and using Eqs. (5-17) and (5-18) yields

$$6t_2\left[\frac{2(P_1 - P_2)}{t_2^3} + \frac{P_1'}{t_2^2} + \frac{P_2'}{t_2^2}\right] + 2\left[\frac{3(P_2 - P_1)}{t_2^2} - \frac{2P_1'}{t_2} - \frac{P_2'}{t_2}\right] = 2\left[\frac{3(P_3 - P_2)}{t_3^2} - \frac{2P_2'}{t_3} - \frac{P_3'}{t_3}\right] \quad (5-23)$$

Multiplying by $t_2 t_3$ and collecting terms gives

$$t_3 P_1' + 2(t_3 + t_2)P_2' + t_2 P_3' = \frac{3}{t_2 t_3}\left[t_2^2(P_3 - P_2) + t_3^2(P_2 - P_1)\right] \quad (5-24)$$

which can be solved for P_2', the unknown tangent vector at the internal joint. Again notice that the end values of the parameter t, i.e., t_2 and t_3, occur in the resulting equation.

For n data points the results given above can be generalized to yield n - 1 cubic spline segments with position, slope, and curvature continuity at all the internal joints. The nomenclature for multiple spline segments is shown in Fig. 5-1b. In the general case Eqs. (5-20) and (5-21) apply for any two adjacent data points. The second-derivative continuity condition Eq. (5-24) generalizes to

$$t_{K+2}P_K' + 2(t_{K+2} + t_{K+1})P_{K+1}' + t_{K+1}P_{K+2}' = \frac{3}{t_{K+1}t_{K+2}}\left[t_{K+1}^2(P_{K+2} - P_{K+1}) + t_{K+2}^2(P_{K+1} - P_K)\right] \quad 1 \le K \le n - 2 \quad (5-25)$$

Equation (5-25) applies recursively over all segments. The corresponding matrix equation for all segments of the piecewise cubic is therefore

$$\begin{bmatrix} t_3 & 2(t_2 + t_3) & t_2 & 0 & \\ 0 & t_4 & 2(t_3 + t_4) & t_3 & 0 \\ & & t_5 & 2(t_4 + t_5) & t_4 \\ & & & \cdot & \cdot & \cdot \\ & & & & \cdot & \cdot & \cdot \\ & & & & & \cdot \end{bmatrix} \begin{bmatrix} P_1' \\ P_2' \\ P_3' \\ \cdot \\ \cdot \\ P_n' \end{bmatrix} = \begin{bmatrix} \frac{3}{t_2 t_3}\left[t_2^2(P_3 - P_2) + t_3^2(P_2 - P_1)\right] \\ \frac{3}{t_3 t_4}\left[t_3^2(P_4 - P_3) + t_4^2(P_3 - P_2)\right] \\ \cdot \\ \cdot \\ \cdot \\ \frac{3}{t_{n-1}t_n}\left[t_{n-1}^2(P_n - P_{n-1}) + t_n^2(P_{n-1} - P_{n-2})\right] \end{bmatrix} \quad (5-26)$$

The expansion of Eq. (5-26) gives n - 2 equations in n unknown tangent vectors. When the two *end* tangent vectors P_1' and P_n' are specified, then the system of equations is determinant. Thus, to generate a curve the position vectors P_i, $1 \le i \le n$, along with P_1' and P_n', are specified. Then Eq. (5-26) is used to calculate the intermediate tangent vectors P_2', P_3', . . ., P_{n-1}'. This calculation is most conveniently accomplished by matrix inversion (cf Sec. 5-5). The tangent vectors are then used to calculate the B_i coefficients given by the generalized form of Eqs. (5-13), (5-14), (5-17), and (5-18), for each curve segment, e.g.,

$$B_1 = P_K \quad (5-27)$$

$$B_2 = P_K' \quad (5-28)$$

$$B_3 = \frac{3(P_{K+1} - P_K)}{t_{K+1}^2} - \frac{2P_K'}{t_{K+1}} - \frac{P_{K+1}'}{t_{K+1}} \quad (5\text{-}29)$$

$$B_4 = \frac{2(P_K - P_{K+1})}{t_{K+1}^3} + \frac{P_K'}{t_{K+1}^2} + \frac{P_{K+1}'}{t_{K+1}^2} \quad (5\text{-}30)$$

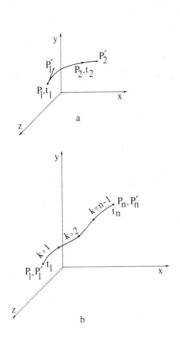

Figure 5-1 Cubic spline.

Finally, each cubic segment is generated by use of Eq. (5-10), with $0 \leq t \leq t_{max}$. Before the curve can be generated, the maximum parameter value t_{max} for each segment, i.e., t_2, t_3, . . . , t_n, must be chosen. This choice will affect the curve smoothness.

Continuity of second derivatives at the internal joints does not in itself produce a smooth spline in the sense of minimum curvature along the curve. To obtain a minimum, and hence maximum smoothness, the coefficients B_3 and B_4 must be minimized for each segment by choosing the correct values of the parameter range within each segment. This additional computational effort is normally not required. Simpler methods for choosing t_{max} can be used to generate curves smooth enough for most practical purposes.

One approach is to set the maximum parameter values equal to the chord lengths between successive data points. This has proven to give acceptably smooth curves for graphical display. A second approach is to normalize the variation by choosing $t_{max} = 1.0$ for each cubic segment. As can be seen from the previous equations, each choice of t_{max} will produce different coefficient values and, hence, different curves through the given data points. As the *magnitude* of the tangent vectors is changed, the slope of the cubic segments *between* data points is changed. On the other hand, the *direction* of the tangent vectors controls the shape of the cubic segments at their *end points*.

5-4 NORMALIZED PARAMETERS

In spite of the approximate smoothness of the resulting curve, normalized parameter ranges for all cubic segments of a spline curve can be used when defining a curve. When this approach is used, $0 \leq t \leq 1$ for all spans and Eq. (5-26) can be rearranged in the form

$$
\begin{bmatrix} 4 & 1 & 0 & 0 & \cdots & \\ 1 & 4 & 1 & 0 & 0 & \cdots \\ 0 & 1 & 4 & 1 & 0 & \cdots \\ \cdot & 0 & 1 & 4 & 1 & 0 \cdot \\ & \cdot & \cdot & \cdot & \cdot & \\ & & \cdot & \cdot & \cdot & \\ \cdot & \cdots & 0 & 1 & 4 \end{bmatrix}
\begin{bmatrix} P_2' \\ P_3' \\ \cdot \\ \cdot \\ \cdot \\ \cdot \\ P_{n-1}' \end{bmatrix}
=
\begin{bmatrix} 3(P_3 - P_1) - P_1' \\ 3(P_4 - P_2) \\ 3(P_5 - P_3) \\ \cdot \\ \cdot \\ \cdot \\ 3(P_n - P_{n-2}) - P_n' \end{bmatrix}
\tag{5-31}
$$

The four coefficients for each parametric cubic equation, given by Eqs. (5-27) and (5-30), can be expressed in matrix form as

$$
\begin{bmatrix} B_4 \\ B_3 \\ B_2 \\ B_1 \end{bmatrix}
=
\begin{bmatrix} 2 & -2 & 1 & 1 \\ -3 & 3 & -2 & -1 \\ 0 & 0 & 1 & 0 \\ 1 & 0 & 0 & 0 \end{bmatrix}
\begin{bmatrix} P_K \\ P_{K+1} \\ P_K' \\ P_{K+1}' \end{bmatrix}
\qquad 1 \le K \le n - 1
\tag{5-32}
$$

With the normalized formulation the tridiagonal matrix in Eq. (5-31) need only be inverted once to determine the tangent vectors at the internal joints. For a set of n position vectors, this represents a considerable savings of computer time. However, if the position vectors are not uniformly distributed, experience indicates that the resulting curves are not as smooth as when each segment parameter length is made equal to its local chord. The normalized formation does find use in creating cubic boundary curves for three-dimensional surface patches (see Chapter 6).

Although parametric cubics have many advantages for representing and manipulating curves, there are also disadvantages which limit their usefulness. Parametric cubics never reduce exactly to a circular arc, and so true circles can only be approximated. Also, they do not closely approximate mathematical curves which are asymptotic. Nevertheless, they are widely used for many applications, expecially in the shipbuilding and aircraft industries.

5-5 Boundary Conditions

When Eq. (5-26) is used to determine the tangent vectors at the internal joints of a curve defined by n points, a nonsquare matrix with n - 2 rows and n columns results. The tangent vector column matrix contains n rows and the coefficient column matrix contains n - 2 rows. Thus Eq. (5-26) may be written in the form

$$
[\overline{M}] [P'] = [B]
\tag{5-33}
$$

where

$$\overline{M} \text{ is an } n - 2 \times n \text{ matrix}$$
$$P' \text{ is an } n \times 1 \text{ matrix}$$
$$B \text{ is an } n - 2 \times 1 \text{ matrix}$$

The only nonzero terms on each row of the nonsquare $[\overline{M}]$-matrix are $\overline{M}(J, J-1)$, $\overline{M}(J, J)$, and $\overline{M}(J, J+1)$ for $2 \le J \le n - 1$. Hence the expanded form of Eq. (5-33) is

$$\begin{bmatrix} \overline{M}(2,1) & \overline{M}(2,2) & & & & \\ & \overline{M}(3,2) & \overline{M}(3,3) & \cdot & & \\ & & & \cdot & & \\ & & & & \cdot & \\ & & & & & \cdot \\ & & \overline{M}(N-1, N-1) & \overline{M}(N-1, N) \end{bmatrix} \begin{bmatrix} P'(K,1) \\ P'(K,2) \\ \cdot \\ \cdot \\ \cdot \\ P'(K,N) \end{bmatrix} = \begin{bmatrix} B(K,2) \\ B(K,3) \\ \cdot \\ \cdot \\ \cdot \\ B(K,N-1) \end{bmatrix} \quad (5\text{-}34)$$

A square $[M]$-matrix is necessary to obtain a unique solution for the unknown tangent vectors. The required square matrix M can be created by specifying boundary conditions at each end of the total piecewise cubic curve as shown below. In this case Eq. (5-33) may be written as

$$[M][P'] = [B] \quad (5\text{-}35)$$

where M is the required square matrix. Then the internal tangent vectors $(P'_2, \ldots, P'_{n-1})$ are given by

$$[P'] = [M]^{-1}[B] \quad (5\text{-}36)$$

where $[M]^{-1}$ is the inverse of $[M]$. Once the P'-values are known, B_i-values for each segment are calculated using Eqs. (5-27) and (5-30).

Many choices exist for specifying the end boundary conditions for a piecewise cubic curve. Several different choices may be desirable if only a few data points are known or if physical constraints require accurate control of the curve shape at the ends. The most direct solution is obtained by specifying the two end tangent vectors P'_1 and P'_n of the total piecewise spline. This boundary condition is called the clamped end condition in Ref. 5-2, and the encastered spline in Ref. 5-3. The complete matrix equation for the cubic spline curve is then given by

$$(5\text{-}37)$$

$$\begin{bmatrix} 1 & & & & & \\ M(2,1) & M(2,2) & & & & \\ & M(3,2) & M(3,3) & \cdot & & \\ & & \cdot & \cdot & & \\ & & \cdot & \cdot & & \\ & & \cdot & \cdot & & \\ & & M(N-1, N-1) & M(N-1, N) & \\ & & & & 1 \end{bmatrix} \begin{bmatrix} P'(K,1) \\ P'(K,2) \\ P'(K,3) \\ \cdot \\ \cdot \\ \cdot \\ P'(K,N-1) \\ P'(K,N) \end{bmatrix} = \begin{bmatrix} B(K,1) \\ B(K,2) \\ B(K,3) \\ \cdot \\ \cdot \\ \cdot \\ B(K,N-1) \\ B(K,N) \end{bmatrix}$$

This equation implies that $P'(K,1) = B(K,1)$ as is required. Notice that the resulting square $[M]$-matrix is also tridiagonal. This system of equations can readily be solved for the unknown tangent vectors $P'(K,2)...P'(K,N-1)$. Since this $[M]$-matrix is tridiagonal, the solution can be obtained very concisely by means of recursion formulas. This procedure is used in the algorithm which appears in Appendix C.

Other end conditions will increase the number of nonzero terms in the first and last rows of the M-matrix. For example, consider the mathematical end condition that $d^2P/dt^2 = 0$. This condition is called either relaxed or natural. Setting Eq. (5-22) equal to zero for the first span ($K = 1$), with $t = 0$, and using Eq. (5-17) leads to

$$P_1' + \frac{1}{2} P_2' = \frac{3}{2} \frac{(P_2 - P_1)}{t_2} \qquad (5\text{-}38)$$

If the same end condition is used for the last span ($K = N - 1$), with $t = t_n$, then with the help of Eqs. (5-29) and (5-30) one obtains

$$2P_{n-1}' + 4P_n' = \frac{6}{t_n}(P_n - P_{n-1}) \qquad (5\text{-}39)$$

It follows that the nonzero terms in the first row of the square $[M]$-matrix are $M(1,1) = 1.0$ and $M(1,2) = 0.5$. The nonzero terms in the last row are $M(N,N-1) = 2.0$ and $M(N,N) = 4.0$. In the $[B]$-matrix, $B(K,1)$ equals the right side of Eq. (5-38) and $B(K,N)$ equals the right side of Eq. (5-39). Notice that this relaxed (natural) end condition also produces a tridiagonal $[M]$-matrix.

Two other end conditions of practical use are the cyclic end condition and the anticyclic end condition. A cyclic spline can be used to produce a closed curve or a portion of a curve which repeats at intervals. It is based on the following end condition specifications

$$P_1'(0) = P_n'(t_n) \qquad (5\text{-}40)$$

and

$$P_1''(0) = P_n''(t_n) \qquad (5\text{-}41)$$

i.e., the slope and curvature at the beginning and end of the curve are equal.

Recalling Eqs. (5-16) and (5-28) to (5-30) the condition expressed by Eq. (5-40) yields

$$P_1' - P_{n-1}' = 2\left[\frac{3(P_n - P_{n-1})}{t_n^2} - \frac{2P_{n-1}'}{t_n} - \frac{P_n'}{t_n}\right]t_n + 3\left[\frac{2(P_{n-1} - P_n)}{t_n^3} + \frac{P_{n-1}'}{t_n^2} + \frac{P_n'}{t_n^2}\right]t_n \quad (5\text{-}42)$$

Similarly the condition expressed by Eq. (5-41) yields

$$2\left[\frac{3(P_2 - P_1)}{t_2^2} - \frac{2P_1'}{t_2} - \frac{P_2'}{t_2}\right] = 2\left[\frac{3(P_n - P_{n-1})}{t_n^2} - \frac{2P_{n-1}'}{t_n} - \frac{P_n'}{t_n}\right] + 6\left[\frac{2(P_{n-1} - P_n)}{t_n^3} + \frac{P_{n-1}'}{t_n^2} + \frac{P_n'}{t_n^2}\right]t_n \quad (5\text{-}43)$$

These two equations can be combined to yield a single equation which when combined with the M-matrix yields a $(n - 1) \times (n - 1)$ square matrix. Note that the order of the square matrix has been reduced by one. This is because the slope and curvature conditions imposed at two of the n points are no longer independent. Thus, there are only $n - 1$ independent slopes to be determined.

We combine Eqs. (5-42) and (5-43) by multiplying Eq. (5-43) by t_n and subtracting it from Eq. (5-42). This results in

$$P_1' - P_{n-1}' - 2\left[\frac{3(P_2 - P_1)}{t_2^2} - \frac{2P_1'}{t_2} - \frac{P_2'}{t_2}\right]t_n = 3\left[\frac{2(P_{n-1} - P_n)}{t_n^3} + \frac{P_{n-1}'}{t_n^2} + \frac{P_n'}{t_n^2}\right]t_n^2 - 6\left[\frac{2(P_{n-1} - P_n)}{t_n^3} + \frac{P_{n-1}'}{t_n^2} + \frac{P_n'}{t_n^2}\right]t_n^2 \quad (5\text{-}44)$$

Recalling that $P_1' = P_n'$ and rearranging the terms yields

$$2(1 + \frac{t_n}{t_2})P_1' + P_1'\frac{t_n}{2t_2} + P_{n-1}' = 3(P_2 - P_1)\frac{t_n}{t_2^2} - 3(P_{n-1} - P_n)\frac{1}{t_n} \quad (5\text{-}45)$$

Using this result allows writing Eq. (5-35) as

$$\begin{bmatrix} 2(1 + \frac{t_n}{t_2}) & \frac{t_n}{t_2} & 0 & . & & 1 \\ M(2,1) & M(2,2) & M(2,3) & . & & \\ & M(3,2) & M(3,3) & . & & \\ & & & . & & \\ & & & . & & \\ & & & . & & \\ & & & & M(N-1,N-1) \end{bmatrix} \begin{bmatrix} P'(K,1) \\ P'(K,2) \\ P'(K,3) \\ . \\ . \\ . \\ P'(K,N-1) \end{bmatrix} = \begin{bmatrix} B(K,1) \\ B(K,2) \\ B(K,3) \\ . \\ . \\ . \\ B(K,N-1) \end{bmatrix} \quad (5\text{-}46)$$

Normal Gaussian elimination or other matrix inversion methods can be used to invert the nontridiagonal matrix in Eq. (5-46).

Notice that the P' and B matrices are now $(n - 1) \times 1$ matrices as required for matrix multiplication in Eq. (5-46).

The anticylic spline is similar to the cyclic spline, except that

$$P_1'(0) = -P_n'(t_n)$$

and

$$P_1''(0) = -P_n''(t_n)$$

Following that same procedure used to derive Eq. (5-45) yields

$$2(1 + \frac{t_n}{t_2})P_1' + P_2'\frac{t_n}{t_2} - P_{n-1} = 3(P_2 - P_1)\frac{t_n}{t_2^2} + 3(P_{n-1} - P_n)\frac{1}{t_n} \quad (5\text{-}47)$$

Equation (5-47) shows that the only effect of imposing the anticyclic end conditions is to change the one in the $M(1,N - 1)$ position of the M-matrix for the cyclic spline boundary conditions (cf Eq. 5-46) to a minus one, as well as the sign on the second term of $B(K,N-1)$. This type of spline is useful for producing parallel end spans with end tangent vectors which are equal in magnitude but opposite in direction (cf Fig. 5-2b).

The cubic spline end conditions considered above are summarized in Table 5-1.

Table 5-1

End Conditions for Cubic Splines

End Condition Requirement	M-matrix Nonzero Elements in First and Last Rows	$B(K,1)$ $B(K,N)$
1. Clamped (encastered) specify $P'(0)$, $P'(t_n)$	$M(1,1) = 1 \quad M(N,N) = 1$	$B(K,1) = P_1'$ $B(K,N) = P_n'$
2. Relaxed (natural) require $d^2\bar{P}/dt^2 = 0$	$M(1,1) = 1 \quad M(N,N-1) = 2$ $M(1,2) = 0.5 \quad M(N,N) = 4$	$B(K,1) = (3/2)(P_2 - P_1)(1/t_2)$ $B(K,N) = 6(P_n - P_{n-1})(1/t_n)$
3. Cyclic require $\left.\dfrac{d\bar{P}}{dt}\right|_{\substack{t=0 \\ K=1}} = \left.\dfrac{d\bar{P}}{dt}\right|_{\substack{t=t_n \\ K=N-1}}$ and $\left.d^2\bar{P}/dt^2\right|_{\substack{t=0 \\ K=1}} = \left.d^2\bar{P}/dt^2\right|_{\substack{t=t \\ K=N-1}}$	$M(1,1) = 2(1 + t_n/t_2)$ $M(1,2) = t_n/t_2$ $M(1,N-1) = 1$	$B(K,1) = 3(P_2 - P_1)(t_n/t_2)$ $\quad -3(P_{n-1} - P_n)(1/t_n)$ $B(K,N):$ undefined
4. Anti-cyclic require $\left.\dfrac{d\bar{P}}{dt}\right|_{\substack{t=0 \\ K=1}} = \left.-\dfrac{d\bar{P}}{dt}\right|_{\substack{t=t_n \\ K=N-1}}$ and $\left.d^2\bar{P}/dt^2\right|_{\substack{t=0 \\ K=1}} = -\left.\dfrac{d^2\bar{P}}{dt^2}\right|_{\substack{t=t_n \\ K=N-1}}$	$M(1,1) = 2(1 + t_n/t_2)$ $M(1,2) = t_n/t_2$ $M(1,N-1) = -1$	$B(K,1) = 3(P_2 - P_1)(t_n/t_2)$ $\quad +3(P_{n-1} - P_n)(1/t_n)$ $B(K,N):$ undefined

Cubic splines will have continuous first and second derivatives with any of these end conditions. However, if the number of data points is large, the computation time required to invert the [M]-matrix can be excessive when cyclic spline or anticyclic splines are generated. Additional spline end conditions are discussed in Refs. 5-3 and 5-4.

Comparisons of the effects of the various end conditions is shown in Fig. 5-2. These results were obtained with the SPLINE subroutine given in Appendix C. In Fig. 5-2a, the "clamped" curve has a specified slope of $dy/dx = (dy/dt)/(dx/dt)$ equal to -1 at the beginning and a slope of $+1$ at the end. The other curve has relaxed boundary conditions so that $d^2p/dt^2 = 0$ at each end point. There is a significant variation in curve shape, especially near the beginning. Both curves consist of three cubic spans through the four indicated data points. The computer program generates 10 intermediate points per span for this particular output.

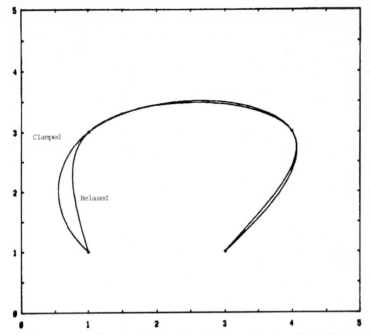

Figure 5-2a Comparison of clamped and relaxed end conditions.

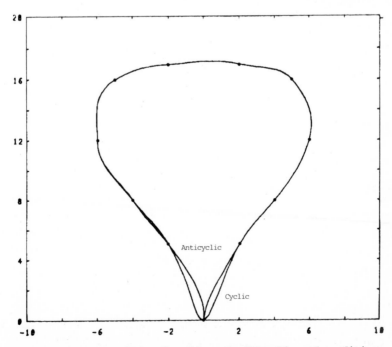

Figure 5-2b Comparison of cyclic and anticyclic end conditions.

Figure 5-2b shows two closed curves, a curve with cyclic end conditions through the 12 data points, the first and last point being identical at x = 0, y = 0, and a curve, also closed, with an anticyclic end condition at x = y = 0. Notice that the direction of the initial end tangent vector is vertically upward, while the direction of the final end tangent vector is vertically downward.

Figure 5-2c compares a relaxed end boundary condition to a cyclic end condition. This illustrates how a cyclic end condition can be used with an open curve. However, the direction of the initial end tangent vector on the curve with cyclic end conditions is the same as the direction of the final end tangent vector.

Example 5-1:   CUBIC SPLINES

Assume that the three position vectors P_1 [0 0], P_2 [1 2], and P_3 [3 2] are known. We wish to determine a cubic spline fit through these points using relaxed end conditions. We base t_{max} on the chord lengths of each span.

To begin we first calculate the chord distances t_2 and t_3:

$$t_2 = \sqrt{(x_2 - x_1)^2 + (y_2 - y_1)^2} = \sqrt{(1)^2 + (2)^2} = \sqrt{5}$$

$$t_3 = \sqrt{(x_3 - x_2)^2 + (y_3 - y_2)^2} = \sqrt{(3-1)^2 + (0)^2} = 2$$

Using Eq. (5-26) and the relaxed end condition Eqs. (5-38) and (5-39), the matrix equation required to find the internal derivative P_2' is

$$\begin{bmatrix} 1 & 0.5 & 0 \\ 2 & 8.472 & 2.236 \\ 0 & 2 & 4 \end{bmatrix} \begin{bmatrix} P_1' \\ P_2' \\ P_3' \end{bmatrix} = \begin{bmatrix} \frac{3}{2\sqrt{5}} (P_2 - P_1) \\ \frac{3}{2\sqrt{5}}[5(P_3 - P_2) + 4(P_2 - P_1)] \\ 3(P_3 - P_2) \end{bmatrix}$$

Solving for the derivatives by inverting the 3 x 3 square matrix and multiplying yields

$$\begin{bmatrix} P_1' \\ P_2' \\ P_3' \end{bmatrix} = \begin{bmatrix} 1.1574 & -0.0787 & 0.0440 \\ -0.3148 & 0.1574 & -0.08798 \\ 0.1574 & -0.0787 & 0.2940 \end{bmatrix} \begin{bmatrix} 0.671(P_2 - P_1) \\ 0.671[5(P_3 - P_2) + 4(P_2 - P_1)] \\ 3(P_3 - P_2) \end{bmatrix}$$

Thus,

$$P_1' = 0.5654(P_2 - P_1) - 0.132(P_3 - P_2)$$
$$= 0.5654[1\ 2] - 0.132[2\ 0]$$
$$= [0.3013\ 1.1308]$$

$$P'_2 = 0.2112(P_2 - P_1) + 0.2641(P_3 - P_2)$$
$$= 0.2112[1\ 2] + 0.2641[2\ 0]$$
$$= [0.7394\ 0.4224]$$

$$P'_3 = -0.1056(P_2 - P_1) + 0.618(P_3 - P_2)$$
$$= -0.1056[1\ 2] + 0.618[2\ 0]$$
$$= [1.1305\ -0.2111]$$

Recalling Eqs. (5-11) and (5-27) to (5-30) allows calculation of the cubic spline segments. For the first segment

$$P(t) = B_1 + B_2 t + B_3 t^2 + B_4 t^3$$

and

$$B_1 = P_1 = [0\ 0]$$

$$B_2 = P'_1 = [0.3013\ 1.1308]$$

$$B_3 = \frac{3}{5}(P_2 - P_1) - \frac{2P'_1}{\sqrt{5}} - \frac{P'_2}{\sqrt{5}}$$
$$= 0.6[1\ 2] - 0.8944[0.3013\ 1.1308] - 0.4472[0.7394\ 0.4224] = [0\ 0]$$

$$B_4 = \frac{2}{5\sqrt{5}}(P_1 - P_2) + \frac{P'_1}{5} + \frac{P'_2}{5}$$
$$= 0.17889[-1\ -2] + 0.2[0.3013\ 1.1308] + 0.2[0.7394\ 0.4224]$$
$$= [0.0293\ -0.0472]$$

Choosing $t/t_2 = 1/3$, $2/3$ yields t = 0.745, 1.4907, and

$$P(0.745) = [0\ 0] + 0.745[0.3013\ 1.1305] + (0.745)^2[0\ 0] + (0.745)^3[0.0293\ -0.0472]$$
$$= [0.2366\ 0.8227]$$

and similarly

$$P(1.4907) = [0.5462\ 1.5289]$$

For the second span, Eqs. (5-27) and (5-30) yield

$$B_1 = P_2 = [1\ 2]$$

$$B_2 = P'_2 = [0.7394\ 0.4224]$$

$$B_3 = \frac{3(P_3 - P_2)}{4} - \frac{2P'_2}{2} - \frac{P'_3}{2} = [0.19535\ -0.31685]$$

$$B_4 = \frac{2(P_2 - P_3)}{8} + \frac{P'_2}{4} + \frac{P'_3}{4} = [-0.03253\ 0.05283]$$

Again choosing $t/t_3 = 1/3$, $2/3$ yields t = 2/3, 4/3, and Eq. (5-11) gives

$$P(2/3) = [1.573\ 2.1579]$$
$$P(4/3) = [2.256\ 2.125]$$

The results are plotted in Fig. 5-3. It should be noted that it is not necessary to invert the matrix to obtain the internal derivatives. Equations (5-24), (5-38), and (5-39) can be easily solved by substitution to yield the required results.

An algorithm for generating cubic spline fits for n known data points is given in Appendix C.

It is possible to make various modifications to the above technique which may offer improvement for certain applications. For example, in Ref. 5-5, Manning describes an algorithm in which the shape of the curve is controlled by varying the tangent vector magnitudes at the data points (knots) through which the curve passes. This technique has found application in computer-aided footwear design.

Another method for improving curve smoothness for explicit cubic splines was reported by Denman (Ref. 5-6). His technique requires an interactive numerical search and the use of Gaussian quadrature integration. Details are described in the cited reference. The unique feature of this method is that the end conditions are automatically selected based upon a minimization criterion. It has been used in the automobile industry.

A technique used to smooth out undesirable oscillations which sometimes occur with cubic spline curves is the use of splines under tension. Oscilla- tions occur since the cubic spline is influenced locally by each data point

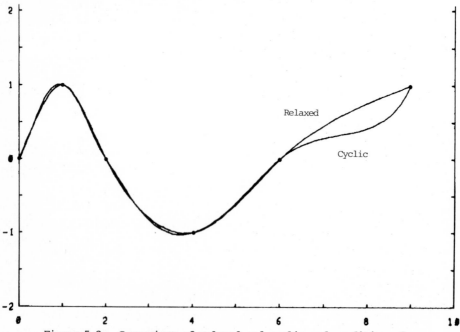

Figure 5-2c Comparison of relaxed and cyclic end conditions for open curves.

along the curve, and the third derivative is only piecewise constant. Dis-
continuities in third derivatives can
thus induce unwanted inflection points
at certain locations along the curve.

Consider a physical spline supported
by ducks at certain points. If the
thin, flexible beam has small oscillations, one way to remove them would be
to apply tension to the ends of the beam
to smooth out the spline. A mathematical spline under tension is an approximation to this procedure. Theory and
applications for this technique are discussed in Refs. 5-7 and 5-8.

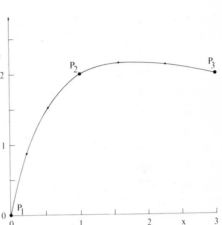

5-6 PARABOLIC BLENDING

Figure 5-3   Results of cubic spline
fit for Example 5-1.

The technique for parabolic blending presented here was first suggested
by A. W. Overhauser (Ref. 5-9). The interpolation scheme considers four consecutive points simultaneously. A smooth curve between the two interior points is
generated by blending two overlapping parabolic segments. The first parabolic
segment is defined by the first three points, and the last three points of the
set of four define the second parabolic segment.

Consider four consecutive points in space specified by the position vectors
P_3, P_4, P_5, and P_6. Two overlapping parabolas $P(r)$ and $Q(s)$ between these
points are shown in Fig. 5-4. Each parabola goes through three points and each
is defined relative to its own local coordinate system. The parabola $P(r)$
through P_3, P_4, and P_5 is governed by the following equation, relative to the
ur-coordinate system

$$u = P(r) = \alpha r (d - r) \tag{5-48}$$

where as shown in Fig. 5-4 r is measured along the chord length $P_3 P_5$ and u is
measured perpendicular to r in the plane defined by P_3, P_4, and P_5. The chord
length between P_3 and P_5 is d. A parabola can be completely specified by two
end points P_3, P_5, and a third point P_4 on the curve. The value of the constant
α is chosen such that the parabola $P(r)$ passes through P_4.

In a similar manner, the parabola $Q(s)$ is defined so as to pass through
the points P_4, P_5, and P_6. The equation is

$$v = Q(s) = \beta s (e - s) \qquad (5-49)$$

Here s is measured along the chord length $P_4 P_6$, v is perpendicular to s in the plane defined by P_4, P_5, and P_6, and β is chosen such that the parabola passes through P_5. The chord length between P_4 and P_6 is e.

The parameter t is now chosen as the distance measured along the chord length between P_4 and P_5. A curve C(t), which is a blend of the two overlapping parabolas, is constructed between P_4 and P_5 by use of an interpolation scheme. The blending curve C(t) is defined as

$$C(t) = [1 - (\frac{t}{t_o})]P(r) + [\frac{t}{t_o}]Q(s) \qquad (5-50)$$

where t_o is the distance between P_4 and P_5. The coefficients of P(r) and Q(s) act as blending functions, varying linearly between 1.0 and 0, and 0 and 1.0 respectively.

The position vectors P_3, P_4, P_5, and P_6 above are specified in terms of the Cartesian xyz-coordinate system, whereas the blending parabolas P(r) and Q(s) are specified in terms of a local coordinate system. To derive the parametric, parabolic equations in terms of the xyz-coordinate system, the geometry shown in Fig. 5-5 is helpful. In Fig. 5-5a, $P_4 J$ is perpendicular to the chord between P_3 and P_5. Thus, the ur-plane can be defined by the vector dot product

$$(P_4 - J) \cdot (P_5 - P_3) = 0 \qquad (5-51)$$

If J is located in the ur-plane at r = xd, then in the xyz=coordinate system

$$J = P_3 + x(P_5 - P_3) \qquad (5-52)$$

and Eq. (5-51) may be written

$$\{P_4 - [P_3 + x(P_5 - P_3)]\} \cdot (P_5 - P_3) = 0 \quad (5-53)$$

Solving for x in the xyz-coordinate system yields

$$x = \frac{(P_4 - P_3) \cdot (P_5 - P_3)}{(P_5 - P_3)^2} \qquad (5-54$$

$$= \frac{(P_4 - P_3) \cdot (P_5 - P_3)}{d^2}$$

With this information the vector equation for a point P on the parabola P(r), relative to the xyz-coordinate system, is given by

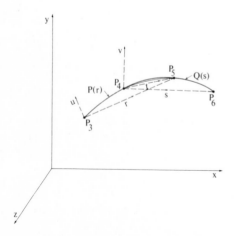

Figure 5-4 Parabolic blending.

$$P(r) = P_3 + \frac{r}{d}(P_5 - P_3) + \alpha r(d - r)(P_4 - J) \tag{5-55}$$

or after using Eq. (5-52) for J,

$$P(r) = P_3 + \frac{r}{d}(P_5 - P_3) + \alpha r(d - r)[(P_4 - P_3) - x(P_5 - P_3)] \tag{5-56}$$

It remains to determine α and the parametric equation for $r(t)$. Since in the ur-coordinate system $P(xd) = P_4$, it follows that the vector equation for $P_4 - J$ is

$$P_4 - J = \alpha xd(d - xd)(P_4 - J)$$

or

$$\alpha = \frac{1}{d^2 x(1 - x)} \tag{5-57}$$

The required relationship for $r = r(t)$ can be obtained from the geometry shown in Fig. 5-5. It follows that

$$r = xd + t\cos\theta \tag{5-58}$$

where

$$\cos\theta = (P_5 - P_4) \cdot (\frac{P_5 - P_3}{t_o d}) \tag{5-59}$$

For the parabola $Q(s)$, similar equations can be derived using Fig. 5-5b. For the parabola $Q(s)$, the relationship $s = s(t)$ is

$$s = t\cos\theta = t[(P_5 - P_4) \cdot (\frac{P_6 - P_4}{t_o e})] \tag{5-60}$$

and

$$Q(s) = P_4 - \frac{s}{e}(P_6 - P_4) + \beta s(e - s)[(P_5 - P_4) - x(P_6 - P_4)] \tag{5-61}$$

Once the points are specified, the procedure is to calculate x using Eq. (5-54) and then α using Eq. (5-57). For a given value of t, r is given by Eqs. (5-58) and (5-59). Finally, points on the curve, $P(r)$, are calculated using Eq. (5-56). This procedure is then repeated for the $Q(s)$ parabola.

To continue generating a curve through additional points, a blending curve $C_i(t_i)$ is formed between each adjacent pair of points. This creates a continuous curve which is also continuous in first derivative at the internal data points. These first derivatives can be easily determined if Eq. (5-50) is rewritten as

$$C(t) = P(t) + (\frac{t}{t_o})[Q(t) - P(t)] \tag{5-62}$$

Then

$$\frac{dC}{dt} = \frac{dP}{dt} + (\frac{t}{t_o})(\frac{dQ}{dt} - \frac{dP}{dt}) + (\frac{1}{t_o})(Q - P) \tag{5-63}$$

At point P_4 on the blending curve, $t = 0$ and $P = Q$. Thus

$$(\frac{dC}{dt})_{P_4} = (\frac{dP}{dt})_{P_4}$$

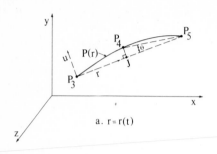

a. r = r(t)

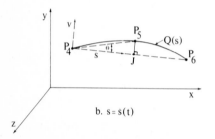

b. s = s(t)

Figure 5-5   Geometric relationships r(t) and s(t).

That is, the slope of the blending curve equals the slope of the parabola P(r) at P_4. Likewise, at P_5 on the blending curve, $t = t_0$ and $P = Q$. Thus,

$$\left(\frac{dC}{dt}\right)_{P_5} = \left(\frac{dQ}{dt}\right)_{P_5}$$

The equation for the blending curve C(t) is cubic when expressed in terms of the basic Cartesian coordinate system. For this reason it can produce a point of inflection within an interval. However, the blending cubic which defines the curve between points P_4 and P_5 does not pass through P_3 and P_6. This behavior makes parabolic blending a different interpolation scheme than one which passes a cubic through four points on a curve. According to Overhauser (Ref. 5-9), this characteristic guarantees that spurious wiggles are not introduced during the curve definition.

Parabolic blending can be used only for internal segments of a curve. The two end segments must each be a single parabola, defined through the first and last three data points respectively (cf Sec. 4-9). The distance between these points can be smaller than that for other segments in order to carefully specify the shape of the curve at its end points. Also, closely spaced points can be used in regions of high curvature.

The technique of parabolic blending offers a different approach to curve definition and generation. In the cubic spline technique discussed previously, it was necessary to define the complete set of points and two end tangent vectors before the curve was generated. In parabolic interpolation, only three points are needed to start a curve. These define the initial parabolic segment between points P_1 and P_3 passing through P_2. A fourth point can then be added and the cubic blending segment between points P_2 and P_3 determined as shown above. Successive points may be added, one by one, and these determine the continuous cubic blending curve segments that make up the interior part of the curve. If the shape is not correct, the last point or points can be deleted and a new shape defined by using alternate points.

When an artist, stylist, or designer sketches, he or she uses short, overlapping strokes to produce the contour desired. This is not unlike the technique that can be used with parabolic blending. Once the sketch is defined in a computer, then the vectors defining the points can be quickly displayed in a variety of ways. In some applications it may be desirable to sketch a shape by using parabolic blending and then use the resulting junction points as data for other techniques.

Example 5-2: PARABOLIC BLENDING

Assume that the position vectors $P_3[0,0]$, $P_4[1,1]$, $P_5[3,2]$, and $P_6[4,3]$ are known. We wish to determine a curve between the two points P_4 and P_5 using parabolic blending. The procedure is

1. For each span composed of three points
   a. calculate x
   b. calculate α or β
   c. calculate r or s for given t
2. Calculate the blended curve

For the first span Eq. (5-54) yields

$$x = \frac{(P_4 - P_3) \cdot (P_5 - P_3)}{(P_5 - P_3)^2} = \frac{(i + j) \cdot (3i + 2j)}{(9 + 4)} = \frac{3 + 2}{13} = 0.3846$$

Equation (5-57) yields

$$\alpha = \frac{1}{d^2 x(1 - x)} = \frac{1}{(13)(0.3846)(1 - 0.3846)} = 0.325$$

Recalling Eq. (5-58) we first calculate

$$t_o = \sqrt{(2)^2 + (1)^2} = \sqrt{5}$$

$$\cos\theta = \frac{(P_5 - P_4) \cdot (P_5 - P_3)}{t_o d}$$

$$= \frac{(2i + j) \cdot (3i + 2j)}{\sqrt{5}\sqrt{13}} = \frac{6 + 2}{\sqrt{5}\sqrt{13}} = \frac{8}{\sqrt{5}\sqrt{13}} = 0.9923$$

and

$$r = xd + t\cos\theta = 0.3846\sqrt{13} + \frac{8t}{\sqrt{5}\sqrt{13}} = 1.3867 + 0.9923t$$

For $t/t_o = 1/3$, $t = 0.745$, which yields $r = 2.126$. Equation (5-56) then yields

$$P(r) = P_3 + \frac{r}{d}(P_5 - P_3) + \alpha r(d - r)[(P_4 - P_3) - x(P_5 - P_3)]$$

$$P(2.126) = P_3 + 0.5896(P_5 - P_3) + 1.0223[(P_4 - P_3) - 0.3846(P_5 - P_3)]$$

$$= [0\ 0] + 0.5896[3\ 2] + 1.0223[[1\ 1] - 0.3846[3\ 2]]$$

$$= [0\ 0] + [1.7688\ 1.1792] + 1.0223[-0.1538\ 0.2308]$$

$$P(2.126) = [1.612 \ 1.415]_{t/t_o} = 1/3$$

For $t/t_o = 2/3$, $t = 1.4907$, and $r = 2.8659$, Eq. (5-56) then yields

$$P(2.8659) = [2.279 \ 1.7487]|_{t/t_o = 2/3}$$

For the second span

$$x = \frac{(P_5 - P_4) \cdot (P_6 - P_4)}{(P_6 - P_4)^2} = \frac{8}{13} = 0.6154$$

$$\beta = 0.325$$

$$t_o = \sqrt{5}$$

$$e = \sqrt{13}$$

$$\cos\theta = \frac{(P_5 - P_4) \cdot (P_6 - P_4)}{t_o e} = 0.9923$$

$$s = t\cos\theta = 0.9923t$$

For $t/t_0 = 1/3$, $t = 0.745$, and $s = 0.7392$, Eq. (5-61) yields

$$Q(s) = P_4 + \frac{s}{e}(P_6 - P_4) + \beta s(e - s)[(P_5 - P_4) - x(P_6 - P_4)]$$

$$= P_4 + 0.205(P_6 - P_4) + 0.6887[(P_5 - P_4) - 0.6154(P_6 - P_4)]$$

$$= [1.721 \ 1.251]|_{t/t_o = 1/3}$$

and for $t/t_o = 2/3$, $t = 1.4907$ and $s = 1.479$, Eq. (5-61) yields

$$Q(1.479) = [2.3882 \ 1.584]|_{t/t_o = 2/3}$$

Equation (5-62) may now be used to blend the two parabolas to yield the desired curve between P_4 and P_5:

$$C(t) = (1 - \frac{t}{t_o})P(r) + (\frac{t}{t_o})Q(s)$$

for $t/t_o = 1/3$,

$$C(0.745) = \frac{2}{3}P(2.126) + \frac{1}{3}Q(0.7392)$$

$$= [1.648 \ 1.361]$$

and for $t/t_o = 2/3$,

$$C(1.4907) = \frac{1}{3}P(2.8659) + \frac{2}{3}Q(1.479)$$

$$= [2.352 \ 1.6393]$$

The results are shown plotted in Fig. 5-6.

An algorithm which will implement the parabolic blending technique described above is given in Appendix C.

5-7 Bezier Curves

The previously discussed methods for three-dimensional-curve generation have been constrained to pass through all the specified data points; i.e., they are curve fitting techniques. In many cases excellent results are achieved with these methods. There are, however, certain drawbacks which render these methods ineffective for interactive "ab initio" curve design. This is due to the fact that control of the curve shape by numerical specification of both direction and magnitude of tangent derivatives does not provide the intuitive "feel" required for curve design; i.e., there is not always an obvious relation between the numbers and the curve shape. In addition, the cubic curve fitting

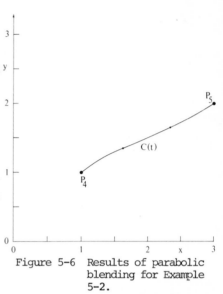

Figure 5-6 Results of parabolic blending for Example 5-2.

technique specifies a curve of unique order, which does not vary from spline to spline. In order to increase flexibility, more points must be input, creating more splines which are all still of cubic order.

An alternate method of curve description has been described by Bezier (Refs. 5-10, 5-11, and 5-12) which allows the user a much greater feel for the relation between input and output. This enables him to use the program as an artist, stylist or designer, varying curve shape and order by the use of easily controlled input parameters until the output matches the desired shape.

A Bezier curve is associated with the "vertices" of a polygon which uniquely define the curve shape. Only the first and last vertices of the polygon actually lie on the curve; however, the other vertices define the derivatives, order, and shape of the curve. Thus, the curve is defined by an open polygon, as shown in Fig. 5-7. Since the curve shape will tend to follow the polygon shape, changing the vertices of this polygon gives the user a much greater intuitive feeling for input/output relationships. All that is necessary to increase the order of any curve segment is to specify another interior vertex. This greatly increases flexibility and overcomes many of the difficulties of the cubic spline fitting and parabolic blending techniques. Furthermore, local control is easy with Bezier curves. Any change in the vertices of a span will only effect the curve within that span. The rest of the curve will remain

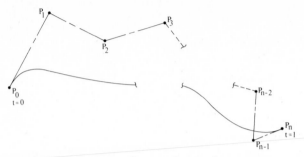

Figure 5-7   Nomenclature for Bezier curves.

unaffected.

The mathematical basis of the Bezier curve is a polynomial blending function which interpolates between the first and last vertices.   The Bezier polynomial is related to the Bernstein polynomial.   Thus, the Bezier curve is said to have a Bernstein basis.   The basis function is given by

$$J_{n,i}(t) = \binom{n}{i} t^{i} (1 - t)^{n-i} \tag{5-64}$$

where

$$\binom{n}{i} = \frac{n!}{i!\,(n-i)!} \tag{5-65}$$

with n being the degree of the polynomial and i the particular vertex in the ordered set (from 0 to n).   In general an nth order polynomial is specified by n + 1 vertices.   The curve points are then given by

$$P(t) = \sum_{i=0}^{n} P_{i} J_{n,i}(t) \quad 0 \leq t \leq 1 \tag{5-66}$$

where P_{i} contains the vector components of the various vertices.   At the starting point of a curve segment,

$$J_{n,0}(0) = \frac{n!\,(1)\,(1 - 0)^{n-0}}{n!} = 1 \tag{5-67}$$

At the end point of a curve segment,

$$J_{n,n}(1) = \frac{n!\,(1)^{n} (0)^{n-n}}{n!\,(1)} = 1 \tag{5-68}$$

Equations (5-67) and (5-68) along with Eq. (5-66) show that $P(0) = P_{0}$ and $P(1) = P_{n}$; i.e., the vertices P_{0} and P_{n} lie on the actual curve segment at the starting point and the end point respectively.

Another characteristic of the interpolation function is that maximum values occur at t = i/n.   This maximum is given by Ref. 5-12 as

$$J_{n,i}\left(\frac{i}{n}\right) = \binom{n}{i} \frac{i^{i} (n - i)^{n-i}}{n^{n}} \tag{5-69}$$

For example, for a cubic,

$$J_{3,1}\left(\frac{1}{3}\right) = \frac{4}{9}$$

and

$$J_{3,2}(\tfrac{2}{3}) = \frac{4}{9}$$

As an example, consider cubic Bezier curves, as shown in Fig. 5-8. For this case $n = 3$. Assume equal increments in the parameter t for the segment, say, $t = 0$, 1/3, 2/3, 1. Then using Eqs. (5-64) and (5-65) yields

$$J_{3,1}(t) = \frac{3!}{1!\,(2!)}\,t(1-t)^2 = 3t(1-t)^2$$

and

$$J_{3,2}(t) = \frac{3!}{2!\,(1!)}\,t^2(1-t) = 3t^2(1-t)$$

The results are tabulated in Table 5-2. Using Table 5-2 and Eq. (5-66)

$$P(\tfrac{1}{3}) = \frac{8}{27}P_0 + \frac{4}{9}P_1 + \frac{2}{9}P_2 + \frac{1}{27}P_3$$

Thus, to create a cubic curve segment, it is only necessary to specify the the four polygon vertices and then calculate points along the curve for $0 \le t \le 1.0$ using Eqs. (5-64) and (5-68).

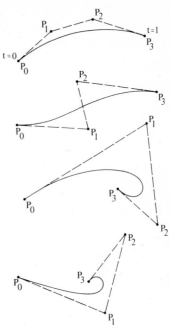

Figure 5-8   Bezier polygons for cubics.

Table 5-2

Results for Bezier Curve

i	$J_{n,i}$	0	1/3	2/3	1	
				$n = 3$		
0		1	8/27	1/27	0	$J_{3,0} = (1-t)^3$
1		0	4/9	2/9	0	$J_{3,1} = 3t(1-t)^2$
2		0	2/9	4/9	0	$J_{3,2} = 3t^2(1-t)$
3		0	1/27	8/27	1	$J_{3,3} = t^3$

as shown above. It is not necessary to explicitly consider parametric derivatives. A user can quickly learn to predict the shape of a curve which will be generated by a certain polygonal shape. Various Bezier cubic curve segments are shown in Fig. 5-8.

Although it is not necessary to consider curve derivatives in generating individual Bezier curves, maintaining continuity of slope and curvature when joining two Bezier curves requires consideration of these derivatives.   The rth derivative at the starting point is given by

$$P^r(0) = \frac{n!}{(n-r)!} \sum_{i=0}^{r} (-1)^{r-i} \binom{r}{i} P_i \qquad (5\text{--}70)$$

and at the end point by

$$P^r(1) = \frac{n!}{(n-r)!} \sum_{i=0}^{r} (-1)^{i} \binom{r}{i} P_{n-i} \qquad (5\text{--}71)$$

Thus, the first derivatives at the end points are

$$P'(0) = n(P_1 - P_0) \qquad (5\text{--}72)$$

and

$$P'(1) = n(P_n - P_{n-1}) \qquad (5\text{--}73)$$

This illustrates that the first derivative of the Bezier curve at the initial and final points is tangent to the initial and final polygon segments, i.e., the end slopes are fixed by the direction of the line joining the two end vertices.

Similarly the second derivatives are

$$P''(0) = n(n-1)(P_0 - 2P_1 + P_2)$$

and $\qquad (5\text{--}74)$

$$P''(1) = n(n-1)(P_n - 2P_{n-1} + P_{n-2})$$

These results illustrate that the second derivative of the Bezier curve at the initial and final points depends on the nearest two polygon segments or on the nearest three polygon vertices.   In general the rth derivatives at an end point or starting point are determined by the end or starting point and its r neighboring polygon vertices.

Continuity conditions between adjacent Bezier curves can thus be simply specified.   If one Bezier curve of order n is defined by vertices P_i and an adjacent Bezier curve of order m by vertices Q_i, then first derivative continuity at the joint is obtained when

$$P'(1) = gQ'(0)$$

where g is a scaler.   Using Eqs. (5--72) and (5--73)

$$Q_1 - Q_0 = \left(\frac{n}{m}\right)(P_n - P_{n-1}) \qquad (5\text{--}75)$$

Since the curve must be continuous at the joint, $Q_0 = P_n$.   Thus, the end of one segment is equal to the starting slope of the next segment when the three points Q_1, P_n, P_{n-1} are collinear.   For the particular case of two adjacent cubic Bezier curves (cf Fig. 5-9), n = m = 3.   If both direction and magnitude of the joint tangents are to be equal, Eq. (5--75) yields

$$Q_1 - Q_0 = P_3 - P_2 = Q_1 - P_3$$

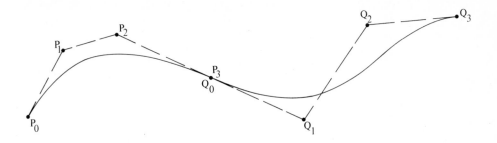

Figure 5-9   First-order continuity in Bezier cubic segments.

Thus

$$Q_1 + P_2 = 2P_3$$

That is, P_3 is the midpoint of P_2Q_1. Note that continuity of slope only requires that P_3 lie on P_2Q_1 somewhere between P_2 and Q_1.

For the same P and Q curves above, second derivative continuity is given by

$$m(m - 1)(Q_0 - 2Q_1 + Q_2) = n(n - 1)(P_{n-2} - 2P_{n-1} + P_n) \qquad (5-76)$$

As a practical matter it may be necessary to increase the order of the curve, i.e., increase the number of polygon vertices to maintain higher order derivative continuity. This is frequently easier than splitting the overall curve into smaller segments and maintaining lower orders, say cubic, within the segment. This flexibility of increasing the order of curve segments to get better control of the curve shape is one of the major advantages of the Bezier method.

Example 5-3:   BEZIER CURVE

Assume that $P_0[1\ 1]$, $P_1[2\ 3]$, $P_2[4\ 3]$, and $P_3[3\ 1]$ are the position vectors of a Bezier polygon.

Recall Eqs. (5-64) to (5-66)

$$P(t) = \sum_{i=0}^{n} P_i J_{n,i}(t)$$

where $J_{n,i}(t) = \binom{n}{i} t^i (1 - t)^{n-i}$ and $\binom{n}{i} = \dfrac{n!}{i!(n-i)!}$. Here n = 3, since we have 4 vertices. Hence

$$\binom{n}{i} = \frac{6}{i!(3-i)!}$$

and

$$J_{3,0}(t) = (1)t^0(1 - t)^3 = (1 - t)^3$$
$$J_{3,1}(t) = 3t(1 - t)^2$$
$$J_{3,2}(t) = 3t^2(1 - t)$$

$$J_{3,3}(t) = t^3$$

Thus

$$P(t) = P_0 J_{3,0} + P_1 J_{3,1} + P_2 J_{3,2} + P_3 J_{3,3}$$

A table of $J_{n,1}$ for various values of t is given below.

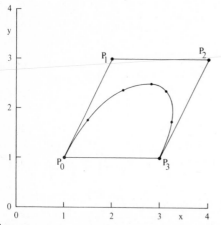

Table 5-3

Coefficients for a Bezier Curve

t	$J_{3,0}$	$J_{3,1}$	$J_{3,2}$	$J_{3,3}$
0	1	0	0	0
0.15	0.614	0.325	0.0574	0.0034
0.35	0.275	0.444	0.239	0.043
0.5	0.125	0.375	0.375	0.125
0.65	0.043	0.239	0.444	0.275
0.85	0.0034	0.0574	0.325	0.614
1	0	0	0	1

Figure 5-10   Results for Bezier curve segment for Example 5-3. Finally

$$P(0) = P_0 = [1\ 1]$$

$$P(0.15) = 0.614P_0 + 0.325P_1 + 0.0574P_2 + 0.0034P_3 = [1.5\ 1.765]$$

$$P(0.35) = 0.275P_0 + 0.444P_1 + 0.239P_2 + 0.043P_3 = [2.248\ 2.367]$$

$$P(0.5) = 0.125P_0 + 0.375P_1 + 0.375P_2 + 0.125P_3 = [2.75\ 2.5]$$

$$P(0.65) = 0.043P_0 + 0.239P_1 + 0.444P_2 + 0.275P_3 = [3.122\ 2.367]$$

$$P(0.85) = 0.0034P_0 + 0.0574P_1 + 0.325P_2 + 0.614P_3 = [3.248\ 1.765]$$

$$P(1) = P_3 = [3\ 1]$$

These points are plotted along with the defining polygon in Fig. 5-10.

An algorithm which may be used to calculate Bezier curve segments given the position vectors of the polygon vertices is given in Appendix C.

5-8   B-SPLINE CURVES

From a mathematical point of view, a curve which is generated by using the vertices of a defining polygon is dependent on some interpolation or approximation scheme to establish the relationship between the curve and the polygon. This scheme is provided by the choice of a basis or weighting function. As noted in the previous section, the Bernstein basis produces Bezier curves generated by Eq. (5-66). These have several useful properties.

Two characteristics of the Bernstein basis, however, limit the flexibility of the resulting curves. First the number of specified polygon vertices fixes the order of the resulting polynomial which defines the curve. For example, a cubic curve must be defined by a polygon with four vertices and three spans. A polygon with six vertices will always produce a fifth-degree curve. The only way to reduce the order of the curve is to reduce the number of vertices, and conversely the only way to increase the order of the curve is to increase the number of vertices.

The second limiting characteristic is due to the global nature of the Bernstein basis. This means that the value of the weighting function $J_{n,i}(t)$ given by Eq. (5-64) is nonzero for all parameter values over an entire span of the curve. Since any point on a Bezier curve is a result of weighting the values of all defining vertices, a change in one vertex is felt throughout the entire span. Practically, this eliminates the ability to produce a local change within a span.

For example, since the end slopes of a Bezier curve are established by the directions of the first and last polygon sides, it is possible to change the middle vertex of a five-point polygon without changing the *direction* of the end slopes. However, the shape of the total curve is affected due to the global nature of the Bernstein basis. This lack of local span control can be detrimental in some applications.

There is another basis, called the B-spline basis, which contains the Bernstein basis as a special case. This basis is generally nonglobal. The nonglobal behavior of B-spline curves is due to the fact that each vertex P_i is associated with a unique basis function. Thus, each vertex affects the shape of a curve only over a range of parameter values where its associated basis function is nonzero. The B-spline basis also allows the order of the resulting curve to be changed without changing the number of defining polygon vertices. The theory for B-splines was first suggested by Schoenberg (Ref. 5-13). A recursive definition useful for numerical computation was published by Cox (Ref. 5-14), and by de Boor (Ref. 5-15). Reisenfeld (Ref. 5-16) applied the B-spline basis to curve definition.

If we again let $P(t)$ be the position vectors along the curve, as a function of the parameter t, a curve generated by the use of the B-spline basis is given by

$$P(t) = \sum_{i=0}^{n} P_i N_{i,k}(t) \qquad (5-77)$$

where the P_i are the n + 1 defining polygon vertices.

For the ith normalized B-spline basis curve of order k, the weighting functions $N_{i,k}(t)$ are defined by the recursion formulas

$$N_{i,1}(t) = \begin{cases} 1 \text{ if } x_i \leq t < x_{i+1} \\ 0 \text{ otherwise} \end{cases}$$

and

$$N_{i,k}(t) = \frac{(t - x_i)N_{i,k-1}(t)}{x_{i+k-1} - x_i} + \frac{(x_{i+k} - t)N_{i+1,k-1}(t)}{x_{i+k} - x_{i+1}} \tag{5-78}$$

The values of x_i are elements of a knot vector which is discussed below. The parameter t varies from 0 to t_{max} along the curve $P(t)$.

An additional variable must be used for B-spline curves to account for the inherent added flexibility. This is achieved by use of a knot vector. A knot vector is simply a series of real integers x_i, such that $x_i \leq x_{i+1}$ for all x_i. Examples of knot vectors are [0 1 2 3 4] and [0 0 0 1 1 2 3 3 3]. The values of x_i are considered to be parametric knots. They can be used to indicate the range of the parameter t used to generate a B-spline curve with $0 \leq t \leq t_{max}$.

Recall that the parameter range for a Bezier curve was arbitrarily chosen to be $0 \leq t \leq 1$ for a Bezier curve of any order. We now deviate from this convention and use a knot vector to specify the parameter variation for the curve. For example, the vector [0 1 2 3 4] indicates that the parameter t varies from 0 to 4. The number of intermediate knot vectors depends on the number of spans in the defining polygon. A duplicate intermediate knot value indicates that a multiple vertex (span of zero length) occurs at a point, and an intermediate knot value in triplicate indicates three concurrent vertices (two zero-length spans). The actual point on a B-spline curve which corresponds to the value of a parametric knot ($t = x_i$) is called a geometric knot. It is convenient to use evenly spaced knots with unit separation between noncoincident knots. This gives integer values for the components of the knot vector. In addition to the knot vector values, the order of the curve must be specified. If the order k equals the number of polygon vertices, and there are no multiple vertices, then a Bezier curve will be generated. As the order decreases, the curve produced lies closer to the defining polygon. When k = 2 the generated curve is a series of straight lines which are identical to the defining polygon.

The order of a curve is reflected in the knot vector that is used to generate the curve. It is necessary to specify knots of multiplicity k at both the beginning and the end of the knot set. For example, consider a five-point polygon (n + 1 = 5) with no duplicate vertices. When there are no duplicate vertices, the parameter t varies from 0 to n - k + 2 over the entire curve.

For a third-order curve defined by five vertices, the value of t_{max} =
4 - 3 + 2 = 3. The complete knot vector, using multiplicity of 3 at each end,
is then given by [0 0 0 1 2 3 3 3]. A second-order curve for the same defining
polygon has a knot vector [0 0 1 2 3 4 4], and a fourth-order curve has
[0 0 0 0 1 2 2 2 2]. If seven polygon vertices are used a third-order curve is
desired, then the knot vector is [0 0 0 1 2 3 4 5 5 5].

As a final example, consider a polygon of four distinct vertices. The knot
vector for a second-order curve is [0 0 1 2 3 3]. Now, if the two center vertices are made to coincide so that a multiple knot occurs between the two end
knots, the knot vector for the second-order curve is [0 0 1 1 2 2].

If smoothness is based on continuity of higher order derivatives, the
order of the curve determines how "smooth" the curve is. For example, a fourth
order curve is continuous in first and second derivative, as well as position,
along the entire curve.

The B-spline curve is mathematically defined as a polynomial spline function of order k (degree k - 1) since it satisfies the following two conditions:

The function P(t) is a polynomial of degree k - 1 on each interval
$(x_i \leq t \leq x_{i+1})$.

P(t) and its derivatives of order 1, 2, . . . , k - 2 are all continuous
over the entire curve.

Thus, a fourth order B-spline curve is a piecewise cubic spline.

Due to the flexibility of B-spline curves, different types of control
"handles" can be used to change the shape of a curve. Control can be achieved
by changing the integer order k for $2 \leq k \leq n + 1$, by use of repeating vertices,
or by changing the number and/or position of nonrepeating vertices in the defining polygon. These effects are illustrated in the following six figures.

Figure 5-11 shows three B-spline curves of different order, each defined
by the same four polygon vertices given by $\begin{bmatrix} 0 & 0 \\ 3 & 9 \\ 6 & 3 \\ 9 & 6 \end{bmatrix}$. The second-order curve
creates three straight lines between the four vertices, the fourth-order curve
corresponds to the Bezier curve for the polygon set, and the third-order curve
produces a looser curve between the two end points. Notice that all three
curves have the same end slopes, determined by the slope of the first and last
spans of the defining polygon. As the order of a curve increases, the resulting
shape looks less like the defining polygon shape. Thus, increasing the order
tightens the curve.

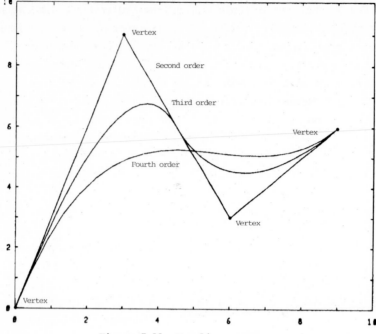

Figure 5-11 B-spline curves.

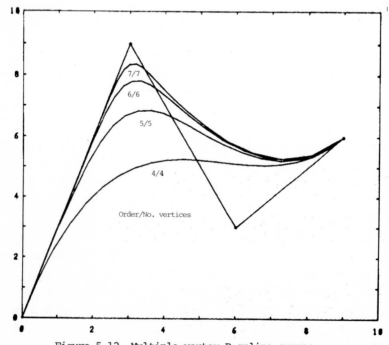

Figure 5-12 Multiple vertex B-spline curves.

Figure 5-12 shows the effect of multiple vertices in the defining polygon. For each of the four curves shown, the order of the curve is equal to the number of vertices in the defining polygon. The lower curve in Fig. 5-12 is identical to the lower curve in Fig. 5-11, a fourth-order curve defined by four polygon vertices. The second curve in Fig. 5-12 is a fifth-order curve with a double vertex at [3,9]. The third curve is a sixth-order curve with a triple vertex at [3,9]. The final seventh-order curve has a defining polygon given by

$$\begin{bmatrix} 0 & 0 \\ 3 & 9 \\ 3 & 9 \\ 3 & 9 \\ 3 & 9 \\ 6 & 3 \\ 9 & 6 \end{bmatrix}$$

e.g., four multiple vertices at [3 9]. This figure clearly shows how a curve can be pulled closer to a specific vertex position by use of multiple vertices while maintaining the same end slopes for each curve. On the other hand, decreasing the order pulls the curve closer to all polygon vertices.

In Fig. 5-13 the defining vertex is

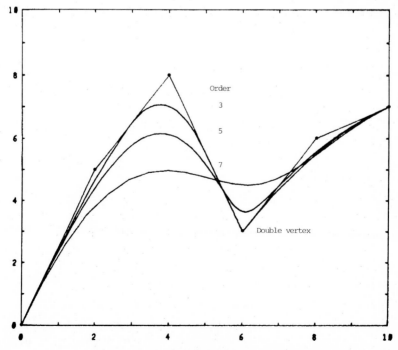

Figure 5-13 Multiple knot B-spline curves.

$$\begin{bmatrix} 0 & 0 \\ 2 & 5 \\ 4 & 8 \\ 6 & 3 \\ 6 & 3 \\ 8 & 6 \\ 10 & 7 \end{bmatrix}$$

for each curve. That is, we keep a double vertex at the fourth element in the polygon. Here the curve is altered by changing the order of each curve, keeping the defining polygon constant. The first curve is of order seven, equal to the number of vertices in the polygon. The second curve is of order five. This curve shape is closer to the polygon shape, especially near the double vertex. The third curve is of order 3. Notice that a "knuckle" occurs at the double vertex since the slope and curvature are discontinuous. A duplicate vertex is required to create a knuckle in a third-order curve. A triple vertex creates a knuckle in a fourth order curve. This ability is a common requirement in ship design.

Figure 5-14 demonstrates how local changes can be made without affecting the entire shape of a curve. Each curve is a fifth-order curve, defined by a seven-point polygon with no multiple vertices. The only difference between

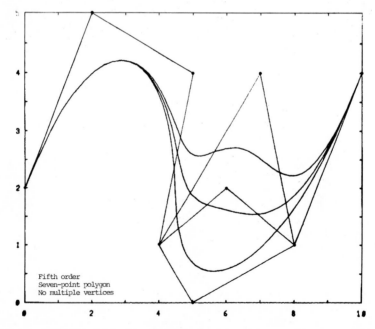

Figure 5-14 Local control of B-spline curves.

each curve is that the fifth vertex is moved to a new position, as shown in the figure. It can be seen that the first part of each curve is unchanged. This behavior is a result of the nonglobal (local) nature of the B-spline basis.

Figure 5-15 shows curves of order 2 through 6, generated by a six-point polygon with no multiple vertices. The fourth order curve is a cubic spline. The B-spline curve technique allows a cubic spline to be generated with four or more polygon vertices. Since there are six vertices in this polygon, the sixth-order curve is the Bezier curve. The third-order curve may be of special interest since it is tangent to the midpoints of the internal polygon spans. This characteristic is also shown in Fig. 5-16, where a third-order curve is generated with an eight-point polygon.

Example 5-4:   B-SPLINE CURVE

Consider the same four polygon position vectors used in the previous example for a Bezier curve. These are $P_0[1\ 1]$, $P_1[2\ 3]$, $P_2[4\ 3]$, and $P_3[3\ 1]$. The knot vector set for a second-order curve defined by four polygon vertices is [0 0 1 2 3 3], where we denote $x_0 = 0$, $x_1 = 0$, $x_2 = 1$, ..., $x_5 = 3$.

When using Eq. (5-78) the convention $0/0 = 0$ is applied. The $N_{i,k}$ values needed are

$$N_{0,2}(t) = \frac{(t - 0)N_{0,1}(t)}{x_1 - x_0} + \frac{(x_2 - t)N_{1,1}(t)}{x_2 - x_1}$$

$$N_{1,2}(t) = \frac{(t - 0)N_{1,1}(t)}{x_2 - x_1} + \frac{(x_3 - t)N_{2,1}(t)}{x_3 - x_2}$$

$$N_{2,2}(t) = \frac{(t - 1)N_{2,1}(t)}{x_3 - x_1} + \frac{(x_4 - t)N_{3,1}(t)}{x_4 - x_3}$$

$$N_{3,2}(t) = \frac{(t - 2)N_{3,1}(t)}{x_4 - x_3} + \frac{(x_5 - t)N_{4,1}(t)}{x_5 - x_4}$$

Specifically, for $t = 0$, $N_{0,2}(0) = 0(1)/0 + (1 - 0)(1)/1 = 1.0$ and $N_{1,2}(t) = 0(1)/1 + (2 - 0)(0)/1 = 0$. For $t = 0.5$ we find $N_{1,2}(t) = 0.5(1)/1 + (2 - 0.5)(0)/1 = 0.5$, and for $t = 1$ we calculate $N_{3,2}(1) = -1(0)/1 + 2(0)/0 = 0$. Other values of $N_{i,k}$ are found in a similar manner. Table 5-4 gives the complete results. By using the values of $N_{i,j}$ given in Table 5-4, points on the second-order curve can be determined. From Eq. (5-77), in general,

$$P(t) = P_0N_{0,2} + P_1N_{1,2} + P_2N_{2,2} + P_3N_{3,2}$$

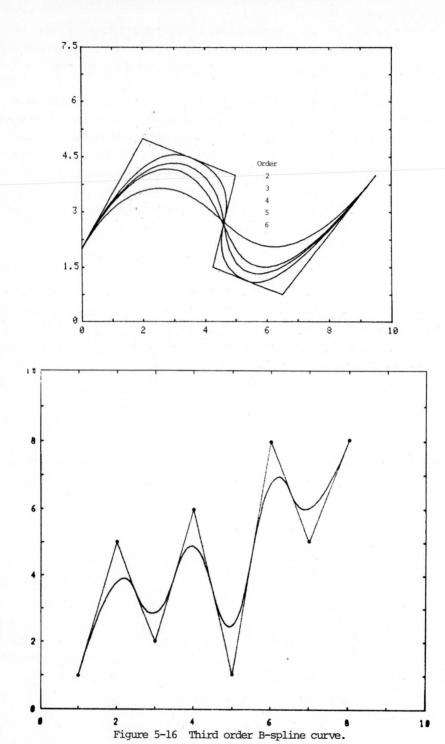

Figure 5-16 Third order B-spline curve.

Table 5-4

Weighting Functions for a Second-Order B-Spline

$N_{i,j}$ \ t	0	0.5	1.0	1.5	2	2.5	3
$N_{0,2}$	1	0.5	0	0	0	0	0
$N_{1,2}$	0	0.5	1	0.5	0	0	0
$N_{2,2}$	0	0	0	0.5	1	0.5	0
$N_{3,2}$	0	0	0	0	0	0.5	1

For t = 0,

$$P(0) = P_0(1) + P_1(0) + P_2(0) + P_3(0) = P_0$$

Similarly

$$P(0.5) = P_0(0.5) + P_1(0.5) + P_2(0) + P_3(0) = 0.5(P_0 + P_1)$$

$$P(1) = P_0(0) + P_1(1) + P_2(0) + P_3(0) = P_1$$

$$P(1.5) = P_0(0) + P_1(0.5) + P_2(0.5) + P_3(0) = 0.5(P_1 + P_2)$$

In a like manner the last three points are $P(2) = P_2$, $P(2.5) = 0.5(P_2 + P_3)$, and $P(3) = P_3$. These points obviously fall on the straight lines joining the polygon vertices.

Now, if the order of the curve is increased from two to four for the same four defining polygon vertices, a Bezier curve will be obtained since the order now equals the number of vertices. The knot vector set (with t_{max} = 3 - 4 + 2 = 1) is [0 0 0 0 1 1 1 1]. Values of the weighting functions given by Eq. (5-78) are

$$N_{0,4}(t) = \frac{(t - 0)N_{0,3}(t)}{0 - 0} + \frac{(1 - t)N_{1,3}(t)}{1 - 0}$$

$$N_{1,4}(t) = \frac{(t - 0)N_{1,3}(t)}{1 - 0} + \frac{(1 - t)N_{2,3}(t)}{1 - 0}$$

$$N_{2,4}(t) = \frac{(t - 0)N_{2,3}(t)}{1 - 0} + \frac{(1 - t)N_{3,3}(t)}{1 - 0}$$

$$N_{3,4}(t) = \frac{(t - 0)N_{3,3}(t)}{1 - 0} + \frac{(1 - t)N_{4,3}(t)}{1 - 1}$$

Proceeding with the required $N_{i,3}$ evaluations,

$$N_{0,3}(t) = \frac{(t - 0)N_{0,2}(t)}{0 - 0} + \frac{(1 - t)N_{1,2}(t)}{0 - 0}$$

$$N_{1,3}(t) = \frac{(t - 0)N_{1,2}(t)}{0 - 0} + \frac{(1 - t)N_{2,2}(t)}{1 - 0}$$

$$N_{2,3}(t) = \frac{(t - 0)N_{2,2}(t)}{1 - 0} + \frac{(1 - t)N_{3,2}(t)}{1 - 0}$$

$$N_{3,3}(t) = \frac{(t - 0)N_{3,2}(t)}{1 - 0} + \frac{(1 - t)N_{4,2}(t)}{1 - 1}$$

$$N_{4,3}(t) = \frac{(t - 1)N_{4,2}(t)}{1 - 1} + \frac{(1 - t)N_{5,2}(t)}{1 - 1}$$

These $N_{i,3}$ equations in turn require $N_{i,2}$ values given by

$$N_{0,2}(t) = \frac{(t - 0)N_{0,1}(t)}{0 - 0} + \frac{(0 - t)N_{1,1}(t)}{0 - 0}$$

$$N_{1,2}(t) = \frac{(t - 0)N_{1,1}(t)}{0 - 0} + \frac{(0 - t)N_{2,1}(t)}{0 - 0}$$

$$N_{2,2}(t) = \frac{(t - 0)N_{2,1}(t)}{0 - 0} + \frac{(1 - t)N_{3,1}(t)}{1 - 0}$$

$$N_{3,2}(t) = \frac{(t - 0)N_{3,1}(t)}{1 - 0} + \frac{(1 - t)N_{4,1}(t)}{1 - 1}$$

$$N_{4,2}(t) = \frac{(t - 1)N_{4,1}(t)}{1 - 1} + \frac{(1 - t)N_{5,1}(t)}{1 - 1}$$

$$N_{5,2}(t) = \frac{(t - 1)N_{5,1}(t)}{1 - 1} + \frac{(1 - t)N_{6,1}(t)}{1 - 1}$$

Let us evaluate the point on the curve at $t = 0.5$. Since the parameter variation as specified by the knot vector falls between $0 \le t \le 1$ for this case, the value $P(0.5)$ should correspond to the value $P(0.5)$ found in the Bezier example in Sec. 5-7. For $t = 0.5$, $N_{0,1} = N_{1,1} = N_{2,1} = N_{4,1} = N_{5,1} = N_{6,1} = 0$, and $N_{3,1} = 1.0$. Thus, $N_{0,2} = N_{1,2} = N_{4,2} = N_{5,2} = 0$, and

$$N_{2,2}(0.5) = 0 + \frac{(0.5)(1)}{1} = 0.5$$

$$N_{3,2}(0.5) = \frac{(0.5)(1)}{1} + 0 = 0.5$$

Working backward it follows that $N_{0,3} = N_{4,3} = 0$, and

$$N_{1,3} = 0 + \frac{(0.5)(0.5)}{1} = 0.25$$

$$N_{2,3} = \frac{(0.5)(0.5)}{1} + \frac{(0.5)(0.5)}{1} = 0.50$$

$$N_{3,3} = \frac{(0.5)(0.5)}{1} + 0 = 0.25$$

Likewise

$$N_{0,4} = 0 + \frac{(0.5)(0.25)}{1} = 0.125$$

$$N_{1,4} = \frac{(0.5)(0.25)}{1} + \frac{(0.5)(0.5)}{1} = 0.375$$

$$N_{2,4} = \frac{(0.5)(0.5)}{1} + \frac{0.5(0.25)}{1} = 0.375$$

$$N_{3,4} = \frac{(0.5)(0.25)}{1} + 0 = 0.125$$

Finally, the point on the curve at t = 0.5 is given by Eq. (5-77) as

$$P(0.5) = P_0 N_{0,4} + P_1 N_{1,4} + P_2 N_{2,4} + P_3 N_{3,4}$$

or

$$P(0.5) = [1\ 1]0.125 + [2\ 3]0.375 + [4\ 3]0.375 + [3\ 1]0.125$$

$$= [2.75\ 2.5]$$

The x-component is then $P_x = 2.75$ and the y-component $P_y = 2.5$, which agrees with the Bezier curve results.

Algorithms which will generate the required B-spline basis knot vectors and the corresponding B-spline curves are given in Appendix C.

REFERENCES

5-1 Higdon, A., Ohlsen, E., Stiles, W. and Weese, J., Mechanics of Materials, 2d edition, John Wiley & Sons, Inc., New York, 1967.

5-2 South, N.E., and Kelly, J. P., "Analytic Surface Methods," Ford Motor Company N/C Development Unit, Product Engineering Office, December 1965.

5-3 Nutbourne, A. W., "A Cubic Spline Package Part 2 - The Mathematics," Comput. Aided Des., vol. 5, no. 1, January 1973.

5-4 Adams, J. Alan, "A Comparison of Methods for Cubic Spline Curve Fitting," Comput. Aided Des., vol. 6, pp. 1-9, 1974.

5-5 Manning, J. R., "Computer-Aided Footwear Design: A method of constructing smooth curves," SATRA (Shoe & Allied Trades Research Association - SATRA House, Rockingham Road, Kettering Northants, England) Research Report R.R. 251, December 1972.

5-6 Denman, H. H., "Smooth Cubic Spline Interpolation Functions," Industrial Mathematics, J. Ind. Math. Soc., vol. 21, Part 2, pp. 55-75, 1971.

5-7 Cline, A. K., "Curve Fitting Using Splines Under Tension," Atmos. Tech., no. 3, pp. 60-65, 1973.

5-8 Schweikert, D. C., "An interpolation curve using a spline in tension," J. Math. Phys., vol. 45, pp. 312-317, 1966.

5-9 Overhauser, A. W., "Analytic Definition of Curves and Surfaces by Parabolic Blending," Technical Report No. SL68-40, Ford Motor Company Scientific Laboratory, May 8, 1968.

5-10   Bezier, P.E., Emploi des Machines a Commande Numerique, Masson et Cie, Paris, 1970. Translated by Forrest, D. R. and Pankhurst, A. F. as Bezier, P.F., Numerical Control Mathematics and Applications, John Wiley & Sons, Inc., London, 1972.

5-11   Bezier, P.E., "Example of an Existing System in the Motor Industry: The Unisurf System," Proc. Roy. Soc. (London), vol. A321, pp. 207-218, 1971.

5-12   Forrest, A. R., "Interpolation and Approximation by Bezier Polynomials, " CAD Group Doc. No. 45, UML, Cambridge University, October 1970.

5-13   Schoenberg, I. J., "Contributions to the Problem of Approximation of Equidistant Data by Analytic Functions," Q. Appl. Math., vol. 4, 1946, pp. 45-99; 112-141.

5-14   Cox, M. G., "The Numerical Evaluation of B-Splines," Nathional Physical Laboratory DNAC 4, August 1971.

5-15   de Boor, Carl, "On Calculating with B-Splines," J. Approx. Theory, vol. 6, pp. 50-62, 1972.

5-16   Riesenfeld, R. F., "Application of B-Spline Approximation to Geometric Problems of Computer Aided Design," Available at U. of Utah, UTEC-CSc-73-126

and

Gordon, W. J., Reisenfeld, R. F., "Bernstein-Bezier Methods for the Computer-Aided Design of Free Form Curves and Surfaces," J. ACM, vol. 21, pp. 293-310, 1974.

CHAPTER 6

SURFACE DESCRIPTION AND GENERATION

6-1 INTRODUCTION

Surfaces and surface representation play a critical role in most design and manufacturing processes. The design and manufacture of automobiles, aircraft, ships, machine parts, glassware, and clothing are obvious examples. The traditional way of representing a surface is to use multiple orthogonal projections. However, many complex surfaces cannot be efficiently represented in this manner. The development of interactive computer-aided design techniques along with that of numerically controlled machine tools has lead to the development of more effective methods of surface representation. Here we are not concerned with computer representation of just the pictorial aspects of a surface, but rather the mathematical description of shape from which either drawings or numerical controlled machine tool tapes can be obtained. The feasibility of producing a surface directly from a computer stored representation of that surface has been demonstrated by Bezier (Ref. 6-1), Sabin (Ref. 6-2), Peters (Ref. 6-3), and others.

Various techniques of analytically and numerically representing a three-dimensional surface are discussed below. To begin the discussion we consider a simple spherical surface.

6-2   SPHERICAL SURFACES

Some properties of curves which are useful in surface definition can be demonstrated by considering a surface of known analytical description. To this end consider a spherical surface. Specific curves on the surface are defined by planes which intersect the sphere. As an example consider the intersection of a unit sphere and the plane defined by the surface $z = \cos\phi_1 = a_1$. This is shown in Fig. 6-1a. The resulting curve is a parallel of latitude. The equation for the parallel of latitude is obtained by solving the two surface equations simultaneously. The nonparametric equation for a unit sphere is

$$x^2 + y^2 + z^2 = 1.0 \qquad (6-1)$$

Thus,

$$x^2 + y^2 = 1 - a_1^2$$

defines the intersection.

In Fig. 6-1b, the plane at $\theta = \theta_0$ which intersects the sphere is defined by

$$x\sin\theta_0 - y\cos\theta_0 = 0$$

or

$$c_1 x - b_1 y = 0 \qquad (6-2)$$

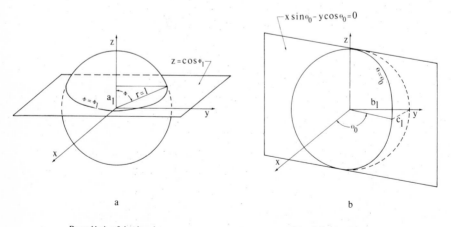

a

Parallel of latitude

b

Meridian of longitude

Figure 6-1   Intersections of a plane and sphere.

The resulting intersection of the plane and the sphere yields a meridian of longitude. Solving Eqs. (6-1) and (6-2) simultaneously yields the equation for the resulting curve, i.e.,

$$y^2 [(\frac{b_1}{c_1})^2 + 1] + z^2 = 1.0$$

A spherical surface patch can be formed by four planes intersecting the sphere, as shown in Fig. 6-2. This creates two parallels of latitude and two meridians of longitude for the patch boundaries. The vector equation for the resulting surface patch $S(\theta, \phi)$ is

$$S = (\cos\theta\sin\phi)\vec{e}_1 + (\sin\phi\sin\theta)\vec{e}_2 + (\cos\phi)\vec{e}_3 \qquad (6-3)$$

where $\vec{e}_1$, $\vec{e}_2$, and $\vec{e}_3$ are unit vectors in the rectangular coordinate system, and S is a position vector on the surface of the sphere as shown in Fig. 6-2. This surface patch can be thought of as the locus of a point in three-dimensional space which moves with two degrees of freedom controlled by the two parameter variables θ and ϕ.

A parametric representation of the unit spherical surface is

$$x = \cos\theta\sin\phi \qquad (6-4)$$
$$y = \sin\theta\sin\phi$$
$$z = \cos\phi$$

Notice that two parameters θ and ϕ are required for the parametric representation of a surface. The patch shown in Fig. 6-2 is defined between $0 \leq \theta \leq \pi/2$ and $\pi/4 \leq \phi \leq \pi/2$. From Fig. 6-2 we see that the surface patch is defined by the four boundary curves AB, BC, CD, and DA. For the spherical patch these are circular arcs. Further analysis of Fig. 6-2 shows that the shape of a boundary curve can be described by specifying the tangent vectors at the end of each curve, i.e., the eight tangent vectors at the end of each of the corner points A, B, C, and D. For a known analytical surface these end tangent vectors can be obtained by differentiating the equation describing the surface. For the spherical surface shown in Fig. 6-2 these are

$$\frac{\partial S}{\partial \theta} = -(\sin\theta\sin\phi)\vec{e}_1 + (\cos\theta\sin\phi)\vec{e}_2 \qquad (6-5)$$

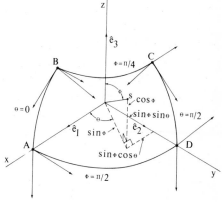

Figure 6-2   Spherical surface patch.

$$\frac{\partial S}{\partial \phi} = (\cos\theta\cos\phi)\vec{e}_1 + (\sin\theta\cos\phi)\vec{e}_2 - (\sin\phi)\vec{e}_3 \qquad (6\text{-}6)$$

At corner A, $\theta = 0$, $\phi = \pi/2$, and

$$\frac{\partial S}{\partial \theta} = \vec{e}_2$$

$$\frac{\partial S}{\partial \phi} = -\vec{e}_3$$

The magnitude of each of these tangent vectors is unity. At corner C, $\phi = \pi/4$, $\theta = \pi/2$, and

$$\frac{\partial S}{\partial \theta} = -\frac{1}{\sqrt{2}}\vec{e}_1$$

$$\frac{\partial S}{\partial \phi} = \frac{1}{\sqrt{2}}\vec{e}_2 - \frac{1}{\sqrt{2}}\vec{e}_3$$

Here the magnitude of $\partial S/\partial \theta$ is $1/\sqrt{2}$, and the magnitude of $\partial S/\partial \phi$ is

$$\sqrt{(1/\sqrt{2})^2 + (1/\sqrt{2})^2} = 1.0$$

The tangent vectors at all four corners are shown in Fig. 6-2 and are given in Table 6-1.

Table 6-1

Tangent Vectors for the Spherical
Surface of Fig. 6-2

Point	$\partial S/\partial \theta$	$\lvert \partial S/\partial \theta \rvert$	$\partial S/\partial \phi$	$\lvert \partial S/\partial \phi \rvert$
A	$\vec{e}_2$	1	$-\vec{e}_3$	1
B	$\frac{1}{\sqrt{2}}\vec{e}_2$	$\frac{1}{\sqrt{2}}$	$\frac{1}{\sqrt{2}}\vec{e}_1 - \frac{1}{\sqrt{2}}\vec{e}_3$	1
C	$-\frac{1}{\sqrt{2}}\vec{e}_1$	$\frac{1}{\sqrt{2}}$	$\frac{1}{\sqrt{2}}\vec{e}_2 - \frac{1}{\sqrt{2}}\vec{e}_3$	1
D	$-\vec{e}_1$	1	$-\vec{e}_3$	1

The cross derivatives, or twist vectors, at the corners are also useful in describing the boundaries of a surface patch. For the unit spherical patch these are

$$\frac{\partial}{\partial \phi}\left(\frac{\partial S}{\partial \theta}\right) = \frac{\partial}{\partial \theta}\left(\frac{\partial S}{\partial \phi}\right) = -(\sin\theta\cos\phi)\vec{e}_1 + (\cos\theta\cos\phi)\vec{e}_2 \qquad (6\text{-}7)$$

The magnitude of the twist vector is

$$\left\lvert \frac{\partial^2 S}{\partial \theta \partial \phi} \right\rvert = \sqrt{\sin^2\theta\cos^2\phi + \cos^2\theta\cos^2\phi} = \cos\phi \qquad (6\text{-}8)$$

Note at corner A, $\partial^2 S/\partial \theta \partial \phi = 0$ and at corner C, $\partial^2 S/\partial \theta \partial \phi = -(1/\sqrt{2})\vec{e}_1$. The twist vectors and their magnitudes for the corners of the spherical and surface patch are shown in Table 6-2.

Table 6-2

Twist Vectors for the Spherical
Surface of Fig. 6-2

Point	$\partial/\partial\phi\,(\partial S/\partial\theta)$	$\lvert\partial/\partial\theta\,(\partial S/\partial\theta)\rvert$
A	0	0
B	$1/\sqrt{2}\ \vec{e}_2$	$1/\sqrt{2}$
C	$-1/\sqrt{2}\ \vec{e}_1$	$1/\sqrt{2}$
D	0	0

Surface normals can also be used to indicate the shape and orientation
of a surface patch. The surface normals are given by the vector cross product
of two tangent vectors. For the spherical patch,

$$N = \frac{\partial S}{\partial\theta} \times \frac{\partial S}{\partial\phi} = \begin{vmatrix} \vec{e}_1 & \vec{e}_2 & \vec{e}_3 \\ -\sin\theta\sin\phi & \cos\theta\sin\phi & 0 \\ \cos\theta\cos\phi & \sin\theta\cos\phi & -\sin\phi \end{vmatrix} \tag{6-9}$$

It follows that at corners A and D, $N = -\vec{e}_2$, at corner B, $N = -1/2\,(\vec{e}_1 + \vec{e}_3)$ and
at corner C, $N = -1/2\,(\vec{e}_2 + \vec{e}_3)$. The normals at corners B and C are shown in
Fig. 6-2. The *outward* drawn normals for the surface patch are the negatives of
these values.

A unit surface normal is defined by $\vec{n} = N/\lvert N\rvert$. Expanding Eq. (6-9) gives

$$N = -(\cos\theta\sin^2\phi)\vec{e}_1 - (\sin\theta\sin^2\phi)\vec{e}_2 - (\sin\phi\cos\phi)\vec{e}_3 \tag{6-10}$$

and

$$\lvert N\rvert = \sqrt{\cos^2\theta\sin^4\phi + \sin^2\theta\sin^4\phi + \sin^2\phi\cos^2\phi} = \sin\phi \tag{6-11}$$

Thus,

$$\vec{n} = -(\cos\theta\sin\phi)\vec{e}_1 - (\sin\theta\sin\phi)\vec{e}_2 - (\cos\phi)\vec{e}_3 \tag{6-12}$$

where

$$\lvert\vec{n}\rvert = 1.0 \tag{6-13}$$

A final vector operation which is useful for surface description is the
dot product. For the surface patch under consideration,

$$\frac{\partial S}{\partial\theta} \cdot \frac{\partial S}{\partial\phi} = [(-\sin\theta\sin\phi)\vec{e}_1 + (\cos\theta\sin\phi)\vec{e}_2] \cdot [(\cos\theta\cos\phi)\vec{e}_1 + (\sin\theta\cos\phi)\vec{e}_2 - (\sin\phi)\vec{e}_3] = 0 \tag{6-14}$$

Since the dot product of these tangents vectors equals zero, the two tangent
vectors are perpendicular to one another. Thus, lines of ϕ = constant (parallels of latitude) are perpendicular to lines of θ = constant (meridians of

longitude) on the surface.

Having used a spherical surface to illustrate a number of useful concepts for surfaces, e.g., tangent vectors, twist vectors and surface normals, we now consider methods for describing more arbitrary surfaces.

6-3   PLANE SURFACES

Some of the techniques for surface representation are most conveniently described by considering a plane surface.   In this section we restrict ourselves to a four-sided plane surface.   The four sides defining the surface are four parametric curves or lines which connect the four corners and form the shape of the boundaries.

As shown by Eq. (6-4) in the previous section, it is possible to express points which fall on a surface in terms of two parameters.   Let these two parameters be u and w.   The expression for the plane surface is then

$$x = f(u,w) \qquad\qquad (6\text{-}15)$$
$$y = g(u,w)$$

The functions in Eqs. (6-15) are chosen such that the four boundary curves are described by the following four conditions:

$$u = c_1 \quad c_1 \le w \le c_2 \qquad\qquad (6\text{-}16)$$
$$u = c_2 \quad c_1 \le w \le c_2$$
$$w = c_1 \quad c_1 \le u \le c_2$$
$$w = c_2 \quad c_1 \le u \le c_2$$

This defines a square in the uw-plane, as shown in Fig. 6-3.   The functions which represent the actual surface are those which map this square in the uw-plane into the desired surface in the xy-plane.

The derivatives of the point functions x and y as defined by Eqs. (6-15) are

$$dx = \frac{\partial x}{\partial u}du + \frac{\partial x}{\partial w}dw$$

and

$$dy = \frac{\partial y}{\partial u}du + \frac{\partial y}{\partial w}dw$$

These equations can be written in matrix form as

$$\begin{bmatrix} dx \\ dy \end{bmatrix} = \begin{bmatrix} \frac{\partial x}{\partial u} & \frac{\partial x}{\partial w} \\ \frac{\partial y}{\partial u} & \frac{\partial y}{\partial w} \end{bmatrix} \begin{bmatrix} du \\ dw \end{bmatrix} \qquad\qquad (6\text{-}17)$$

Equation (6-17) relates a differential change in the uw-plane to the corresponding differential change in the xy-plane.

Example 6-1: PLANE SURFACE

Consider the surface in the xy-plane defined by two parametric equations given by

$$x = 3u + w$$
$$y = 2u + 3w + uw$$

with boundaries specified by

$$u = 0 \quad 0 \leq w \leq 1.0$$
$$u = 1 \quad 0 \leq w \leq 1.0$$
$$w = 0 \quad 0 \leq u \leq 1.0$$
$$w = 1 \quad 0 \leq u \leq 1.0$$

This surface is shown in Fig. 6-4a. The equations for the boundaries can be obtained by substituting the appropriate u and w values. They are

$$u = 0 \quad y = 3x$$
$$u = 1 \quad y = 4x-10$$
$$w = 0 \quad y = (\tfrac{2}{3})x$$
$$w = 1 \quad y = x + 2$$

The derivatives which appear in the Eq. (6-17) are $\partial x/\partial u = 3$, $\partial x/\partial w = 1$, $\partial y/\partial u = 2 + w$, and $\partial y/\partial w = 3 + u$. From these partial derivatives the slopes of the boundaries can be found. It follows that

$$\frac{dy}{dx} = \frac{\partial y/\partial u}{\partial x/\partial u} = \frac{2 + w}{3}$$

along w = constant, and

$$\frac{dy}{dx} = \frac{\partial y/\partial w}{\partial x/\partial w} = \frac{3 + u}{1}$$

along u = constant. These slopes can be verified in Fig. 6-4a.

If desired, additional parametric lines may be added to help represent the surface patch. For example, when u = 1/2 the equation for this parametric line is y = (14x - 17)/4. When w = 1/2, the parametric line is y = (10x + 13)/12. These two surface parametric lines are shown as dashed lines in Fig. 6-4a.

Similar calculations can be made for an expression for a planar surface written as

$$u = f(x,y) \tag{6-18}$$
$$w = g(x,y)$$

Figure 6-4b shows the surface defined by

$$u = \frac{y^2}{x}$$

$$w = \frac{x^2}{y}$$

The boundaries are given by

$$u = 1 \quad 1 \le w \le 4$$
$$u = 4 \quad 1 \le w \le 4$$
$$w = 1 \quad 1 \le u \le 4$$
$$w = 4 \quad 1 \le u \le 4$$

The equations for each boundary curve are indicated in Fig. 6-4b. Many other types of curves, such as conic sections, cubic splines, Bezier polynomials, or B-spline curves can be used to define the boundaries of surfaces.

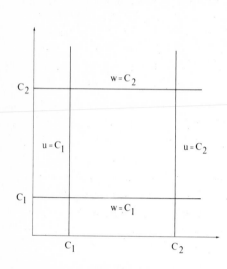

Figure 6-3   Parametric surface rectangle.

6-4   Curved Surface Representation

Before proceeding with the details of the representation of curved three-dimensional surfaces, it is necessary to make several decisions. First, we assume a surface representation based on a vector-valued parametric concept. There are several reasons for this. This type of representation is axis-independent: it avoids infinite slope values with respect to some arbitrary axis system, it allows the unambiguous representation of multivalued surfaces or space functions, it facilitates the representation of space curves in homogeneous coordinates, and it is compatible with the use of the three-dimensional homogeneous coordinate transformations discussed in Chapter 3.

We will assume that a surface may be represented in a piecewise fashion; i.e., a surface is composed of a number of patches which are joined together in some fashion at the boundaries. No attempt will be made to represent a complete surface analytically.

In order to efficiently represent a surface, some notational details are necessary. For consistency we represent a curve as a vector-valued function of a single variable; i.e., the curve $P(t)$ is

$$P(t) = [x(t) \ y(t)]$$

for a planar curve and

$$P(t) = [x(t) \ y(t) \ z(t)]$$

for a space curve. Here t is a parameter. As we have seen in the previous two sections, representation of a surface requires two parameter values. Thus, we assume that a surface may be represented by a bivariate vector-valued

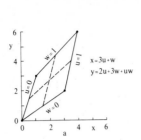 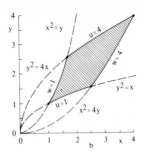

Figure 6-4 Plane surfaces.

function

$$P(u,w) = [x(u,w) \ y(u,w) \ z(u,w)]$$

A curve on this surface may be represented by fixing either u or w, e.g., $P(u_i,w)$ represents a curve along $u = u_i$ = constant, and $P(u,w_i)$ represents a curve along $w = w_i$ = constant. A curve on the surface $P(u,w)$ may also be represented by specifying some relationship between the two parameters, e.g., $f(u,w) = 0$. This relationship might define the intersection of a plane with a surface patch, for example.

A point on the surface may be represented by specifying values of both parameters, i.e., $P(u_i, w_i)$, or by specifying two independent relationships between the parameters, say, $f(u,w) = 0$ and $g(u,w) = 0$. Note that the latter representation does not necessarily define a single fixed point.

We will consider that a surface patch can be built up from known data; i.e., we consider a surface to be constructive. With this in mind we adopt the following convention:

P is the vector obtained from known or input design data.

Q is the vector defining the surface constructed from the input data P.

Thus, P and Q coincide only at the specified data points.

6-5 BILINEAR SURFACES

One of the simplest surfaces is the bilinear surface. Consider that the four corner points of the surface are given in the u,w-plane by $P(0,0)$, $P(0,1)$, $P(1,0)$, and $P(1,1)$, the corners of the unit square. We wish to construct a bivariate function or bilinear surface $Q(u,w)$ where $(u,w\epsilon[0,1])$ allows us to linearly-interpolate any point on the surface. This yields

$$Q(u,w) = P(0,0)(1-u)(1-w) + P(0,1)(1-u)w + P(1,0)u(1-w) + P(1,1)uw \quad (6-19)$$

or

$$Q(u,w) = [(1-u) \ u] \begin{bmatrix} P(0,0) & P(0,1) \\ P(1,0) & P(1,1) \end{bmatrix} \begin{bmatrix} 1-w \\ w \end{bmatrix}$$

which is shown in Fig. 6-5.   Here it is easy to verify that

$$Q(0,0) \equiv P(0,0), \text{ etc.}$$

Also, a point in the center of the surface (u = w = 0.5) is simply

$$Q(0.5, \ 0.5) = \frac{[P(0,0) + P(0,1) + P(1,0) + P(1,1)]}{4}$$

In general, a bilinear surface and the position vectors of the corner points of the surface are three dimensional.   This is perhaps easier to see if we write Eq. (6-19) in a more compact matrix form.   In particular,

$$Q(x(u,w), \ y(u,w), \ z(u,w)) = UP$$

where Q is a position vector on the interpolated surface, P is the matrix of

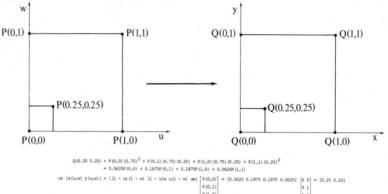

$$Q(0.25 \ 0.25) = P(0,0)(0.75)^2 + P(0,1)(0.75)(0.25) + P(1,0)(0.75)(0.25) + P(1,1)(0.25)^2$$
$$= 0.5625P(0,0) + 0.1875P(0,1) + 0.1875P(1,0) + 0.0625P(1,1)$$

$$\text{or } [x(u,w) \ y(u,w)] = [(1-u)(1-w) \ (1-u)w \ u(1-w) \ uw] \begin{bmatrix} P(0,0) \\ P(0,1) \\ P(1,0) \\ P(1,1) \end{bmatrix} = [0.5625 \ 0.1875 \ 0.1875 \ 0.0625] \begin{bmatrix} 0 & 0 \\ 0 & 1 \\ 1 & 0 \\ 1 & 1 \end{bmatrix} = [0.25 \ 0.25]$$

Figure 6-5a   Planar bilinear surface.

position vectors of the corner points, and U = [(1 - u)(1 - u)w u(1 - w) uw].

An example using two-dimensional position vectors is shown in Fig. 6-5a. An example of a three-dimensional bilinear surface is shown in Fig. 6-5b.   In Fig. 6-5b the assumed three-dimensional position vectors were four of the eight corners of a unit cube.

An algorithm which will create a bilinear surface patch is given in Appendix C.

6-6 LOFTED OR RULED SURFACES

Lofted or ruled surfaces are frequently associated with the aircraft or shipbuilding industries.   To obtain a lofted or ruled surface, assume that two boundary curves associated with the opposite sides of the unit square in the u,w-plane are known, say, P(u,0) and P(u,1).   These may be defined using any of the techniques discussed in Chapter 5.   A ruled or lofted surface is then obtained by linearly interpolating between these two curves, as shown in Fig. 6-6. The interpolation scheme is

$$Q(u,w) = P(u,0)(1 - w) + P(u,1)w \qquad (6-20)$$

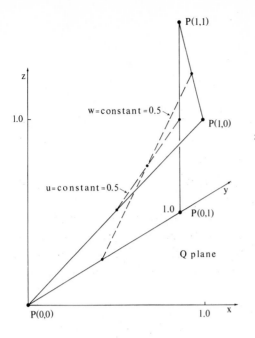

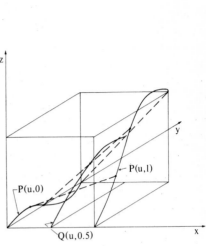

Figure 6-6 Lofted Surface.

$$[x(u,w),\ y(u,w),\ z(u,w)]$$

$$= [(1-u)(1-w)\ (1-u)w\ u(1-w)\ uw] \begin{bmatrix} P(0,0) \\ P(0,1) \\ P(1,0) \\ P(1,1) \end{bmatrix}$$

$$= [(1-u)(1-w)\ (1-u)w\ u(1-w)\ uw] \begin{bmatrix} 0\ 0\ 0 \\ 0\ 1\ 0 \\ 1\ 0\ 1 \\ 0\ 1\ 1 \end{bmatrix}$$

Figure 6-5b Three-dimensional
bilinear surface.

Again note that

$$Q(0,0) = P(0,0),\ \text{etc.}$$

Further note that the edges of the interpolated surface and the given data curves
are coincident, i.e.,

$$Q(u,0) = P(u,0)$$

$$Q(u,1) = P(u,1)$$

Alternately we can assume that $P(0,w)$
and $P(1,w)$ are known. The lofted surface is then given by

$$Q(u,w) = P(0,w)(1-u) + P(1,w)u \qquad (6\text{-}21)$$

Again it is easy to show that

$$Q(0,0) = P(0,0),\ \text{etc.}$$

Example 6-2: LOFTED SURFACE

Two curves $P(u,0)$ and $P(u,1)$ are given by cubic spline segments (cf
Sec. 5-3).

We wish to find the equation for the lofted surface between these two
boundaries. The cubic spline segments are assumed to have clamped ends.
Assume for

$$P(u,0) \qquad \text{and} \quad P(u,1)$$

$$
\begin{aligned}
P_1 &= [0\ 0\ 0] & P_1 &= [1\ 0\ 0] \\
P_2 &= [0\ 1\ 0] & P_2 &= [1\ 1\ 1] \\
P_1' &= [0\ 1\ 1] & P_1' &= [0\ 1\ 1] \\
P_2' &= [0\ 1\ 1] & P_2' &= [0\ 1\ -1]
\end{aligned}
$$

Hence, using Eq. (5-19),

$$P(u,0) = [0\ 0\ 0] + [0\ 1\ 1]u + [0\ 0\ -3]u^2 + [0\ 0\ 2]u^3$$

$$P(u,1) = [1\ 0\ 0] + [0\ 1\ 1]u + [0\ -0.6213\ 0.7929]u^2 + [0\ 0.2929\ -0.707]u^3$$

Equation (6-20) then yields

$$Q(u,w) = [w\ 0\ 0] + [0\ 1\ 1]u + [0\ -0.6213w\ (-3 + 3.7929w)]u^2 + [0\ 0.2929w\ (2 - 2.707w)]u^3$$

This is the surface shown in Fig. 6-6.

6-7 LINEAR COONS SURFACE

If the four boundary curves $P(u,0)$, $P(u,1)$, $P(0,w)$, and $P(1,w)$ are known, then it might be assumed that a simple sum of the lofted surfaces Eqs. (6-20) and (6-21) in the two directions would yield the desired result. If this is done, then

$$Q(u,w) = P(u,0)(1 - w) + P(u,1)w + P(0,w)(1 - u) + P(1,w)u \qquad (6-22)$$

However, examination of Eq. (6-22) at the corners of the surface patch yields

$$Q(0,0) = P(0,0) + P(0,0), \text{ etc.}$$

and at the edges,

$$Q(0,w) = P(0,0)(1 - w) + P(0,1)w + P(0,w)$$

neither of which corresponds to the original data as they should.

Examination of Eq. (6-22) shows that the problem occurs because the corner points are counted twice, since $P(0,0)$ is contained in both the $P(u,0)$ and $P(0,w)$ boundary curves.

The correct result can be obtained by subtracting the excess contribution to the surface due to duplication of the corner points. This yields

$$Q(u,w) = P(u,0)(1 - w) + P(u,1)w + P(0,w)(1 - u) + P(1,w)u \qquad (6-23)$$

$$- P(0,0)(1 - u)(1 - w) - P(0,1)(1 - u)w - P(1,0)u(1 - w) - P(1,1)uw$$

An example of such a surface is shown in Fig. 6-7. It can be readily shown that at the corner,

$$Q(0,0) = P(0,0)$$
$$\text{etc.}$$

and along the boundaries,

$$Q(0,w) = P(0,w)$$
$$Q(u,1) = P(u,1)$$

$$\text{etc.}$$

which implies that the interpolation is correct at the corners and boundaries. This linear blend of the four boundary curves is the simplest Coons surface. A more general Coons surface is discussed in Sec. 6-17 and Ref. 6-4. In vector notation, Eq. (6-22) may be written as

$$Q(u,w) = [(1-u) \ u] \begin{bmatrix} P(0,w) \\ P(1,w) \end{bmatrix} + [P(u,0) \ P(u,1)] \begin{bmatrix} 1 - w \\ w \end{bmatrix} - [(1-u) \ u] \begin{bmatrix} P(0,0) & P(0,1) \\ P(1,0) & P(1,1) \end{bmatrix} \begin{bmatrix} 1 - w \\ w \end{bmatrix}$$

or more compactly as

$$Q(u,w) = [1 - u \ u \ 1] \begin{bmatrix} -P(0,0) & -P(0,1) & P(0,w) \\ -P(1,0) & -P(1,1) & P(1,w) \\ P(u,0) & P(u,1) & 0 \end{bmatrix} \begin{bmatrix} 1 - w \\ w \\ 1 \end{bmatrix} \quad (6\text{-}24)$$

The functions $(1 - u)$, u, $(1 - w)$, and w are called blending functions because they blend the boundary curves to produce the internal shape of the surface.

Example 6-3: LINEAR COONS SURFACE

Let the four boundary "curves" be the diagonals of four of the sides of a unit cuve as shown in Fig. 6-7. We wish to find the center point on a linear Coons surface between these boundaries.

For the center point on the surface, Eq. (6-24) yields

$$Q_x(0.5,0.5) = [0.5 \ 0.5 \ 1] \begin{bmatrix} 0 & 0 & 0 \\ -1 & -1 & 1 \\ 0.5 & 0.5 & 0 \end{bmatrix} \begin{bmatrix} 0.5 \\ 0.5 \\ 1 \end{bmatrix}$$

$$= [0.5 \ 0.5 \ 1] \begin{bmatrix} 0 \\ 0 \\ 0.5 \end{bmatrix} = 0.5$$

$$Q_y(0.5,0.5) = [0.5 \ 0.5 \ 1] \begin{bmatrix} 0 & -1 & 0.5 \\ 0 & -1 & 0.5 \\ 0.5 & 0.5 & 0 \end{bmatrix} \begin{bmatrix} 0.5 \\ 0.5 \\ 1 \end{bmatrix}$$

$$= [0.5 \ 0.5 \ 1] \begin{bmatrix} 0 \\ 0 \\ 0.5 \end{bmatrix} = 0.5$$

$$Q_z(0.5,0.5) = [0.5 \ 0.5 \ 1] \begin{bmatrix} -1 & 0 & 0.5 \\ 0 & -1 & 0.5 \\ 0.5 & 0.5 & 0 \end{bmatrix} \begin{bmatrix} 0.5 \\ 0.5 \\ 1 \end{bmatrix}$$

$$= [0.5 \ 0.5 \ 1] \begin{bmatrix} 0 \\ 0 \\ 0.5 \end{bmatrix} = 0.5$$

Other points on the surface are calculated in a similar manner.

An **algorithm** which will generate a
linear Coons surface as described by
Eq. (6-24) is given in Appendix C.

6-8 BICUBIC SURFACE PATCH

The previous sections have discussed
the representation and description of
simple surface patches from a conceptual
point of view. We now turn our attention
to some practical aspects. One of the
more useful patch descriptions uses parametric cubics for the edge curves $P(u,0)$,
$P(u,1)$ and $P(0,w)$, $P(1,w)$ and the blending functions. The blending functions
for this scheme are derived below.

From our previous work (cf Sec. 5-3)
recall that the form of a parametric
cubic is (cf Eq. (5-11))

$$P(t) = B_1 + B_2 t + B_3 t^2 + B_4 t^3 \qquad (6-25)$$

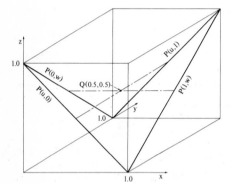

Figure 6-7 Linear Coons surface.

where $P(t)$ is a vector-valued function
having x-, y-, z-components. For convenience we limit the range of the parameter to $0 \leq t \leq 1$, i.e., we use a normalized parametric cubic. For the
boundary curves of a surface, $t = u$ for one pair of curves and $t = w$ for the
other pair.

We now derive the blending functions which will allow interpolation of
the points on the unit square between the two parametric cubics describing the
edge curves, i.e., between $P(0)$ and $P(1)$. There are four unknown coefficients
in Eq. (6-25), and thus we require four independent equations. Recalling that
the derivative of the parametric cubic is

$$P'(t) = B_2 + 2B_3 t + 3B_4 t^2 \qquad (6-26)$$

and letting $t = 0$ or 1 in Eqs. (6-25) and (6-26) yields

$$P(0) = B_1 \qquad (6-27a)$$
$$P(1) = B_1 + B_2 + B_3 + B_4 \qquad (6-27b)$$
$$P'(0) = B_2 \qquad (6-27c)$$
$$P'(1) = B_2 + 2B_3 + 3B_4 \qquad (6-27d)$$

Writing Eqs. (6-27) in matrix form yields

$$\begin{bmatrix} P(0) \\ P(1) \\ P'(0) \\ P'(1) \end{bmatrix} = \begin{bmatrix} 0 & 0 & 0 & 1 \\ 1 & 1 & 1 & 1 \\ 0 & 0 & 1 & 0 \\ 3 & 2 & 1 & 0 \end{bmatrix} \begin{bmatrix} B_4 \\ B_3 \\ B_2 \\ B_1 \end{bmatrix} \tag{6-28}$$

or

$$P = MB \tag{6-29}$$

Solving Eq. (6-29) for the coefficients, i.e., for B, yields

$$B = M^{-1}P \tag{6-30}$$

where

$$M^{-1} = \begin{bmatrix} 2 & -2 & 1 & 1 \\ -3 & 3 & -2 & -1 \\ 0 & 0 & 1 & 0 \\ 1 & 0 & 0 & 0 \end{bmatrix} \tag{6-31}$$

This agrees with Eq. (5-32). Substituting Eq. (6-30) into Eq. (6-25) and re-arranging yields

$$P(u) = F_1(u)P(0) + F_2(u)P(1) + F_3(u)P'(0) + F_4(u)P'(1) \tag{6-32}$$

where in general, with t as the parameter,

$$[F_1(t) \ F_2(t) \ F_3(t) \ F_4(t)] = [t^3 \ t^2 \ t \ 1] \begin{bmatrix} 2 & -2 & 1 & 1 \\ -3 & 3 & -2 & -1 \\ 0 & 0 & 1 & 0 \\ 1 & 0 & 0 & 0 \end{bmatrix} \tag{6-33}$$

The $F_i(t)$'s can be considered as scalar blending functions for the parametric cubic. They blend the quantities P(0), P(1), P'(0), and P'(1) together to form a continuous curve. Figure 6-8 shows these blending functions.

We now utilize these results to generate a bicubic patch. The same procedure that was used to develop the form for the bilinear patch is employed. We first construct surfaces which will satisfy one family of boundary conditions along the edges where $u = 0$ and $u = 1$ and then construct another surface which will satisfy boundary conditions along the edges where $w = 0$ and $w = 1$. We then combine these results to obtain the bicubic patch.

Before proceeding, some notational details are important. For convenience in later work we introduce a superscript notation for the derivatives of position vectors. In particular

$$P^a(u) = \frac{\partial^a P(u)}{\partial u^a}$$

and

$$P^a(u_i) = \frac{\partial^a P(u)}{\partial u^a}\bigg|_{u=u_i}$$

This implies that substitution occurs after differentiation. Higher order derivatives are given by

$$p^{a,b}(u,w) = \frac{\partial^{a+b} P(u,w)}{\partial u^a \partial w^b}$$

and

$$p^{a,b}(u_i,w_j) = \left.\frac{\partial^{a+b} P(u,w)}{\partial u^a \partial w^b}\right|_{\substack{u=u_i \\ w=w_j}}$$

For example,

$$p^{1,1}(u_i,w_j) = \left.\frac{\partial^2 P(u,w)}{\partial u \partial w}\right|_{\substack{u=u_i \\ w=w_j}}$$

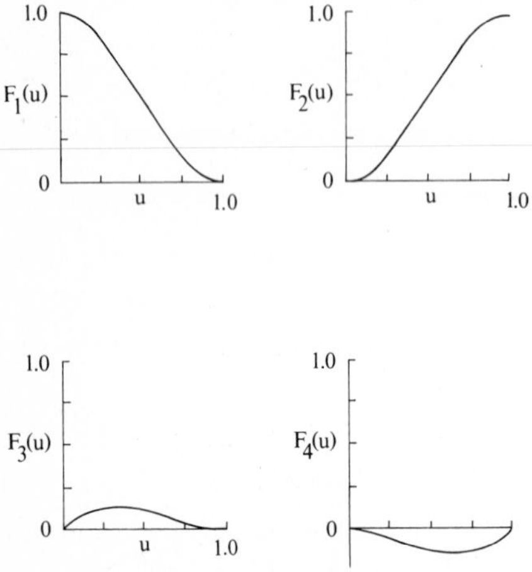

A ruled or lofted surface which will satisfy the boundary conditions along the constant u edges is then represented by

Figure 6-8 Parametric cubic blending functions.

$$Q(u,w) = P(0,w)(1 - 3u^2 + 2u^3) + P(1,w)(3u^2 - 2u^3) + p^{1,0}(0,w)(u - 2u^2 + u^3) + p^{1,0}(1,w)(-u^2 + u^3) \quad (6\text{-}34)$$

Notice that the cubic blending functions previously given in terms of the general parameter t [cf Eq. (6-33)] are used. Here again it is easy to show that along the boundaries Eq. (6-34) reduces to the required result, e.g., when u = 0, Q(u,w) = P(0,w), i.e., the given curve along the u = 0 edge. Similarly a ruled or lofted cubic surface which will satisfy the boundary conditions along the constant w edges is

$$Q(u,w) = P(u,0)(1 - 3w^2 + 2w^3) + P(u,1)(3w^2 - 2w^3) + p^{0,1}(u,0)(w - 2w^2 + w^3) + p^{0,1}(u,1)(-w^2 + w^3) \quad (6\text{-}35)$$

Again it is easy to show that the boundary conditions along the edges are satisfied.

As in the development of the bilinear patch, a simple addition of Eqs. (6-34) and (6-35) will not yield the correct result. Again the corners of the surface would be included twice and in this case the tangent vectors at each corner for the boundary curves and the cross-derivative terms; i.e., the twist vectors at the corners would also be included twice. Thus, we must subtract, weighted in an appropriate manner, these factors to obtain the correct synthesis of the surface. The final result for the bicubic surface patch is

$$Q(u,w) = [F_1(u)\ F_2(u)\ F_3(u)\ F_4(u)] \begin{bmatrix} P(0,0) & P(0,1) & P^{0,1}(0,0) & P^{0,1}(0,1) \\ P(1,0) & P(1,1) & P^{0,1}(1,0) & P^{0,1}(1,1) \\ P^{1,0}(0,0) & P^{1,0}(0,1) & P^{1,1}(0,0) & P^{1,1}(0,1) \\ P^{1,0}(1,0) & P^{1,0}(1,1) & P^{1,1}(1,0) & P^{1,1}(1,1) \end{bmatrix} \begin{bmatrix} F_1(w) \\ F_2(w) \\ F_3(w) \\ F_4(w) \end{bmatrix} \quad (6\text{-}36)$$

Alternately Eq. (6-36) may be written more compactly as

$$Q(u,w) = [u^3\ u^2\ u\ 1] N\ P\ N^T [w^3\ w^2\ w\ 1]^T \quad (6\text{-}37)$$

where N is the square matrix given previously in Eq. (6-31), and P is the square matrix given in Eq. (6-36). N^T is the transpose of N.

Examination of Eqs. (6-36) and (6-37) shows that a bicubic surface patch is defined by the cubic blending functions F_1, F_2, F_3, F_4, four cubic boundary curves, four corner points, eight tangent vectors at the corners, and four twist vectors at the corners.

The 4 x 4 P-matrix may be considered as a boundary condition matrix. It contains only information about corner points, corner tangent vectors, and corner twist vectors. For a given surface patch all the elements in the P-matrix are known constants. Examination of the P-matrix shows that the terms can be classified as

$$P = \begin{bmatrix} \text{Corner} & \vdots & \text{w-tangent} \\ \text{coordinates} & \vdots & \text{vectors} \\ \cdots\cdots\cdots & + & \cdots\cdots \\ \text{u-tangent} & \vdots & \text{Twist} \\ \text{vectors} & \vdots & \text{vectors} \end{bmatrix}$$

Since for the surface patch to be physically reasonable, adjacent boundary curves must intersect at a corner, constraints are placed on the specific function used to represent the boundary curves. For example, at corner A in Fig. 6-9, P(0,w) = P(u,0); at corner B, P(0,w) = P(u,1); at corner C, P(u,1) = P(1,w); and at corner D, P(1,w) = P(u,0).

A complete derivation of the constraints imposed on the blending functions in order that they satisfy certain boundary conditions was derived in Ref. 6-4 and is given in Table 6-1.

The shape of a bicubic patch is controlled by the contents of the 4 x 4 P-matrix, i.e., by the location of the corner position vectors and the magnitude and direction of the corner tangent and twist vectors. Figure 6-10a shows the effect of changing the magnitude but not the direction, of the corner tangent vectors along the (0,w) and (1,w) boundaries. Figure 6-10b shows the effect of changing the direction, but not the magnitude, of these same corner tangent vectors. Figures 6-10c and 6-10d show the effect of adding a twist vector to an initial surface patch with zero twist vectors.

The bicubic surface patch has been successfully used to design surfaces (cf Refs. 6-5 and 6-6). However, several disadvantages exist when using bicubic surface patches in a computer-aided design system. The major disadvantage exists because three different quantities, position, tangent and twist vectors all generally of different orders of magnitude must be specified to describe the surface. For example, for a patch 10 units long, the tangent vectors might have an order of magnitude of 10 units, the twist vectors 100 units, and the position vector 1000 units. Further, the user typically lacks intuition when creating surfaces by changing elements in the defining matrix. For example, the corner tangent vector $P^{0,1}(0,0)$ points toward the interior of the boundary curve, while the corner

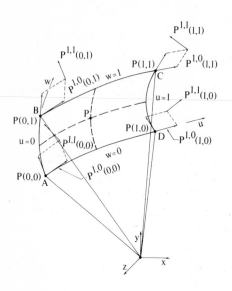

Figure 6-9   Three-dimensional surface patch notation.

Table 6-1

Boundary Condition Imposed Constraints on Surface Blending Functions

	u = 0 or w = 0	u = 1 or w = 1
F_1	1	0
F_2	0	1
F_3	0	0
F_4	0	0
F_1'*	0	0
F_2'	0	0
F_3'	1	0
F_4'	0	1

*Primes indicate differentiation with respect to the independent variable either u or w.

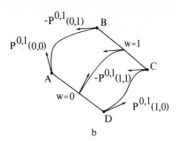

Figure 6-10   Control of bicubic surface patches.

tangent vector $P^{0,1}(0,1)$ points away from the interior of the boundary curve as shown in Fig. 6-11. Also note that incrementing the y-component of the corner tangent vector $P^{0,1}(0,0)$ causes the (0,w) boundary curve to bend up, whereas incrementing the y-component of the corner tangent vector $P^{0,1}(0,1)$ an equal amount has the opposite effect at the (0,1) corner. The same unexpected behavior occurs when incrementing twist vectors. Equal changes in all twist vectors cause opposite surface bends at the (0,1) and (1,0) corners compared with the effect at the (0,0) and (1,1) corners. Thus, manipulating the components of the P boundary condition matrix can be confusing.

An algorithm which will generate the bicubic surface patch described by Eq. (6-37) is given in Appendix C.

6-9 THE F-PATCH

In order to eliminate some of the problems which occur when manipulating bicubic surface patches, a simplified version originally due to Ferguson (cf Ref. 6-7), called an F-patch, is sometimes used. An F-patch is simply a bicubic surface patch with zero twist vectors. Only first-order continuity is possible across the boundaries of an F-patch, because the surface is constrained to leave zero cross derivatives at the corners. This on occasion may lead to

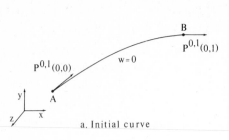

a. Initial curve

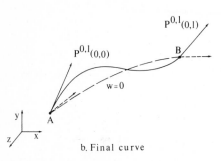

b. Final curve

Figure 6-11 Effect of change in end tangent vectors on the boundary curve shape.

surfaces which are not sufficiently smooth for some applications. Nevertheless, it is easier to construct and modify an F-patch, and they are suitable for many types of surface definition. In particular, F-patches have proven to be useful for axisymmetric surfaces, e.g., vases, cups, bottles, aircraft bodies, etc.

6-10 BEZIER SURFACES

The previous sections have discussed a number of aspects of surface description. In all cases the tacit assumption has been made that the necessary mathematical information such as position, tangent, or twist vectors or blending functions is available. However, providing this information may be extremely difficult for the user, especially a nonmathematical or non-computer-oriented user. A number of schemes have been devised to overcome this difficulty. Probably the most successful of these is the extension of the Bezier curve (cf Sec. 5-7) to surfaces (Ref. 6-8).

The surface equation for a Bezier surface patch can be written in the form of Eq. (6-36). Using the binomial representation of a Bezier curve given in Sec. 5-7, the equation for a surface patch with boundary curves described by four point Bezier polygons, i.e., a 4 x 4-point Bezier surface patch is given by

$$P(u,w) = [(1 - u^3) \quad 3(1 - u)^2 u \quad 3(1 - u)u^2 \quad u^3] [B] \begin{bmatrix} (1 - w)^3 \\ 3(1 - w)^2 w \\ 3(1 - w)w^2 \\ w^3 \end{bmatrix}$$

where

$$B = \begin{bmatrix} B(1,1) & B(1,2) & B(1,3) & B(1,4) \\ B(2,1) & B(2,2) & B(2,3) & B(2,4) \\ B(3,1) & B(3,2) & B(3,3) & B(3,4) \\ B(4,1) & B(4,2) & B(4,3) & B(4,4) \end{bmatrix}$$

The B-tensor is composed of the position vectors of the defining polygon points, as shown in Fig. 6-12. In the Bezier formulation, only the corner points A, B, C, and D actually lie on the surface. The point $B_{1,2}$ defines the slope vector from the first to the second point on the first Bezier polygon in the u-direction. The point $B_{2,1}$ defines the slope vector from the first to the second point on the first Bezier polygon in the w-direction. The points $B_{1,3}$, $B_{2,4}$, $B_{3,4}$, $B_{4,3}$, $B_{4,2}$, and $B_{3,1}$ are used in a similar manner. The points $B_{2,2}$, $B_{2,3}$, $B_{3,3}$, and $B_{3,2}$ interior to the defining polygonal surface are used to define the twist vectors at the corners A, B, C, and D respectively.

As shown in Fig. 6-12 the Bezier surface is completely defined by a net of design points on the polygonal surface. These points serve to define a two-parameter family of Bezier curves on the design surface. To generate a para-

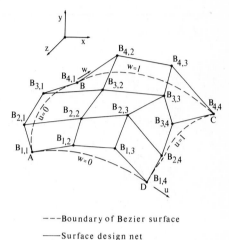

---Boundary of Bezier surface

——Surface design net

Figure 6-12 4 x 4 Bezier surface nomenclature.

metric curve on the Bezier surface shown in Fig. 6-12, let the parametric curve be defined by $0 \le u \le 1.0$ and $w = C_1$, where $0 \le C_1 \le 1.0$. Before this curve can be generated, the elements in the S-tensor given by Eq. (5-53) must be known. For $w = C_1$, the matrix product

$$[B] \begin{bmatrix} (1-w)^3 \\ 3(1-w)^2 w \\ 3(1-w)w^2 \\ w^3 \end{bmatrix}_{w=C_1} = \begin{bmatrix} P_1 \\ P_2 \\ P_3 \\ P_4 \end{bmatrix} \qquad (6\text{-}40)$$

produces four position vectors P_1, P_2, P_3, and P_4 for the Bezier polygon which defines a Bezier curve with a parametric value of $w = C_1$. The point P_1 lies on the surface boundary 0w, and the point P_4 lies on the surface boundary 1w. The points P_2 and P_3 are slope design points which lie off the curve.

Then, the matrix product

$$P(u,C_1) = [(1-u)^3 \quad 3(1-u)^2 u \quad 3(1-u)u^2 \quad u^3] \begin{bmatrix} P_1 \\ P_2 \\ P_3 \\ P_4 \end{bmatrix} \qquad (6\text{-}41)$$

gives the expression for a point on the surface along the curve $w = C_1$. For each value u, Eq. (6-41) gives the corresponding position vector for the point on the surface.

The boundary curves for a Bezier surface can be defined in an analogous manner to the Coons surface boundaries. In fact, a Bezier surface can be placed within the family of generalized Coons surfaces described in Sec. 6-12. For example, along the boundary $u = 0$, $0 \leq w \leq 1.0$, the Bezier curve is

$$C = [B_{1,1} \quad B_{2,1} \quad B_{3,1} \quad B_{4,1}] \begin{bmatrix} (1-w)^3 \\ 3(1-w)^2 w \\ 3(1-w)w^2 \\ w^3 \end{bmatrix} \tag{6-42}$$

or alternately,

$$C = [(1-w)^3 \quad 3(1-w)^2 w \quad 3(1-w)w^2 \quad w^3] \begin{bmatrix} B_{1,1} \\ B_{2,1} \\ B_{3,1} \\ B_{4,1} \end{bmatrix} \tag{6-43}$$

The Bezier boundary curve for $0 \leq u \leq 1.0$, $w = 1.0$ is

$$C = [(1-u)^3 \quad 3(1-u)^2 u \quad 3(1-u)^2 \quad u^3] \begin{bmatrix} B_{4,1} \\ B_{4,2} \\ B_{4,3} \\ B_{4,4} \end{bmatrix} \tag{6-46}$$

The equations for the other two boundary curves can be written directly, with the aid of Fig. 6-12.

It is sometimes desirable to create a surface patch that is not described by a square tensor. This can be used to allow simple curves to be bounded by a complex surface. As an example, the surface shown in Fig. 6-13 has three-point Bezier curve boundaries along $u = 0$ and $u = 1.0$ and five-point Bezier curve boundaries along $w = 0$ and $w = 1.0$. The equation for the boundary along $w = 0$ is given by

$$C = [(1-w)^2 \quad 2(1-w)w \quad w^2] \begin{bmatrix} B_{1,1} \\ B_{1,2} \\ B_{1,3} \end{bmatrix} \tag{6-47}$$

The equation for the boundary along $u = 0$ is

$$C = [(1-u)^4 \quad 4u(1-u)^3 \quad 6u^2(1-u)^2 \quad 4u^3(1-u) \quad u^4] \begin{bmatrix} B_{1,1} \\ B_{2,1} \\ B_{3,1} \\ B_{4,1} \\ B_{5,1} \end{bmatrix} \tag{6-48}$$

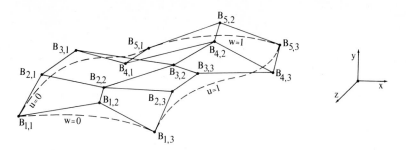

Figure 6-13   3 x 5 Bezier surface.

The surface equation is then given by

$$P(u,w) = [(1-u)^4 \quad 4u(1-u)^3 \quad 6u^2(1-u)^2 \quad 4u^3(1-u) \quad u^4][B]\begin{bmatrix}(1-w)^2 \\ 2(1-w)w \\ w^2\end{bmatrix} \quad (6\text{-}47)$$

A five-point Bezier boundary curve has an advantage over a four-point curve, since a change in the central design point does not effect the slope at either end of the boundary curve. Thus, the surface shape can be changed without disturbing the slope design points, which may then be independently specified to satisfy continuity requirements with adjacent surfaces.

The Bezier surface discussed above can be represented in the form of a Cartesian product surface. In particular the surface is given by

$$Q(u,w) = \sum_{i=0}^{n} \sum_{j=0}^{m} B_{i+1,j+1} J_{n,i}(u) K_{m,j}(w) \qquad (6\text{-}48)$$

where by analogy with Eq. (5-63),

$$J_{n,i} = \binom{n}{i} u^i (1-u)^{n-i} \qquad (6\text{-}49)$$

$$K_{m,j} = \binom{m}{j} w^j (1-w)^{m-j} \qquad (6\text{-}50)$$

and m and n are one less than the number of polygon vertices in the w- and u-directions respectively.

Bezier has been successful in using his technique in a production environment as described in Ref. 6-8. In the Unisurf system at Regie Renault a free-hand curve is first drawn with a pencil in the xy-plane to give y = f(x). A computer controlled drafting machine used as a digitizer receives the input coordinates of the polygon vertices which roughly define the curve. The resulting Bezier curve is then drawn by the computer controlled drafting machine. If modifications are needed, the polygon vertices are adjusted and the curve is redrawn until the designer is satisfied. A three-dimensional curve is obtained by repeating the process to produce z = f(x).

This method is used to define the four boundary curves for a surface framework. The surface definition is then completed by specifying the coordinates of the remaining surface design network points. This data is then input into a computer programmed to produce rotated, scaled, or perspective views of the described surface curves or into a computer controlled cutting machine to produce a three-dimensional model from a block of polystyrene foam.

A. P. Armit (Ref. 6-9) has also developed a design system called MULTIOBJECT which makes use of Bezier surface patches. His system allows easy use of various types of Bezier boundary curves, ranging from a three-point to a seven-point curve definition. This capability is dependent upon the binomial nature of the blending functions. A surface framework of six-point and four-point curves was found useful for many applications. The system allows for curve splitting at any point to produce a pair of continuous curves of the same order as the previous single curve. This system is described in Ref. 6-9 and discussed in detail in Ref. 6-5.

Some of the difficulties associated with Eq. (6-48) as with the Bezier curve are concerned with local control. This is because the movement of one point on the polygonal generating surface will affect the entire Bezier surface. This can be a distinct disadvantage to the designer, especially for detail work. In order to obtain local control a patch must effectively be subdivided. The use of a B-spline basis, i.e., by using B-spline curves as blending functions, eliminates this problem. This is discussed in the next section.

An algorithm which will generate a Cartesian product surface based on Eq. (6-48), using Bezier curves as the blending functions, is given in Appendix C.

6-11 B-SPLINE SURFACES

Implementation of B-spline surfaces can take many forms. Perhaps the simplest is the Cartesian product surface analogous to the Bezier surface of the previous section. For a B-spline surface the corresponding Cartesian product surface is

$$Q(u,w) = \sum_{i=0}^{n} \sum_{j=0}^{m} B_{i+1,j+1} N_{i,k}(u) M_{j,L}(w) \qquad (6-51)$$

where by analogy with Eq. (5-78)

$$N_{i,1}(u) = \begin{cases} 1 \text{ if } x_i \le u < x_{i+1} \\ 0 \text{ otherwise} \end{cases}$$

$$N_{i,k}(u) = \frac{(u - x_i)N_{i,k-1}(u)}{x_{i+k-1} - x_i} + \frac{(x_{i+k} - u)N_{i+1,k-1}(u)}{x_{i+k} - x_{i+1}} \qquad (6-52)$$

and the x_i are the elements of the k knot vector discussed in Sec. 5-8.

Further,

$$M_{j,1}(w) = \begin{cases} 1 \text{ if } y_j \leq w < y_{j+1} \\ 0 \text{ otherwise} \end{cases}$$

$$M_{j,L}(w) = \frac{(w - y_j)M_{j,L-1}(w)}{y_{j+L-1} - y_j} + \frac{(y_{j+L} - w)M_{j+1,L-1}(w)}{y_{j+L} - y_{j+1}} \qquad (6\text{-}53)$$

and the y_i are the elements of the L knot vector discussed in Sec. 5-8, and m and n are one less than the number of vertices in the defining polygons in the u- and w-directions respectively. The $B_{i+1,j+1}$ are the position vectors of the defining polygonal surface, as shown for example in Fig. 6-12.

As with B-spline curves, knot vectors with various degrees of multiplicity can be defined in either the u- or w-directions. However, the above formation requires that each defining polygon in a given direction must have the same degree of multiplicity in a given direction. Alternate formulations could allow various degrees of knot multiplicity in a given direction in order to increase the flexibility of local control. Further discussion of how B-spline curves can be used to form surface patches is given by S. A. Coons, W. J. Gordon, R. F. Riesenfeld, and others in Ref. 6-10.

6-12 GENERALIZED COONS SURFACES

Examination of the results discussed above suggests a more general representation for a surface. Following Forrest (Ref. 6-11) we introduce a general scalar function $\beta_{r,i}(u)$. The $\beta_{r,i}$'s serve to blend the boundary conditions and/or boundary curves to form a surface.

The r subscript indicates that the general blending function is weighted by a single-valued function representing a boundary derivative of order r. For curves, r = 0; for tangent vectors, r = 1; and for curvature or twist vectors, r = 2. The i subscript indicates the position on the unit uw-square of the function being weighted by the $\beta_{r,i}$. Here we assume that $u = u_i$ is implied: e.g.,

$\beta_{0,1}(w)$ is the blending function weighting the curve P(u,1).

$\beta_{0,0}(u)$ is the blending function weighting the curve P(0,w).

Forrest (Ref. 6-10) has pointed out several properties of these blending functions. If a patch is specified by boundary curves alone, then

$$\beta_{0,i}(j) = \delta_{ij}$$

where δ_{ij} is the Kronecker delta, i.e., $\delta_{ij} = 1$, i = j and $\delta_{ij} = 0$, i $\neq$ j.

As an example, recall the equation describing the bilinear surface, i.e.,

$$Q(u,w) = (1 - u)(1 - w)P(0,0) + (1 - u)wP(0,1) + u(1 - w)P(1,0) + uwP(1,1) \quad (6\text{-}19)$$

Now suppose that we replace the linear blending function $(1 - u)$ by $\beta_{0,0}(u)$ but still require that $\beta_{0,0}(0) = 1$ and $\beta_{0,0}(1) = 0$. Further, we replace the linear blending function u by $\beta_{0,1}(u)$ and require $\beta_{0,1}(0) = 0$ and $\beta_{0,1}(1) = 1$, $(1 - w)$ by $\beta_{0,0}(w)$ and require that $\beta_{0,0}(0) = 1$ and $\beta_{0,0}(1) = 0$ and w by $\beta_{0,1}(w)$ with $\beta_{0,1}(0)$ and $\beta_{0,1}(1) = 1$. Equation (6-19) may then be written as

$$Q(u,w) = \beta_{0,0}(u)\beta_{0,0}(w)P(0,0) + \beta_{0,0}(u)\beta_{0,1}(w)P(0,1) + \beta_{0,1}(u)\beta_{0,0}(w)P(1,0) + \beta_{0,1}(u)\beta_{0,1}(w)P(1,1)$$

which may be written as

$$Q(u,w) = \sum_{i=0}^{1} \beta_{0,i}(u)P(i,w) + \sum_{j=0}^{1} \beta_{0,j}(w)P(u,j) - \sum_{i=0}^{1}\sum_{j=0}^{1} \beta_{0,i}(u)\beta_{0,j}(w)P(i,j) \quad (6\text{-}54)$$

Noting that in Eq. (6-54) $r = 0$, we see that these simple bilinear Coons surfaces admit only positional continuity.

The bicubic surfaces discussed in Sec. 6-8 can also be written in a more general form. First let's consider the bicubic lofted surfaces represented by Eqs. (6-34) and (6-35).

In the more general notation Eq. (6-34) may be written as

$$Q_{(u,w)} = P(0,w)\beta_{0,0}(u) + P(1,w)\beta_{0,1}(u) + P^{1,0}(0,w)\beta_{1,0}(u) + P^{1,0}(1,w)\beta_{1,1}(u) = \sum_{i=0}^{1}\sum_{j=0}^{1} \beta_{i,j}(u)\, P^{i,0}(j,w) \quad (6\text{-}55)$$

and Eq. (6-35) as

$$Q(u,w) = P(u,0)\beta_{0,0}(w) + P(u,1)\beta_{0,1}(w) + P^{0,1}(u,0)\beta_{1,0}(w) + P^{0,1}(u,1)\beta_{1,1}(w) = \sum_{i=0}^{1}\sum_{j=0}^{1} \beta_{i,j}(w)P^{0,i}(u,j) \quad (6\text{-}56)$$

where the blending functions, i.e., the β_{ij}'s, obey the relations

$$\frac{\delta^{P}[\beta_{r,i}(u)]}{du^{P}}\bigg|_{u=u_j} = \beta_{r,i}^{P}(u_j) = \delta_{pr} \cdot \delta_{ij}$$

Thus

$$\beta_{0,0}(0) = 1, \ \beta_{0,0}(1) = \beta_{0,0}'(0) = \beta_{0,0}'(1) = 0$$

$$\beta_{1,1}(0) = \beta_{1,1}(1) = \beta_{1,1}'(0) = 0, \ \beta_{1,1}'(1) = 1$$

Comparison of Eqs. (6-55) and (6-56) with Eqs. (6-34), (6-35) and recalling Eq. (6-33) shows that

$$[\beta_{0,0}(u) \ \beta_{0,1}(u) \ \beta_{1,0}(u) \ \beta_{1,1}(u)] = [u^3 \ u^2 \ u \ 1]\begin{bmatrix} 2 & -2 & 1 & 1 \\ -3 & 3 & -2 & -1 \\ 0 & 0 & 1 & 0 \\ 1 & 0 & 0 & 0 \end{bmatrix} = [F_1(u) \ F_2(u) \ F_3(u) \ F_4(u)] \quad (6\text{-}57a)$$

and

$$[\beta_{0,0}(w) \ \beta_{0,1}(w) \ \beta_{1,0}(w) \ \beta_{1,1}(w)] = [w^3 \ w^2 \ w \ 1]\begin{bmatrix} 2 & -2 & 1 & 1 \\ -3 & 3 & -2 & -1 \\ 0 & 0 & 1 & 0 \\ 1 & 0 & 0 & 0 \end{bmatrix} = [F_1(w) \ F_2(w) \ F_3(w) \ F_4(w)] \quad (6\text{-}57b)$$

Turning now to the bicubic surface patch itself, we see that Eq. (6-36) may be written in the general notation as

$$Q(u,w) = \sum_{i=0}^{1} \sum_{r=0}^{1} P^{r,0}(i,w)\beta_{r,i}(u) + \sum_{j=0}^{1} \sum_{s=0}^{1} P^{0,s}(u,j)\beta_{s,j}(w) - \sum_{i=0}^{1} \sum_{j=0}^{1} \sum_{r=0}^{1} \sum_{s=0}^{1} P^{r,s}(i,j)\beta_{r,i}(u)\beta_{s,j}(w) \quad (6\text{-}58)$$

By substitution and/or differentiation it can be shown that at the corners

$$Q(i,j) = P(i,j)$$

$$Q^{1,0}(i,j) = P^{1,0}(i,j)$$

$$Q^{0,1}(i,j) = P^{0,1}(i,j)$$

$$Q^{1,1}(i,j) = P^{1,1}(i,j)$$

and along the boundary curves

$$Q(i,w) = P(i,w)$$

$$Q(u,j) = P(u,j)$$

$$Q^{0,1}(u,j) = P^{0,1}(u,j)$$

$$Q^{1,0}(i,w) = P^{1,0}(i,w)$$

Notice that since $r = 1$ here, normal derivatives can be satisfied across patch boundaries to first order i.e., bicubic patches may be joined with first order continuity across the boundaries.

Forrest (Ref. 6-11) has shown that it is possible to generalize the Coons surface description such that higher order boundary conditions can be satisfied. Assuming that we wish to satisfy normal derivatives to order m_i on $u = u_i$ and to order n_j on $w = w_j$, then the surface boundary curves are given by the functions $P^{r,0}(i,w)$, with $0 \le r \le m_i$, and $P^{0,s}(u,j)$, with $0 \le s \le n_j$, and the blending functions by $\beta_{r,i}(u)$ and $\beta_{s,j}(w)$. The surface equation is then

$$Q(u,w) = \sum_{i=0}^{1} \sum_{r=0}^{m_i} P^{r,0}(i,w)\beta_{r,i}(u) + \sum_{j=0}^{1} \sum_{s=0}^{n_j} P^{0,s}(u,j)\beta_{s,j}(w) - \sum_{i=0}^{1} \sum_{j=0}^{1} \sum_{r=0}^{m_i} \sum_{s=0}^{n_j} P^{r,s}(i,j)\beta_{r,i}(u)\beta_{s,j}(w) \quad 6\text{-}59)$$

where the blending functions have the properties

$$\beta_{r,i}^{P}(u_k) = \delta_{pr} \cdot \delta_{ik} \quad \text{for } 0 \le p \le m_i \quad (6\text{-}60)$$

$$\beta_{s,j}^{P}(u_k) = \delta_{ps} \cdot \delta_{jk} \quad \text{for } 0 \le p \le n_j$$

Equation (6-59) represents the most general form of a Coons surface. It should be noted that most implementations do not utilize this form, but rather one of the special cases discussed previously.

Forrest (Ref. 6-11) points out that if in Eq. (6-59)

$$P^{0,s}(u,j) = \sum_{i=0}^{1} \sum_{r=0}^{m_i} P^{r,s}(i,j)\beta_{r,i}(u)$$

then the last two terms of Eq. (6-59) cancel and the surface equation is

$$Q(u,w) = \sum_{i=0}^{1} \sum_{r=0}^{m_i} p^{r,0}(i,w) \beta_{r,i}(u) \qquad (6\text{-}61)$$

which is a type of ruled or lofted surface. Similarly if

$$p^{r,0}(i,w) = \sum_{j=0}^{1} \sum_{s=0}^{n_j} p^{r,s}(i,j) \beta_{s,j}(w)$$

then the surface equation is

$$Q(u,w) = \sum_{j=0}^{1} \sum_{s=0}^{n_j} p^{0,s}(u,j) \beta_{s,j}(w) \qquad (6\text{-}62)$$

which is a ruled or lofted surface using the alternate boundary conditions.

If both the conditions represented by Eqs. (6-61) and (6-62) are imposed, then the surface equation is

$$Q(u,w) = \sum_{i=0}^{1} \sum_{j=0}^{1} \sum_{r=0}^{m_i} \sum_{s=0}^{n_j} p^{r,s}(i-j) \beta_{r,i}(u) \beta_{s,j}(w) \qquad (6\text{-}63)$$

which is the so-called tensor product or Cartesian product surface. Equation (6-63) is important because it represents the natural extension to surfaces of the common methods of curve approximation. The Cartesian surface represented by Eq. (6-63) or the lofted surfaces represented by Eqs. (6-61) and (6-62) are the most frequently implemented forms of Coons surfaces.

When $m_i = n_j = 1$ and the $\beta_{i,j}$'s are given by Eq. (6-57), Eq. (6-63) represents a bicubic patch, i.e.,

$$Q(u,w) = \sum_{i=0}^{1} \sum_{j=0}^{1} \sum_{r=0}^{1} \sum_{s=0}^{1} p^{r,s}(u,j) \beta_{r,i}(u) \beta_{s,j}(w)$$

Comparison of Eq. (6-63) with Eq. (6-58) shows that it is of a more limited form. In particular, the bicubic surface patch described by Eq. (6-63) depends only on corner information - position, tangent, and twist vectors, along with the cubic blending functions to determine the interior shape of the patch. The bicubic surface patch described by Eq. (6-58) also takes into account the boundary curves which outline the patch when determining the interior shape of the surface patch. The bicubic surface patch described by Eq. (6-58) is thus more general.

Notice that in Eq. (6-56) and its special cases, summation occurs for $i = 0$ and 1, $j = 0$ and 1, i.e., from one boundary curve to the other. This implies that the interior of the surface patch is governed entirely by the boundary curves, corner points, corner tangent and twist vectors, and the blending function. That is, the interior of the surface patch is controlled by the exterior boundary conditions. If, however, we sum from $0 \leq i \leq M$, $0 \leq j \leq N$, then all curves $P(u_i,w)$ and $P(u,w_j)$ between the boundary curves, and in fact any normal derivatives on these curves, are accounted for. This allows specifying interior curves and boundary conditions to assist in controlling the interior shape of the surface patch. In this case the surface is then represented by

$$Q(u,w) = \sum_{i=0}^{M} \sum_{r=0}^{m_i} P^{r,0}(u_i,w)\beta_{r,i}(u) - \sum_{j=0}^{N} \sum_{s=0}^{n_j} P^{0,s}(u,w_j)\beta_{s,j}(w) - \sum_{i=0}^{M} \sum_{j=0}^{N} \sum_{r=0}^{m_i} \sum_{s=0}^{n_j} P^{r,s}(u_i,w_j)\beta_{r,i}(u)\beta_{s,j}(w) \tag{6-64}$$

Here the blending curves satisfy the relations

$$\beta_{r,i}^{P}(u_k) = \delta_{pr} \cdot \delta_{ik} \quad 0 \leq P \leq m_i \quad 0 \leq k \leq m$$

$$\beta_{s,j}^{P}(w_k) = \delta_{ps} \cdot \delta_{jk} \quad 0 \leq P \leq n_j \quad 0 \leq k \leq N$$

Notice that the degree of the interpolated normal derivatives is given by m_i and n_j. Further notice that for $M = N = 1$, Eq. (6-64) reduces to the Coons surface described by Eq. (6-56). Figure 6-14 illustrates the difference between the surfaces described by Eqs. (6-56) and (6-64). Figure 6-14a shows an exterior blended surface. Only the boundary curves $P(u,0)$, $P(u,1)$, $P(0,w)$, and $P(1,w)$ and the corner points, corner tangent, and twist vectors at A, B, C, and D are considered in blending the center of the surface patch. Figure 6-14b shows an interior blended surface where the interior curves $P(u,0.5)$ and $P(0.5,w)$ are also considered.

The generalized lofted surface and the Cartesian product surface can be obtained in a manner analogous to those in the previous section. They are given by

$$Q(u,w) = \sum_{i=0}^{M} \sum_{r=0}^{m_i} P^{r,0}(u_i,w)\beta_{r,i}(u) \quad (6-65)$$

$$Q(u,w) = \sum_{j=0}^{N} \sum_{s=0}^{n_j} P^{0,s}(u,w)\beta_{s,j}(w) \quad (6-66)$$

and

$$Q(u,w) = \sum_{i=0}^{M} \sum_{j=0}^{N} \sum_{r=0}^{m_i} \sum_{s=0}^{n_j} P^{r,s}(u_i,w_s)\beta_{r,i}(u)\beta_{s,j}(w) \quad (6-67)$$

6-13 CONCLUSION

The final two chapters have been an introduction to some of the current methods for curve and surface descriptions. Many other techniques have been suggested and used with varying degrees of success. This is a young and dynamic field with new ideas and techniques constantly

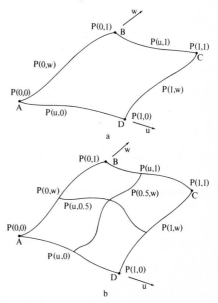

Figure 6-14 Exterior and interior "blended" surfaces.

appearing in the literature.

To actually implement these techniques in a production or design environment requires many more considerations than can be discussed here. Specific
requirements will depend upon the needs of specific applications. Problems
such as joining surface patches, calculating cutter path offsets, determining
intersections of lines and surfaces, designing data and file structures in
which to store and manipulate the information, writing analysis programs to
calculate needed parameters, removing hidden lines and surfaces for proper
graphical display, etc., are the types of requirements that will arise. Some
solutions to these problems can be found in the current computer-aided design
literature. The reader of this book should be able to build upon the foundation presented herein to create a capability to meet his needs.

REFERENCES

6-1 Bezier, P. E., Emploi des Machines a Commande Numerique, Masson et Cie,
     Paris, France, 1970; Bezier, P. E., "Example of an Existing System in the
     Motor Industry: The Unisurf System," Proc. Roy. Soc. (London), Vol. A321,
     pp. 207-218, 1971.

6-2 Sabin, M. A., "An Existing System in the Aircraft Industry. The British
     Aircraft Corporation Numerical Master Geometry System," Proc. Roy. Soc.
     (London), Vol. A321, pp. 197-205, 1971.

6-3 Peters, G. J., "Interactive Computer Graphics Application of the Bi-Cubic
     Parametric Surface to Engineering Design Problems," McDonnell Douglas
     Automation Company. St. Louis, Missouri, presented at Society of Indus-
     trial and Applied Mathematics 1973 National Meeting, Hampton, Va., 18-21
     June 1973.

6-4 Coons, S. A., "Surfaces for Computer-Aided Design of Space Forms," M.I.T.
     Project MAC, MAC-TR-41, June 1967. (Also as AD 663 504).

6-5 Armit, A. P., "Computer Systems for Interactive Design of Three-Dimensional
     Shapes," Ph.D. Thesis, Cambridge University, November 1970.

6-6 Lee, T. M. P., "Analysis of an Efficient Homogeneous Tensor Representation
     of Surfaces for Computer Display," in Advanced Computer Graphics. Edited
     by Parslow, R. D., and Green, R. E., Plenum Press, New York, pp. 1119-1141,
     1971.

6-7 Ferguson, J. C., "Multivariable Curve Interpolation," J. Assoc. Comput.
     Mach., Vol. no. 2, pp. 221-228, April 1964.

6-8 Bezier, P., Numerical Control-Mathematics and Applications, (translated
     by A. R. Forrest), John Wiley & Sons, Inc., London, 1972.

6-9 Armit, A. P., "Multipatch and Multiobject Design Systems," Proc. Roy. Soc. (London), Vol. A321, pp. 235-242, 1971.

6-10 Barnhill, R. E., and Riesenfeld, R. F., "Computer Aided Geometric Design," Academic Press, New York, 1974.

6-11 Forrest, A., "On Coons and other Methods for the Representation of Curved Surfaces," Computer Graphics and Image Processing, Vol. 1, pp. 341-359, 1972.

APPENDIX A

COMPUTER GRAPHICS SOFTWARE

In developing the concepts for a computer graphics software system it is
convenient to divide the overall system into several parts. Two of the obvious
parts are the support computer and the graphics device itself. These are both
hardware. In considering these descriptions a not too narrow view should be
taken. In general, the support computer is the system on which the data base
exists and on which software manipulation of the data base occurs. However, in
some systems this function may be physically split between two or more computer
systems. The graphics device is the hardware which actually produces the picture.
A conceptual view of a computer graphics software system is shown in Fig. A-1.

Two software systems produce an interface between the support computer and
the graphics device. The first is the data base manipulation software. The
mathematical basis for this system is the topic of the main part of the book.
It consists of routines to translate, rotate, clip etc. the data base. Specific
algorithms to perform many of these functions occur later in Appendix C. This
software system is completely device-independent since it is only concerned with
mathematical manipulations.

The second is a software system which provides an interface between the
normal "drawing functions" and the hardware associated with a particular graphics
device. It is this system which causes the necessary codes (information in
terms of binary bits) to be sent to the graphics device to cause that device to

draw lines, plot points, etc. Although as outlined in Secs. A-1 and A-2 below, this software system can be made minimally device-dependent; it cannot be made completely device-independent. Because of this Secs. A-1 and A-2 only conceptually discuss this software system.

A-1 COMPUTER GRAPHICS PRIMITIVES

As pointed out above, when designing or building a computer graphics system it is convenient to define those areas where the support computer must interact with the graphics device. All graphics devices, of course, receive information from the support computer as a data stream composed of binary bits. In particular cases one or more bits may be significant. However, except for very sophisticated users, the composition of this data stream is seldom of interest. It is more convenient to think of the fundamental effects that the data stream has on the graphics device. These fundamental effects are called graphic primitives. They generally fall into three areas: cursor control, device state or mode control, and graphic input. Here cursor is used in a general sense to mean the electron beam on a CRT graphics device, the print head on a teletype, high-speed printer, electrostatic dot matrix printer, or the pen on a pen and ink plotter, etc. We will briefly discuss the graphic primitives associated with each of these areas. From these graphic primitives several compound graphic commands can be developed which are of more general interest. These will be discussed in the next section.

The two graphic primitives associated with cursor control are

> Move the cursor
> Turn the cursor on/off

The function of each of these primitives is self-explanatory.

The graphic primitives associated with device state or mode control are, for example:

> Alphanumeric mode (1)
> Graphics mode (2)

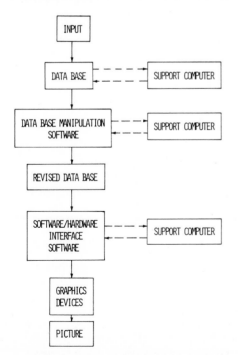

Figure A-1 Conceptual view of a computer graphics software system

Standby mode (3)

Absolute coordinate mode (4)

Relative (incremental) coordinate mode (5)

Erase the screen (6)

Dash line mode (7)

Curved line mode (8)

Local tracking on (9)

Local tracking off (10)

etc.

For some graphics devices, particular modes may not be appropriate and for others additional modes are required. For the latter case a particular example might be a color CRT graphics device where blue, red, and yellow modes would also be required. However, the above list represents those required for a reasonably sophisticated graphics device. Before continuing, a word about the function of each of these various modes or states is in order.

Alphanumeric and graphics modes are generally associated with devices which can interpret a data stream as either alphanumeric characters or graphic elements. Standby mode generally is used to disable the terminal such that it ignores data sent to it and also data generated by interactive devices such as key boards, light pens, etc. Absolute and relative coordinate modes determine whether the coordinates specified in the graphic primitive position command are to be inter-preted as absolute or relative coordinate data. The erase mode is important for storage tube CRT graphics devices. Dashed line mode allows the generation of dashed lines using the hardware characteristics of the graphics device. Curved line mode is used to activate hardware curve generation. Local tracking mode can be used to activate hardware, which allows a visible cursor on a CRT graphics device to follow the movement of an interactive input device such as a light pen or the pen on an analog table.

The graphic primitive associated with graphic input is

read the cursor position.

This primitive assumes that the information supplied is a two-or three-component position vector, i.e., either x,y-pairs or x,y,z-triplets. All interactive computer systems and higher level languages have adequate facilities for accept-ing alphanumeric character input, and hence character input is not considered as a graphic primitive.

From the above we see that there are essentially four graphic primitives which conceptually can be represented either as commands within or subroutines of a higher level language such as BASIC or FORTRAN. These four primitives are

ONOFF (control variable)

MOVE (coordinate, coordinate, <coordinate>)

MODE (control variable)

RC (coordinate, coordinate, <coordinate>)

where < > is used to represent optional variables. The control variable in ONOFF could be an integer with a 0 or 1, indicating that the cursor is either off or on respectively. The control variable in MODE could be an integer assigned a specific meaning, as indicated above in parenthesis to the right of each individual function. These four graphics primitives can be combined into several compound graphic elements which are of more interest to the general user.

A-2 COMPUTER GRAPHIC ELEMENTS

The computer graphic primitives discussed in the previous section can be combined into computer graphic elements. These are generally compound operations; i.e., they generally involve more than one of the graphic primitives. The graphic elements are of more fundamental interest to the user than the graphic primitives. In fact, the user may not be aware of the graphic primitives. Again, as with the graphic primitives, the graphic elements can be placed in three categories: drawing functions, terminal or picture control functions, and interactive device control functions.

The classification method discussed in Sec. 1-6, as well as traditional drawing methods, assist in determining the fundamental drawing elements. A user will want to be able to move the cursor about without drawing, to draw a line, and to plot a point. It is convenient to be able to do this in either absolute or relative coordinates. These ideas lead to six graphic elements:

Move Absolute

Move Relative

Point Absolute

Point Relative

Draw Absolute

Draw Relative

In addition the user will want to be able to print textual material at a specified location in the picture, say,

Text Absolute

Text Relative

In each case it is convenient to consider that the action initiates from the current position of the cursor. Functionally each of these graphic elements can be described in terms of graphic primitives. For example, the Move Absolute algorithm might be

1. Set graphic mode - MODE 2
2. Turn cursor off - ONOFF 0
3. Set absolute coordinate mode - MODE 4
4. Move to the coordinates specified - MOVE (coor., coor., <coor.>)
5. Set alpha mode - MODE 1

The Point Absolute algorithm might be

1. Set graphic mode - MODE 2
2. Turn cursor off - ONOFF 0
3. Set absolute coordinate mode - MODE 4
4. Move to the coordinates specified - MOVE (coor., coor., <coor.>)
5. Turn cursor on - ONOFF 1
6. Turn cursor off - ONOFF 0
7. Set alpha mode - MODE 1

The Draw Absolute algorithm might be

1. Set graphic mode - MODE 2
2. Turn cursor on - ONOFF 1
3. Set absolute coordinate mode - MODE 4
4. Move to the coordinates specified - MOVE (coor., coor., <coor.>)
5. Turn cursor off - ONOFF 0
6. Set alpha mode - MODE 1

and the Text Absolute algorithm might be

1. Set graphic mode - MODE 2
2. Turn cursor off - ONOFF 0
3. Set absolute coordinate mode - MODE 4
4. Move to location - MOVE (coor., coor., <coor.>)
5. Set alpha mode - MODE 1
6. Turn cursor on - ONOFF 1
7. Print characters
8. Turn cursor off - ONOFF 0

The four relative coordinate elements have the same algorithms, except that the third command sets relative mode (MODE 5). The above algorithms set each required graphic primitive every time it is used and leave the graphic device with the cursor off and in alpha mode. This is good insurance. However, an increase in the efficiency of data transmission can be achieved at the expense of some additional complexity. For example, the algorithm for the Point Absolute command might be

1. Is the device in graphic mode? If yes - continue, if no - set graphic mode - MODE 2.
2. Is the cursor off? If yes - continue, if no - turn cursor off - ONOFF 0.
3. Is the device in absolute coordinate mode? If yes - continue, if no - set absolute coordinate mode - MODE 4.
4. Move to the coordinate specified - MOVE (coor., coor., <coor.>).
5. Turn cursor on - ONOFF 1

This scheme requires that a small storage buffer which contains information representing the "state of the device" at the end of the previous graphic command exist. However, the potential exists for reducing the number of data stream elements which must be communicated to the graphic device. Further, analysis of the original algorithm shows that if a method can be devised to anticipate whether the next command will be a graphic command or a nongraphic (alpha) command, then additional efficiencies result. Before continuing it should be noted that although functionally identical, these algorithms might be structured differently for different graphics devices.

Terminal or picture control graphic elements are associated with initializing the graphic device, erasing the screen for storage tube CRT graphics devices, starting and ending frames for refresh CRT graphic devices, and buffering the data stream and on command sending it to the graphics device. For example, the graphic elements

Initialize the Device
Begin Frame
Dump Buffer

could serve these purposes. Functionally, the Initialize the Device command serves to set the default conditions and zero the output buffer; the Begin Frame command serves to erase the screen for storage tube CRT graphic devices, to indicate a new plot for pen and ink devices, and to notify a refresh graphic device that the picture is complete and a new frame must be started. The Dump Buffer command serves to send the stored data stream to the graphics device and leave the device in alpha mode.

From the user's point of view the control of interactive devices must be

more explicit than a simple command to read the cursor position. As discussed
in Sec. 1-5 there are several interactive graphic devices available. As a
minimum the input graphic elements should include

Reading the Cursor Position
Activating an Analog Tablet
Activating a Joy Stick
Activating a Light Pen
Activating Control Dials
Activating Function Switches

Others can be added as is required or a general graphic input element can be
developed. As an example, the algorithm for activating an analog table with
local tracking might be

1. Set graphics mode - MODE 2
2. Set absolute coordinate mode - MODE 4
3. Set local tracking - MODE 9
4. Read the cursor position
5. Read any table switch positions
6. Turn off local tracking - MODE 10
7. Set alpha mode - MODE 1

The other graphic elements would have similar algorithms. Again economies in
the data stream can be obtained by using sophisticated checking procedures for
the various modes, etc.

A-3 CANONICAL SPACE

It is necessary to complete our discussion of graphic systems by considering
the various spaces or coordinate systems which are of interest to both the user
and the system architect.

There are three spaces that are of interest—user space, canonical space,
and device space. User space represents the coordinates or units in which the
application is performed, canonical space is a pseudo space used to obtain
device independence, and device space represents the coordinate system in which
the graphics device must be addressed, e.g., raster points or units for CRT
devices, inches or centimeters for plotters, etc. These are illustrated in
Fig. A-2.

The concept of a canonical or pseudo space is of interest. By using a
standard canonical or pseudo space for all graphic devices, device-independent

graphic software can more easily be obtained. In particular, the picture is first transformed from user space or co-ordinates to the standard canonical space and then transformed from the canonical space to the appropriate device space.

A simple concept for the canonical space assumes that the addressable area is the unit square in the first quadrant; i.e., the addressable area of the pseudo graphic device represented by the canonical space is $0 \leq x_a \leq 1.0$, $0 \leq y_a \leq 1.0$. Although this appears to limit the picture to a square format, this is not necessarily true. The 1.0 x 1.0 square format is assumed for independence among graphics devices and is predicated on the basis that many plotters and most storage tube CRT graphics devices have a square addressable area. However, addressable and viewable areas are not necessarily identical. Frequently the viewable area is a rectangle; e.g., most storage tube CRT graphics devices have a viewable area that is approximately 0.8 of the addressable area in one dimension, most often the vertical dimension. In this case, the viewable area is assumed to be $0 \leq x_v \leq 1.0$ and $0 \leq y_v \leq 0.8$. Further, many plotters have the ability to extend one axis indefinitely. In this case the viewable area is assumed to be $0 \leq x_v \leq a$, where a is some number which is greater than one. One could, of course, argue that the addressable area should then be rectangular. However, unless extreme care was taken with scale factors, distortion of geometric figures would occur; i.e., a circle would be seen as an ellipse. This is, of course, unacceptable for geometric computer graphics.

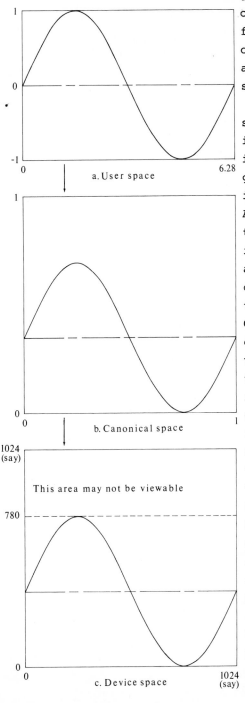

a. User space

b. Canonical space

c. Device space

This area may not be viewable

Figure A-2 Graphic spaces

APPENDIX B

MATRIX OPERATIONS

A few simple rules from matrix algebra are given here for convenience. A *matrix* is simply a rectangular array of numbers which are governed by these rules.

B-1 TERMINOLOGY

The array of numbers which make up a matrix are called its elements. These elements form rows and columns within a matrix. If the number of rows and columns are equal, the matrix is called *square*.

Consider the 4 x 4 square matrix given by

$$\begin{bmatrix} a_{11} & a_{12} & a_{13} & a_{14} \\ a_{21} & a_{22} & a_{23} & a_{24} \\ a_{31} & a_{32} & a_{33} & a_{34} \\ a_{41} & a_{42} & a_{43} & a_{44} \end{bmatrix}$$

The first subscript refers to the matrix row and the second refers to the matrix column. Thus, a_{34} is the element in the third row and fourth column. A matrix of m rows and n columns is one of *order* m x n. In the square matrix above, m = n and the elements a_{11}, a_{22}, a_{33}, and a_{44} are called its *diagonal elements*. The sum of the diagonal elements in a square matrix is called the *trace*.

A *zero matrix* is one in which every element is zero. An *identity matrix* is one in which every element is zero, with the exception of the diagonal elements, which are all unity. An example of a 3 x 3 identity matrix is:

$$\begin{bmatrix} 1 & 0 & 0 \\ 0 & 1 & 0 \\ 0 & 0 & 1 \end{bmatrix}$$

Two matrices are *equal* only when each element in one is equal to the corresponding element in the other; that is, they must be identical.

B-2 ADDITION AND SUBTRACTION

If two matrices are of the same order, then addition and subtraction are defined. To add or substract two matrices, the operation of addition or subtraction is applied to each of the corresponding elements. As an example:

$$\begin{bmatrix} 1 & 2 & 3 \\ 4 & 5 & 6 \\ 7 & 8 & 9 \end{bmatrix} + \begin{bmatrix} 1 & 4 & 7 \\ 2 & 5 & 8 \\ 3 & 6 & 9 \end{bmatrix} = \begin{bmatrix} 2 & 6 & 10 \\ 6 & 10 & 14 \\ 10 & 14 & 18 \end{bmatrix}$$

and

$$\begin{bmatrix} 1 & 2 & 3 \\ 4 & 5 & 6 \\ 7 & 8 & 9 \end{bmatrix} - \begin{bmatrix} 1 & 4 & 7 \\ 2 & 5 & 8 \\ 3 & 6 & 9 \end{bmatrix} = \begin{bmatrix} 0 & -2 & -4 \\ 2 & 0 & -2 \\ 4 & 2 & 0 \end{bmatrix}$$

B-3 MULTIPLICATION

Matrix multiplication is the most useful matrix operation for computer graphics. Consider one matrix of order $n_1 \times m_1$ and a second matrix of order $n_2 \times m_2$. For multiplication of two matrices to be defined, the value of m_1 must equal the value of n_2. That is, the number of columns in the first matrix must equal the number of rows in the second matrix.

The rules for matrix multiplication are best described by the following example. If [A] is a matrix of order 4 x 3 and [B] is a square matrix of order 3 x 3, then the matrix product [A][B] is defined by the following operation.

$$\begin{bmatrix} a_{11} & a_{12} & a_{13} \\ a_{21} & a_{22} & a_{23} \\ a_{31} & a_{32} & a_{33} \\ a_{41} & a_{42} & a_{43} \end{bmatrix} \begin{bmatrix} b_{11} & b_{12} & b_{13} \\ b_{21} & b_{22} & b_{23} \\ b_{31} & b_{32} & b_{33} \end{bmatrix} = \begin{bmatrix} a_{11}b_{11} + a_{12}b_{21} + a_{13}b_{31} & a_{11}b_{12} + a_{12}b_{22} + a_{13}b_{32} & a_{11}b_{13} + a_{12}b_{23} + a_{13}b_{33} \\ a_{21}b_{11} + a_{22}b_{21} + a_{23}b_{31} & a_{21}b_{12} + a_{22}b_{22} + a_{23}b_{32} & a_{21}b_{13} + a_{22}b_{23} + a_{23}b_{33} \\ a_{31}b_{11} + a_{32}b_{21} + a_{33}b_{31} & a_{31}b_{12} + a_{32}b_{22} + a_{33}b_{32} & a_{31}b_{13} + a_{32}b_{23} + a_{33}b_{33} \\ a_{41}b_{11} + a_{42}b_{21} + a_{43}b_{31} & a_{41}b_{12} + a_{42}b_{22} + a_{43}b_{32} & a_{41}b_{13} + a_{42}b_{43} + a_{43}b_{33} \end{bmatrix}$$

Notice that a 4 x 3 matrix multiplied by a 3 x 3 matrix produces a 4 x 3 matrix. In general, a n_1 x m_1 matrix times a n_2 x m_2 matrix, where $m_1 = n_2$, produces a n_1 x m_2 matrix. As a numerical example, consider

$$\begin{bmatrix} 1 & 3 \\ 4 & 2 \\ 1 & 1 \\ 6 & 4 \\ 3 & 2 \end{bmatrix} \begin{bmatrix} 1 & 2 \\ 3 & 4 \end{bmatrix} = \begin{bmatrix} 1+9 & 2+12 \\ 4+6 & 8+8 \\ 1+3 & 2+4 \\ 6+12 & 12+16 \\ 3+6 & 6+8 \end{bmatrix} = \begin{bmatrix} 10 & 14 \\ 10 & 16 \\ 4 & 6 \\ 18 & 28 \\ 9 & 14 \end{bmatrix}$$

The operation of matrix multiplication is not commutative. That is, in general, [A][B] is not equal to [B][A]. Thus, the order (sequence) of multiplication is important. Matrix operations follow the first and second distributive laws; e.g., A(B + C) = AB + AC and (A + B)C = AC + BC. Also, the associative law A(BC) = (AB)C applies.

B-4 DETERMINANT OF A SQUARE MATRIX

The determinant of a square matrix [A] is denoted by $|A|$. The determinant has many useful properties in matrix theory. For our purpose, it is sufficient to illustrate the method for finding the determinant of a 3 x 3 square matrix. If

$$M = \begin{bmatrix} a_{11} & a_{12} & a_{13} \\ a_{21} & a_{22} & a_{23} \\ a_{31} & a_{32} & a_{33} \end{bmatrix}$$

then

$$\begin{vmatrix} a_{11} & a_{12} & a_{13} \\ a_{21} & a_{22} & a_{23} \\ a_{31} & a_{32} & a_{33} \end{vmatrix} = a_{11} \begin{vmatrix} a_{22} & a_{23} \\ a_{32} & a_{33} \end{vmatrix} - a_{12} \begin{vmatrix} a_{21} & a_{23} \\ a_{31} & a_{33} \end{vmatrix} + a_{13} \begin{vmatrix} a_{21} & a_{22} \\ a_{31} & a_{32} \end{vmatrix}$$

$$= a_{11}(a_{22}a_{33} - a_{23}a_{32}) - a_{12}(a_{21}a_{33} - a_{23}a_{31})$$
$$+ a_{13}(a_{21}a_{32} - a_{22}a_{31})$$

This gives a single numerical value for the determinant. Consider the evaluation of

$$\begin{vmatrix} 3 & 9 & 4 \\ 6 & 1 & 8 \\ 2 & 5 & 3 \end{vmatrix}$$

The result is

$$3(3 - 40) - 9(18 - 16) + 4(30 - 2)$$
$$= 3(-37) - 9(2) + 4(28) = -17$$

B-5 INVERSE OF A SQUARE MATRIX

There are many techniques for calculating the inverse of a square matrix. Most computer languages have functions or subroutines which will perform the repetitive calculations necessary to evaluate the elements of the inverse of a given matrix.

In algebra, where single variables are considered, if $ax = y$, then $x = a^{-1}y$, where a^{-1} is simply the reciprocal of a, e.g., $a^{-1} = 1/a$. In matrix algebra, division is not defined and the reciprocal of a matrix does not exist. However, if $[A][X] = [Y]$, then $[X] = [A]^{-1}[Y]$, where $[A]^{-1}$, is called the inverse of the square matrix $[A]$.

A matrix inverse will exist if the matrix is square *and* if the matrix is nonsingular. Thus, not every square matrix has an inverse. However, if the determinant of the square matrix is nonzero and an inverse exists, then that inverse is unique.

The important property of a matrix inverse that is used in this book is that, for any square matrix $[A]$, the equality $[A][A]^{-1} = [I]$ is valid, where $[I]$ is the identity matrix.

Consider the matrix product of the two following 3 x 3 matrices:

$$\begin{bmatrix} 1 & 2 & 3 \\ 1 & 3 & 3 \\ 1 & 2 & 4 \end{bmatrix} \begin{bmatrix} 6 & -2 & -3 \\ -1 & 1 & 0 \\ -1 & 0 & 1 \end{bmatrix} = \begin{bmatrix} 1 & 0 & 0 \\ 0 & 1 & 0 \\ 0 & 0 & 1 \end{bmatrix}$$

If this product is represented by $[A][B] = [I]$, then $[B]$ is equal to $[A]^{-1}$.

APPENDIX C

DATA BASE
MANIPULATION
ALGORITHMS

     The algorithms presented in this section are based on the mathematical discussion presented in the body of the text. They are given as subprograms, written in Dartmouth Sixth Edition BASIC. They can easily be converted to other languages. The algorithms are not intended to be the most efficient possible. They are intended to be instructive. Each of the transformation algorithms assumes that the data base is presented in ordinary coordinates. The algorithm then develops the necessary homogeneous coordinate representation, performs the transformation, and returns to ordinary coordinates. The apparent inefficiency associated with reconversion to ordinary coordinates has been deliberately accepted since experience indicates that users normally will perform one or two transformations, display the result, which requires ordinary coordinates, and then continue. If additional efficiency is required the reader can either modify the algorithms or develop his or her own based on the theory presented in the body of the text.

C-1 AN ALGORITHM FOR TWO-DIMENSIONAL TRANSLATIONS

     An algorithm for an arbitrary translation utilizing homogeneous coordinates is given below as a BASIC language subprogram. It is based on Sec. 2-15.

2DTRANS

```
100 SUB"2DTRANS":P,X(),Y(),M,N          '2-D TRANSLATION
110     'P=NUMBER OF X,Y-PAIRS
120     'X()=ARRAY CONTAINING X-COORDINATES
130     'Y()=ARRAY CONTAINING Y-COORDINATES
140     'M=X TRANSLATION FACTOR
150     'N=Y TRANSLATION FACTOR
160     DIM U(100,3),V(100,3)           '100 POSITION VECTORS
170     MAT U=ZER(P,3)                  'REDIMENSION U&V FILL WITH ZEROS
180     MAT V=ZER(P,3)
190     FOR I=1 TO P                    'SET UP HOMOGENEOUS
200        LET U(I,1)=X(I)              'POSITION VECTORS
210        LET U(I,2)=Y(I)
220        LET U(I,3)=1
230     NEXT I
240     MAT T=ZER(3,3)                  'REDIMENSION T FILL WITH ZEROS
250     LET T(1,1)=T(2,2)=T(3,3)=1      'PLACE 1'S ON DIA OF T MATRIX
260     LET T(3,1)=M                    'SET X TRANSLATION FACTOR
270     LET T(3,2)=N                    'SET Y TRANSLATION FACTOR
280     MAT V=U*T                       'CALC. TRANSLATED POSITION VECTORS
290     FOR I=1 TO P                    'RETURN TO PHYSICAL COOR.
300        LET X(I)=V(I,1)
310        LET Y(I)=V(I,2)
320     NEXT I
330 SUBEND
```

C-2 A Two-Dimensional Scaling Algorithm

A scaling algorithm is given below as a BASIC language subprogram. The algorithm based on Secs. 2-11 and 2-15 provides both local and overall scaling. Thus, distortion of a shape can be accomplished. It utilizes homogeneous coordinates.

2DSCALE

```
100 SUB"2DSCALE":P,X(),Y(),A,D,S        '2-D SCALE
110     'P=NUMBER OF X,Y-PAIRS
120     'X()=ARRAY CONTAINING X-COORDINATES
130     'Y()=ARRAY CONTAINING Y-COORDINATES
140     'A=X STRETCHING FACTOR A>1 STRETCHES A<1 CONTRACTS
150     'D=Y STRETCHING FACTOR D>1 STRETCHES D<1 CONTRACTS
160     'S=OVERALL SCALING S<1 ENLARGES S>1 REDUCES
170     DIM S(100,3),Q(100,3)           '100 POSITION VECTORS
180     MAT S=ZER(P,3)                  'REDIMENSION S&Q FILL WITH ZEROS
190     MAT Q=ZER(P,3)
200     FOR I=1 TO P                    'SET UP HOMOGENEOUS
210        LET S(I,1)=X(I)              'POSITION VECTORS
220        LET S(I,2)=Y(I)
230        LET S(I,3)=1
240     NEXT I
250     MAT T=ZER(3,3)                  'REDIMENSION T FILL WITH ZEROS
260     LET T(1,1)=A                    'SET X STRETCHING FACTOR
270     LET T(2,2)=D                    'SET Y STRETCHING FACTOR
280     LET T(3,3)=S                    'SET OVERALL SCALING
```

```
290    MAT Q=S*T                      'CALC. TRANSFORMED POINTS
300    FOR I=1 TO P                   'CALC. PHYSICAL COOR.
310       LET X(I)=Q(I,1)/Q(I,3)
320       LET Y(I)=Q(I,2)/Q(I,3)
330    NEXT I
340 SUBEND
```

C-3 A Two-Dimensional Reflection Algorithm

A simple algorithm to reflect about either the x- or y-axis is given below as a BASIC language subprogram. This routine depends on the analysis of Sec. 2-5 and uses homogeneous coordinates. This operation is also frequently referred to as mirror image.

2DREFLT

```
100 SUB"2DREFLT":P,X(),Y(),N          '2-D REFLECTION
110    'P=NUMBER OF X,Y-PAIRS
120    'X()=ARRAY CONTAINING X-COORDINATES
130    'Y()=ARRAY CONTAINING Y-COORDINATES
140    'N=REFLECTION CODE 1=X-AXIS, 2=Y-AXIS
150    DIM S(100,3),Q(100,3)          '100 POSITION VECTORS
160    MAT S=ZER(P,3)                 'REDIMENSION S&Q FILL WITH ZEROS
170    MAT Q=ZER(P,3)
180    FOR I=1 TO P                   'SET UP HOMOGENEOUS
190       LET S(I,1)=X(I)             'POSITION VECTORS
200       LET S(I,2)=Y(I)
210       LET S(I,3)=1
220    NEXT I
230    MAT T=ZER(3,3)                 'REDIMENSION T FILL WITH ZEROS
240    IF N=2 THEN 280                'SET UP TRANSFORMATION MATRIX
250    LET T(1,1)=T(3,3)=1
260    LET T(2,2)=-1
270    GO TO 300
280    LET T(2,2)=T(3,3)=1
290    LET T(1,1)=-1
300    MAT Q=S*T                      'CALC. TRANSFORMED POINTS
310    FOR I=1 TO P                   'CALC. PHYSICAL COOR.
320       LET X(I)=Q(I,1)
330       LET Y(I)=Q(I,2)
340    NEXT I
350 SUBEND
```

C-4 A General Two-Dimensional Rotation Algorithm

An algorithm for two-dimensional rotation about an arbitrary point is given below as a BASIC language subroutine. It utilizes the analysis of Sec. 2-16.

2DROT

```
100 SUB"2DROT":P,X(),Y(),T1,M,N          '2-D ROTATION
110     'P=NUMBER OF X,Y-PAIRS
120     'X()=ARRAY CONTAINING X-COORDINATES
130     'Y()=ARRAY CONTAINING Y-COORDINATES
140     'T1=ROTATION ANGLE IN DEGREES
150     'M=X TRANSLATION FACTOR
160     'N=Y TRANSLATION FACTOR
170     DIM S(100,3),Q(100,3)            '100 POSITION VECTORS
180     MAT S=ZER(P,3)                   'REDIMENSION S&Q FILL
190     MAT Q=ZER(P,3)                   'WITH ZEROS
200     FOR I=1 TO P                     'SET UP HOMOGENEOUS
210        LET S(I,1)=X(I)               'POSITION VECTORS
220        LET S(I,2)=Y(I)
230        LET S(I,3)=1
240     NEXT I
250     LET T2=T1/57.2957795             'CONVERT TO RADIANS
260     MAT T=ZER(3,3)                   'REDIMENSION T FILL WITH ZEROS
270     LET T(1,1)=T(2,2)=COS(T2)        'SET TRANSFORMATION MATRIX
280     LET T(1,2)=SIN(T2)
290     LET T(2,1)=-SIN(T2)
300     LET T(3,1)=-M*(COS(T2)-1)+N*SIN(T2)
310     LET T(3,2)=-M*SIN(T2)-N*(COS(T2)-1)
320     LET T(3,3)=1
330     MAT Q=S*T                        'CALC. TRANSFORMED POINTS
340     FOR I=1 TO P                     'CALC. PHYSICAL COOR.
350        LET X(I)=Q(I,1)
360        LET Y(I)=Q(I,2)
370     NEXT I
380 SUBEND
```

C-5 A Three-Dimensional Scaling Algorithm

An algorithm for three-dimensional scaling is given as a BASIC language subprogram. It is based on Eq. (3-4).

3DSCALE

```
100 SUB"3DSCALE":P,X(),Y(),Z(),A,E,J,S  '3-D SCALE
110     'P=NUMBER OF X,Y,Z-TRIPLETS
120     'X()=ARRAY CONTAINING X-COORDINATE
130     'Y()=ARRAY CONTAINING Y-COORDINATE
140     'Z()=ARRAY CONTAINING Z-COORDINATE
150     'A=X STRETCHING FACTOR A>1 STRETCHES, A<1 CONTRACTS
160     'E=Y STRETCHING FACTOR E>1 STRETCHES, E<1 CONTRACTS
170     'J=Z STRETCHING FACTOR J>1 STRETCHES, J<1 CONTRACTS
180     'S=OVERALL SCALING S>1 ENLARGES S<1 REDUCES
190     DIM U(100,4),V(100,4)            '100 POSITION VECTORS
200     MAT U=ZER(P 4)                   'REDIMENSION U&V FILL WITH ZEROS
210     MAT V=ZER(P,4)
220     FOR I=1 TO P                     'SET UP HOMOGENEOUS
230        LET U(I,1)=X(I)               'POSITION VECTORS
240        LET U(I,2)=Y(I)
250        LET U(I,3)=Z(I)
260        LET U(I,4)=1
270     NEXT I
280     MAT T=ZER(4,4)                   'REDIMENSION T FILL WITH ZEROS
290     LET T(1,1)=A                     'SET X STRETCHING FACTOR
300     LET T(2,2)=E                     'SET Y STRETCHING FACTOR
```

```
310      LET T(3,3)=J                    'SET Z STRETCHING FACTOR
320      LET T(4,4)=1/S                  'SET OVERALL STRETCHING FACTOR
330      MAT V=U*T                       'CALC. TRANSFORMED POINTS
340      FOR I=1 TO P                    'CALC. PHYSICAL COOR.
350         LET X(I)=V(I,1)/V(I,4)
360         LET Y(I)=V(I,2)/V(I,4)
370         LET Z(I)=V(I,3)/V(I,4)
380      NEXT I
390 SUBEND
```

C-6 An Algorithm for Three-Dimensional Rotation About the x-Axis

The algorithm given below as a BASIC language subprogram allows rotation of the position vectors of an object about the x-axis. It utilizes homogeneous coordinates.

3DXROT

```
100 SUB"3DXROT":P,X(),Y(),Z(),T1        '3-D ROTATION ABOUT X-AXIS
110     'P=NUMBER OF X,Y,Z-TRIPLETS
120     'X()=ARRAY CONTAINING X-COORDINATES
130     'Y()=ARRAY CONTAINING Y-COORDINATES
140     'Z()=ARRAY CONTAINING Z-COORDINATES
150     'T1=ROTATION ANGLE IN DEGREES
160     DIM U(100,4),V(100,4)           '100 POSITION VECTORS
170     MAT U=ZER(P,4)                  'REDIMENSION U&V FILL WITH ZEROS
180     MAT V=ZER(P,4)
190     FOR I=1 TO P                    'SET UP HOMOGENEOUS
200        LET U(I,1)=X(I)              'POSITION VECTORS
210        LET U(I,2)=Y(I)
220        LET U(I,3)=Z(I)
230        LET U(I,4)=1
240     NEXT I
250     LET T2=T1/57.2957795            'CONVERT TO RADIANS
260     MAT T=ZER(4,4)                  'REDIMENSION T FILL WITH ZEROS
270     LET T(1,1)=T(4,4)=1             'SET UP TRANSFORMATION MATRIX
280     LET T(2,2)=T(3,3)=COS(T2)
290     LET T(2,3)=SIN(T2)
300     LET T(3,2)=-T(2,3)
310     MAT V=U*T                       'CALC. TRANSFORMED POINTS
320     FOR I=1 TO P                    'CALC. PHYSICAL COOR.
330        LET X(I)=V(I,1)
340        LET Y(I)=V(I,2)
350        LET Z(I)=V(I,3)
360     NEXT I
370 SUBEND
```

C-7 An Algorithm for Three Dimensional Rotation About the y-Axis

The algorithm given below as a BASIC language subprogram allows rotation of the position vectors of an object about the y-axis. It utilizes homogeneous coordinates.

3DYROT

```
100 SUB"3DYROT":P,X(),Y(),Z(),T1          '3-D ROTATION ABOUT Y-AXIS
110     'P=NUMBER OF X,Y,Z-TRIPLETS
120     'X()=ARRAY CONTAINING X-COORDINATES
130     'Y()=ARRAY CONTAINING Y-COORDINATES
140     'Z()=ARRAY CONTAINING Z-COORDINATES
150     'T1=ROTATION ANGLE IN DEGREES
160     DIM U(100,4),V(100,4)             ·100 POSITION VECTORS
170     MAT U=ZER(P,4)                    'REDIMENSION U&V FILL WITH ZEROS
180     MAT V=ZER(P,4)
190     FOR I=1 TO P                      'SET UP HOMOGENEOUS
200         LET U(I,1)=X(I)               'POSITION VECTORS
210         LET U(I,2)=Y(I)
220         LET U(I,3)=Z(I)
230         LET U(I,4)=1
240     NEXT I
250     LET T2=T1/57.2957795              'CONVERT TO RADIANS
260     MAT T=ZER(4,4)                    'REDIMENSION T FILL WITH ZEROS
270     LET T(1,1)=T(3,3)=COS(T2)
280     LET T(3,1)=SIN(T2)
290     LET T(1,3)=-T(3,1)
300     LET T(2,2)=T(4,4)=1
310     MAT V=U*T                         'CALC. TRANSFORMED POINTS
320     FOR I=1 TO P                      'CALC. PHYSICAL COOR.
330         LET X(I)=V(I,1)
340         LET Y(I)=V(I,2)
350         LET Z(I)=V(I,3)
360     NEXT I
370 SUBEND
```

C-8 An Algorithm for Three Dimensional Rotation About the z-Axis

The algorithm given below as a BASIC language subprogram provides for three-dimensional rotation about the z-axis.

3DZROT

```
100 SUB"3DZROT":P,X(),Y(),Z(),T1          '3-D ROTATION ABOUT Z-AXIS
110     'P=NUMBER OF X,Y,Z-TRIPLETS
120     'X()=ARRAY CONTAINING X-COORDINATES
130     'Y()=ARRAY CONTAINING Y-COORDINATES
140     'Z()=ARRAY CONTAINING Z-COORDINATES
150     'T1=ROTATION ANGLE IN DEGREES
160     DIM U(100,4),V(100,4)             '100 POSITION VECTORS
170     MAT U=ZER(P,4)                    'REDIMENSION U&V FILL WITH ZEROS
180     MAT V=ZER(P,4)
190     FOR I=1 TO P                      'SET UP HOMOGENEOUS
200         LET U(I,1)=X(I)               'POSITION VECTORS
210         LET U(I,2)=Y(I)
220         LET U(I,3)=Z(I)
230         LET U(I,4)=1
240     NEXT I
250     LET T2=T1/57.2957795              'CONVERT TO RADIANS
260     MAT T=ZER(4,4)                    'REDIMENSION T FILL WITH ZEROS
270     LET T(1,1)=T(2,2)=COS(T2)
280     LET T(1,2)=-SIN(T2)
```

```
290    LET T(2,1)=-T(1,2)
300    LET T(3,3)=T(4,4)=1
310    MAT V=U*T                    'CALC. TRANSFORMED POINTS
320    FOR I=1 TO P                 'CALC. PHYSICAL COOR.
330       LET X(I)=V(I,1)
340       LET Y(I)=V(I,2)
350       LET Z(I)=V(I,3)
360    NEXT I
370 SUBEND
```

C-9 AN ALGORITHM FOR THREE-DIMENSIONAL REFLECTIONS

An algorithm which will perform three-dimensional reflections through the coordinate planes xy, xz, or yz is given below as a BASIC language subprogram. Reflections about other planes can be obtained by a combination of rotation and reflection.

3DREFLT

```
100 SUB"3DREFLT":P,X(),Y(),Z(),N     '3-D REFLECTIONS
110    'P=NUMBER OF X,Y,Z-TRIPLETS
120    'X()=ARRAY CONTAINING X-COORDINATES
130    'Y()=ARRAY CONTAINING Y-COORDINATES
140    'Z()=ARRAY CONTAINING Z-COORDINATES
150    'N=REFLECTION CODE: 1=XY-PLANE, 2=YZ-PLANE, 3=XZ-PLANE
160    DIM U(100,4),V(100,4)         ·100 POSITION VECTORS
170    MAT U=ZER(P,4)                'REDIMENSION U&V FILL WITH ZEROS
180    MAT V=ZER(P,4)
190    FOR I=1 TO P                  'SET UP HOMOGENEOUS
200       LET U(I,1)=X(I)            'POSITION VECTORS
210       LET U(I,2)=Y(I)
220       LET U(I,3)=Z(I)
230       LET U(I,4)=1
240    NEXT I
250    MAT T=ZER(4,4)                'REDIMENSION T FILL WITH ZEROS
260    IF N=2 THEN 310               'SET UP TRANSFORMATION MATRIX
270    IF N=3 THEN 340
280    LET T(1,1)=T(2,2)=T(4,4)=1
290    LET T(3,3)=-1
300    GO TO 360
310    LET T(4,4)=T(3,3)=T(2,2)=1
320    LET T(1,1)=-1
330    GO TO 360
340    LET T(1,1)=T(3,3)=T(4,4)=1
350    LET T(2,2)=-1
360    MAT V=U*T                     'CALC. TRANSFORMED POINTS
370    FOR I=1 TO P                  'CALC. PHYSICAL COOR.
380       LET X(I)=V(I,1)
390       LET Y(I)=V(I,2)
400       LET Z(I)=V(I,3)
410    NEXT I
420 SUBEND
```

C-10 An Algorithm for Three-Dimensional Translation

An algorithm for translation in three dimensions is given below as a BASIC language subprogram. It makes use of homogeneous coordinates.

3DTRANS

```
100 SUB"3DTRANS":P,X(),Y(),Z(),L,M,N   '3-D TRANSLATION
110    'P=NUMBER OF X,Y,Z-TRIPLETS
120    'X()=ARRAY CONTAINING X-COORDINATES
130    'Y()=ARRAY CONTAINING Y-COORDINATES
140    'Z()=ARRAY CONTAINING Z-COORDINATES
150    'L=X TRANSLATION FACTOR
160    'M=Y TRANSLATION FACTOR
170    'N=Z TRANSLATION FACTOR
180    DIM U(100,4),V(100,4)            '100 POSITION VECTORS
190    MAT U=ZER(P,4)                   'REDIMENSION U&V FILL WITH ZEROS
200    MAT V=ZER(P,4)
210    FOR I=1 TO P                     'SET UP HOMOGENEOUS
220       LET U(I,1)=X(I)               'POSITION VECTORS
230       LET U(I,2)=Y(I)
240       LET U(I,3)=Z(I)
250       LET U(I,4)=1
260    NEXT I
270    MAT T=ZER(4,4)                   'REDIMENSION T FILL WITH ZEROS
280    LET-T(1,1)=T(2,2)=1              'PLACE 1'S ON DIAG. OF T-MATRIX
290    LET T(3,3)=T(4,4)=1
300    LET T(4,1)=L                     'SET X TRANSLATION FACTOR
310    LET T(4,2)=M                     'SET Y TRAMSLATION FACTOR
320    LET T(4,3)=N                     'SET Z TRANSLATION FACTOR
330    MAT V=U*T                        'CALC. TRANS POSITION VECTORS
340    FOR I=1 TO P                     'CALC. PHYSICAL COOR.
350       LET X(I)=V(I,1)
360       LET Y(I)=V(I,2)
370       LET Z(I)=V(I,3)
380    NEXT I
390 SUBEND
```

C-11 An Algorithm for Three-Dimensional Rotation About Any Arbitrary Axis in Space

An algorithm which will produce a three-dimensional rotation about an arbitrary axis in space is given below as a BASIC language subprogram. It is based on Eqs. (3-17) and (3-18).

3DGENROT

```
100 SUB"3DGENROT":P,X(),Y(),Z(),N1,N2,N3,T1   '3-D GENERAL ROTATION
110    'P=NUMBER OF X,Y,Z-TRIPLETS
120    'X()=ARRAY CONTAINING X-COORDINATES
130    'Y()=ARRAY CONTAINING Y-COORDINATES
140    'Z()=ARRAY CONTAINING Z-COORDINATES
150    'N1=DIRECTION COSINE OF ROTATION AXIS W.R.T. X-DIRECTION
```

```
160    'N2=DIRECTION COSINE OF ROTATION AXIS W.R.T. Y-DIRECTION
170    'N3=DIRECTION COSINE OF ROTATION AXIS W.R.T. Z-DIRECTION
180    'T1=ROTATION ANGLE IN DEGREES
190    DIM U(100,4),V(100,4)            '100 POSITION VECTORS
200    MAT U=ZER(P,4)                   'REDIMENSION U&V FILL WITH ZEROS
210    MAT V=ZER(P,4)
220    FOR I=1 TO P                     'SET UP HOMOGENEOUS
230       LET U(I,1)=X(I)               'POSITION VECTORS
240       LET U(I,2)=Y(I)
250       LET U(I,3)=Z(I)
260       LET U(I,4)=1
270    NEXT I
280    MAT T=ZER(4,4)                   'REDIMENSION T FILL WITH ZEROS
290    LET T2=T1/57.2957795             'CONVERT T1 TO RADIANS
300    LET T(4,4)=1                     'SET UP TRANSFORMATION MATRIX
310    LET T(1,1)=N1*N1+(1-N1*N1)*COS(T2)
320    LET T(1,2)=N1*N2*(1-COS(T2))+N3*SIN(T2)
330    LET T(1,3)=N1*N3*(1-COS(T2))-N2*SIN(T2)
340    LET T(2,1)=N1*N2*(1-COS(T2))-N3*SIN(T2)
350    LET T(2,2)=N2*N2+(1-N2*N2)*COS(T2)
360    LET T(2,3)=N2*N3*(1-COS(T2))+N1*SIN(T2)
370    LET T(3,1)=N1*N3*(1-COS(T2))+N2*SIN(T2)
380    LET T(3,2)=N2*N3*(1-COS(T2))-N1*SIN(T2)
390    LET T(3,3)=N3*N3+(1-N3*N3)*COS(T2)
400    MAT V=U*T                        'CALC. TRANSFORMED POINTS
410    FOR I=1 TO P                     'CALC. PHYSICAL COOR.
420       LET X(I)=V(I,1)
430       LET Y(I)=V(I,2)
440       LET Z(I)=V(I,3)
450    NEXT I
460 SUBEND
```

C-12 AN AXONOMETRIC PROJECTIVE ALGORITHM

An algorithm for a simple orthographic projection onto a zero plane perpendicular to any of the three orthogonal axes is given below as a BASIC language
subprogram.

PROJ

```
100 SUB"PROJ":P,X(),Y(),Z(),N          'PROJECTION
110    'P=NUMBER OF X,Y,Z-TRIPLETS
120    'X()=ARRAY CONTAINING X-COORDINATES
130    'Y()=ARRAY CONTAINING Y-COORDINATES
140    'Z()=ARRAY CONTAINING Z-COORDINATES
150    'N=CODE NUMBER INDICATING PERPENDICULAR AXIS:
160    '1=X-AXIS, 2=Y-AXIS, 3=Z-AXIS
170    DIM U(100,4),V(100,4)            '100 POSITION VECTORS
180    MAT U=ZER(P,4)                   'REDIMENSION U&V FILL WITH ZEROS
190    MAT V=ZER(P,4)
200    FOR I=1 TO P                     'SET UP HOMOGENEOUS
210       LET U(I,1)=X(I)               'POSITION VECTORS
220       LET U(I,2)=Y(I)
230       LET U(I,3)=Z(I)
240       LET U(I,4)=1
250    NEXT I
260    MAT T=ZER(4,4)                   'REDIMENSION T FILL WITH ZEROS
```

```
270     LET T(1,1)=T(2,2)=1         'PUT 1'S ON ALL DIA ELEMENTS
280     LET T(3,3)=T(4,4)=1
290     IF N=3 THEN 350             'SET APPROPRIATE DIAGONAL TERM=0
300     IF N=2 THEN 330
310     LET T(1,1)=0
320     GO TO 360
330     LET T(2,2)=0
340     GO TO 360
350     LET T(3,3)=0
360     MAT V=U*T                   'CALC. TRANSFORMED POINTS
370     FOR I=1 TO P                'CALC. PHYSICAL COOR.
380        LET X(I)=V(I,1)
390        LET Y(I)=V(I,2)
400        LET Z(I)=V(I,3)
410     NEXT I
420 SUBEND
```

C-13 A Dimetric Projective Algorithm

An algorithm which implements the specific dimetric transformation given in Eq. (3-26) and assuming projection onto the z = 0 plane is given below as a BASIC language subprogram.

DIMETRIC

```
100 SUB"DIMETRIC":P,X(),Y(),Z()     'DIMETRIC PROJECTION
110     'P=NUMBER OF X,Y,Z-TRIPLETS
120     'X()=ARRAY CONTAINING X-COORDINATES
130     'Y()=ARRAY CONTAINING Y-COORDINATES
140     'Z()=ARRAY CONTAINING Z-COORDINATES
150     DIM U(100,4),V(100,4)       '100 POSITION VECTORS
160     MAT U=ZER(P,4)              'REDIMENSION U&V FILL WITH ZEROS
170     MAT V=ZER(P,4)
180     FOR I=1 TO P                'SET UP HOMOGENEOUS
190        LET U(I,1)=X(I)          'POSITION VECTORS
200        LET U(I,2)=Y(I)
210        LET U(I,3)=Z(I)
220        LET U(I,4)=1
230     NEXT I
240     MAT T=ZER(4,4)              'REDIMENSION T FILL WITH ZEROS
250     LET T(1,1)=0.925820         'SET UP TRANSFORMATION MATRIX
260     LET T(1,2)=0.133631
270     LET T(2,3)=0.353553
280     LET T(1,3)=-0.353553
290     LET T(2,2)=0.935414
300     LET T(3,1)=0.377964
310     LET T(3,2)=-0.327327
320     LET T(3,3)=0.866025
330     LET T(4,4)=1
340     MAT V=U*T                   'CALC. TRANSFORMATION
350     FOR I=1 TO P                'CALC. PHYSICAL COOR.
360        LET X(I)=V(I,1)
370        LET Y(I)=V(I,2)
380        LET Z(I)=V(I,3)
390     NEXT I
400     CALL "PROJ":P,X(),Y(),Z(),3 'PROJECT ON TO Z=0 PLANE
410 SUBEND
```

C-14 An Isometric Projective Algorithm

An algorithm which implements the isometric transformation discussed in Sec. 3-10 [i.e., Eq. (3-26) with θ = 35.264° and ϕ = 45°] and assuming projection on the z = 0 plane is given below as a BASIC language subprogram.

ISOMET

```
100 SUB"ISOMET":P,X(),Y(),Z()        'ISOMETRIC PROJECTION
110    'P=NUMBER OF X,Y,Z-TRIPLETS
120    'X()=ARRAY CONTAINING X-COORDINATES
130    'Y()=ARRAY CONTAINING Y-COORDINATES
140    'Z()=ARRAY CONTAINING Z-COORDINATES
150    DIM U(100,4),V(100,4)         '100 POSITION VECTORS
160    MAT U=ZER(P,4)                'REDIMENSION U&V FILL WITH ZEROS
170    MAT V=ZER(P,4)
180    FOR I=1 TO P                  'SET UP HOMOGENEOUS
190       LET U(I,1)=X(I)            'POSITION VECTORS
200       LET U(I,2)=Y(I)
210       LET U(I,3)=Z(I)
220       LET U(I,4)=1
230    NEXT I
240    MAT T=ZER(4,4)                'REDIMENSION T FILL WITH ZEROS
250    LET T(1,1)=T(3,1)=0.707107    'SET UP TRANSFORMATION MATRIX
260    LET T(1,2)=0.408248
270    LET T(3,2)=-0.408248
280    LET T(1,3)=-0.577353
290    LET T(3,3)=0.577353
300    LET T(2,2)=0.816497
310    LET T(2,3)=0.577345
320    LET T(4,4)=1
330    MAT V=U*T                     'CALC. TRANSFORMATION
340    FOR I=1 TO P                  'CALC. PHYSICAL COOR.
350       LET X(I)=V(I,1)
360       LET Y(I)=V(I,2)
370       LET Z(I)=V(I,3)
380    NEXT I
390    CALL "PROJ":P,X(),Y(),Z(),3   'PROJECT ONTO Z=0 PLANE
400 SUBEND
```

C-15 An Algorithm for Perspective Transformations

An algorithm which will generate a general perspective view is given below as a BASIC language subprogram.

PERSPEC

```
100 SUB"PERSPEC":P1,X(),Y(),Z(),P,Q,R  'PERSPECTIVE TRANSFORMATION
110    'P1=NUMBER OF X,Y,Z-TRIPLETS
120    'X()=ARRAY CONTAINING X-COORDINATES
```

```
130    'Y()=ARRAY-CONTAINING Y-COORDINATES
140    'Z()=ARRAY CONTAINING Z-COORDINATES
150    'P=X-AXIS POINT OF PROJECTION
160    'Q=Y-AXIS POINT OF PROJECTION
170    'R=Z-AXIS POINT OF PROJECTION
180    DIM U(100,4),V(100,4)            '100 POSITION VECTORS
190    MAT U=ZER(P1,4)                  'REDIMENSION U&V FILL WITH ZEROS
200    MAT V=ZER(P1,4)
210    FOR I=1 TO P1                    'SET UP HOMOGENEOUS210
220       LET U(I,1)=X(I)               'POSITION VECTORS
230       LET U(I,2)=Y(I)
240       LET U(I,3)=Z(I)
250       LET U(I,4)=1
260    NEXT I
270    MAT-T=ZER(4,4)                   'REDIMENSION T-FILL WITH ZEROS
280    LET T(1,1)=T(2,2)=1              'PLACE 1'S ON DIAG. OF T MATRIX
290    LET T(3,3)=T(4,4)=1
300    LET T(1,4)=P                     'SET X PROJECTION POINT
310    LET T(2,4)=Q                     'SET Y PROJECTION POINT
320    LET T(3,4)=R                     'SET Z PROJECTION POINT
330    MAT V=U*T                        'CALC. TRANSFORMATION
340    FOR I=1 TO P1                    'CALC. PHYSICAL COOR.
350       LET X(I)=V(I,1)/V(I,4)
360       LET Y(I)=V(I,2)/V(I,4)
370       LET Z(I)=V(I,3)/V(I,4)
380    NEXT I
390 SUBEND
```

C-16 THREE-DIMENSIONAL RECONSTRUCTION ALGORITHMS

An algorithm to reconstruct three-dimensional coordinates from two perspective projections, say, two photographs, when the matrix transformation elements are known is given below as a BASIC language subprogram. It is based on Eq. (3-48).

3DRECON1

```
100 SUB"3DRECON1":T(,),S(,),X1,Y1,X2,Y2,X(,)   '3-D RECONSTRUCTION-1
110    'T(,)=4*4 TRANSFORMATION MATRIX FOR THE FIRST VIEW
120    'S(,)=4*4 TRANSFORMATION MATRIX FOR THE SECOND VIEW
130    'X1,Y1=COORDINATES OF POINT IN FIRST VIEW
140    'X2,Y2=COORDINATES OF POINT IN SECOND VIEW
150    DIM A(4,3),B(4,1),C(3,4),D(3,3),E(3,3),Y(3,1)
160    MAT X=ZER(3,1)                   'FILL X-MATRIX-WITH ZEROS
170    FOR J=1 TO 3                     'FIND PROJECTION PLANE
180       FOR I=1 TO 4                  'IN T-MATRIX
190          IF T(I,J)<>0 THEN 220
200       NEXT I
210       GO TO 250
220    NEXT J
230    PRINT "TRANS T IS NOT A PROJECTION"
240    GO TO 660
250    ON J GO TO 260,290,320           'ELIMINATE 0-COLUMN
260    LET I1=2                         'FROM EQUATIONS
270    LET I2=3
280    GO TO 340
290    LET I1=1
```

```
300    LET I2=3
310    GO TO 340
320    LET I1=1
330    LET I2=2
340    FOR J=1 TO 3                    'FIND PROJECTION PLANE
350       FOR I=1 TO 4                 'IN S-MATRIX
360          IF S(I,J)<>0 THEN 390
370       NEXT I
380       GO TO 420
390    NEXT J
400    PRINT "TRANS S IS NOT A PROJECTION"
410    GO TO 660
420    ON J GO TO 430,460,490         'ELIMINATE 0-COLUMN
430    LET J1=2                        'FROM EQUATIONS
440    LET J2=3
450    GO TO 510
460    LET J1=1
470    LET J2=3
480    GO TO 510
490    LET J1=1
500    LET J2=2
510    FOR I=1 TO 3                    'SET UP A-MATRIX
520       LET A(1,I)=T(I,I1)-T(I,4)*X1
530       LET A(2,I)=T(I,I2)-T(I,4)*Y1
540       LET A(3,I)=S(I,J1)-S(I,4)*X2
550       LET A(4,I)=S(I,J2)-S(I,4)*Y2
560    NEXT I
570    LET B(1,1)=T(4,4)*X1-T(4,I1)    'SET UP B-MATRIX
580    LET B(2,1)=T(4,4)*Y1-T(4,I2)
590    LET B(3,1)=S(4,4)*X2-S(4,J1)
600    LET B(4,1)=S(4,4)*Y2-S(4,J2)
610    MAT C=TRN(A)                    'TRANSPOSE A
620    MAT D=C*A                       'FORM SQ MAT FROM A & IT'S TRANSPOSE
630    MAT E=INV(D)                    'INVERT SQUARE MATRIX
640    MAT Y=C*B                       'FORM A TRANSPOSE * B
650    MAT X=E*Y                       'OBTAIN SOLUTION
660 SUBEND
```

An algorithm to reconstruct the transformation used to obtain a perspective projection from the known location of six points in the physical and projection spaces is given below as a BASIC language subprogram. It is based on Eq. (3-50) in the normalized form.

3DRECON2

```
100 SUB"3DRECON2":X(,),U(,),T(,)       '3-D RECONSTRUCTION-2
110    'X(,)=6*3 MATRIX CONTAINING THE LOCATIONS OF THE SIX POINTS
120    '     IN PHYSICAL COORDINATES IN ORDER
130    'U(,)=6*2 MATRIX CONTAINING THE LOCATIONS OF THE SAME SIX
140    '     POINTS IN THE PERSPECTIVE VIEW IN THE SAME ORDER
150    'T(,)=THE 4*4 TRANSFORMATION MATRIX
160    DIM A(12,12),B(11,11),C(11,1),D(11,1),E(11,11)
170    MAT T=ZER(4,4)                  'FILL T&A MATRICES WITH ZEROS
180    MAT A=ZER(12,12)
190    FOR I=1 TO 12 STEP 2            'SET UP A-MATRIX
200       LET J=J+1
```

```
210       LET A(I,1)=A(I+1,2)=X(J,1)
220       LET A(I,4)=A(I+1,5)=X(J,2)
230       LET A(I,7)=A(I+1,8)=X(J,3)
240       LET A(I,10)=A(I+1,11)=1
250       LET A(I,12)=U(J,1)
260       LET A(I+1,12)=U(J,2)
270       LET A(I,3)=-X(J,1)*U(J,1)
280       LET A(I+1,3)=-X(J,1)*U(J,2)
290       LET A(I,6)=-X(J,2)*U(J,1)
300       LET A(I+1,6)=-X(J,2)*U(J,2)
310       LET A(I,9)=-X(J,3)*U(J,1)
320       LET A(I+1,9)=-X(J,3)*U(J,2)
330     NEXT I
340     FOR I=1 TO 11                     'SET UP B&C MATRICES
350       FOR J=1 TO 11                   'FORM B-MATRIX
360         LET B(I,J)=A(I,J)
370       NEXT J
380       LET C(I,1)=A(I,12)              'FORM C-MATRIX
390     NEXT I
400     MAT E=INV(B)                      'CALC. TRANS. MATRIX
410     MAT D=E*C
420     LET T(1,1)=D(1,1)
430     LET T(1,2)=D(2,1)
440     LET T(1,4)=D(3,1)
450     LET T(2,1)=D(4,1)
460     LET T(2,2)=D(5,1)
470     LET T(2,4)=D(6,1)
480     LET T(3,1)=D(7,1)
490     LET T(3,2)=D(8,1)
500     LET T(3,4)=D(9,1)
510     LET T(4,1)=D(10,1)
520     LET T(4,2)=D(11,1)
530     LET T(4,4)=1
540 SUBEND
```

C-17 A Stereo Algorithm

An algorithm to generate a stereo pair for an object which has been positioned and rotated to form the desired view and perspective is given below as a BASIC language subprogram.

STEREO

```
100 SUB"STEREO":P1,X(),Y(),Z(),K,E,A(,),B(,)
110     'P1=NUMBER OF POINTS USED TO DEFINE OBJECT
120     'X()=ARRAY CONTAINING X-COORDINATES
130     'Y()=ARRAY CONTAINING Y-COORDINATES
140     'Z()=ARRAY CONTAINING Z-COORDINATES
150         'DIM X(P1),Y(P1),Z(P1) IN MAIN PROGRAM
160     'K=FOCAL LENGTH OF STEREO VIEWER
170     'E=DISTANCE BETWEEN EYES OF OBSERVER (RELATIVE TO OUTPUT SCALE)
180     'A(,)=RESULTING X*-,Y*-COORDINATES FOR LEFT EYE
190         'DIM A(P1,2) IN MAIN PROGRAM
200     'B(,)=RESULTING X*-,Y*-COORDINATES FOR RIGHT EYE
210         'DIM B(P1,2) IN MAIN PROGRAM
220 DIM U(100,4)
230 DIM L(100,4)
```

```
240 DIM R(100,4)
250 DIM P(100,4)
260 DIM Q(100,4)
270     FOR I=1 TO P1                    'SET UP HOMOGENEOUS
280         LET U(I,1)=X(I)              'POSITION VECTORS
290         LET U(I,2)=Y(I)
300         LET U(I,3)=Z(I)
310         LET U(I,4)=1
320     NEXT I
330     MAT T=ZER(4,4)                   'CREATE LEFT-EYE PERSPECTIVE
340     LET T(1,1)=T(2,2)=T(3,3)=T(4,4)=1
350     LET T(3,4)=-1/K
360     LET T(4,1)=K/20
370     MAT L=U*T
380     LET T(4,1)=-K/20                 'CREATE RIGHT-EYE PERSPECTIVE
390     MAT R=U*T
400     LET X2=X6=0
410     LET X3=X7=99999
420     FOR I=1 TO P1
430         LET P(I,4)=Q(I,4)=1          'NORMALIZE RESULTS
440         LET P(I,1)=R(I,1)/R(I,4)
450         LET P(I,2)=R(I,2)/R(I,4)
460         LET Q(I,1)=L(I,1)/L(I,4)
470         LET Q(I,2)=L(I,2)/L(I,4)
480         LET X1=P(I,1)                'FIND X* MAX/MIN FOR L/R EYES
490         LET X5=Q(I,1)
500         IF X1>X3 THEN 520
510         LET X3=X1
520         IF X1<X2 THEN 540
530         LET X2=X1
540         IF X5>X7 THEN 560
550         LET X7=X5
560         IF X5<X6 THEN 580
570         LET X6=X5
580     NEXT I
590     LET D=(X6+X7)/2-(X3+X2)/2        'FIND EYE SEPARATION DISTANCE
600     LET L=D+(E-D)/2
610     MAT T=ZER(4,4)                   'TRANSLATE RIGHT-EYE VIEW
620     LET T(1,1)=T(2,2)=T(3,3)=T(4,4)=1
630     LET T(4,1)=L
640     MAT R=P*T
650     LET T(4,1)=-L                    'TRANSLATE LEFT-EYE VIEW
660     MAT L=Q*T
670     MAT A=ZER(P1,2)
680     MAT B=ZER(P1,2)
690     FOR I=1 TO P1                    'SET UP RETURN MATRIX
700         LET A(I,1)=L(I,1)
710         LET A(I,2)=L(I,2)
720         LET B(I,1)=R(I,1)
730         LET B(I,2)=R(I,2)
740     NEXT I
750 SUBEND
```

C-18 AN ALGORITHM FOR A NONPARAMETRIC CIRCLE

The algorithm given below as a BASIC language subprogram generates a circle based on a nonparametric representation. It is based on the discussion of Sec. 4-5. The algorithm in the next section is recommended for circle generation.

NPCIRCLE

```
100 SUB"NPCIRCLE":H,K,R,N,X(),Y()        'NONPARAMETRIC CIRCLE
110    ' H,K=X&Y COOR. OF CENTER
120    ' R=RADIUS OF CIRCLE
130    ' N=NUMBER OF POINTS DESIRED
140    ' X()=ARRAY CONTAINING THE X-COORDINATES OF CIRCLE
145    ' Y()=ARRAY CONTAINING THE Y-COORDINATES OF CIRCLE
150    ' NOTE:N MUST BE DIVISIBLE BY EIGHT.  IF NOT PROGRAM WILL
160    '       USE NEXT HIGHER NUMBER DIVISIBLE BY EIGHT
170    LET A=INT(N/8)                    'DETERMINE IF DIVISIBLE BY EIGHT
180    IF A=N/8 THEN 210
190    LET N1=(A+1)*8                    'SET N1 DIVISIBLE BY EIGHT
200    GO TO 230
210    LET N1=N
230    MAT X=ZER(N1+1)
240    MAT Y=ZER(N1+1)
250    LET D=R*(1-1/SQR(2))/(N1/8)       'CALC. INCREMENT
260    LET X(1)=R                        'CALC. INITIAL POINT
270    LET Y(1)=0
280    FOR I=1 TO N1                     'CALC. POINTS AROUND ORIGIN
290       IF I=1 THEN 370                'DETERMINE SECT. FOR CALC.
300       IF ABS(X(I))<0.0005 THEN 320
310       GO TO 340
320       IF Y(I)>0 THEN 440
330       GO TO 590
340       IF Y(I)<0.0005 THEN 500
350       IF X(I)<0.0005 THEN 430
360       IF Y(I)>=R/SQR(2)-0.0005 THEN 400
370       LET X(I+1)=X(I)-D              'CALC. POINTS 0-45 DEG.
380       LET Y(I+1)=SQR(ABS(R*R-X(I+1)*X(I+1)))
390       GO TO 640
400       LET Y(I+1)=Y(I)+D              'CALC. POINTS 45-90 DEG.
410       LET X(I+1)=SQR(ABS(R*R-Y(I+1)*Y(I+1)))
420       GO TO 640
430       IF Y(I)<=R/SQR(2)+0.0005 THEN 470
440       LET Y(I+1)=Y(I)-D              'CALC. POINTS 90-135 DEG.
450       LET X(I+1)=-SQR(ABS(R*R-Y(I+1)*Y(I+1)))
460       GO TO 640
470       LET X(I+1)=X(I)-D              'CALC. POINTS 135-180 DEG.
480       LET Y(I+1)=SQR(ABS(R*R-X(I+1)*X(I+1)))
490       GO TO 640
500       IF X(I)>-0.0005 THEN 580
510       IF -Y(I)>=R/SQR(2)-0.0005 THEN 550
520       LET X(I+1)=X(I)+D              'CALC. POINTS 180-225 DEG.
530       LET Y(I+1)=-SQR(ABS(R*R-X(I+1)*X(I+1)))
540       GO TO 640
550       LET Y(I+1)=Y(I)-D              'CALC. POINTS 225-270 DEG.
560       LET X(I+1)=-SQR(ABS(R*R-Y(I+1)*Y(I+1)))
570       GO TO 640
580       IF -Y(I)<=R/SQR(2)+0.0005 THEN 620
590       LET Y(I+1)=Y(I)+D              'CALC. POINTS 270-315 DEG.
600       LET X(I+1)=SQR(ABS(R*R-Y(I+1)*Y(I+1)))
610       GO TO 640
620       LET X(I+1)=X(I)+D              'CALC. POINTS 315-360 DEG.
630       LET Y(I+1)=-SQR(ABS(R*R-X(I+1)*X(I+1)))
640    NEXT I
650    FOR I=1 TO N1+1                   'TRANSLATE CIRCLE
660       LET X(I)=X(I)+H
670       LET Y(I)=Y(I)+K
680    NEXT I
730 SUBEND
```

C-19 An Algorithm for a Parametric Circle

An algorithm for a parametric representation of a circle is given as a BASIC language subprogram. It is based on Eqs. (4-28) and (4-29) of Sec. 4-6.

CIRCLE

```
100 SUB"CIRCLE":H,K,R,N,X(),Y()           'PARAMETRIC CIRCLE
110    'H=X-COORDINATE OF CENTER OF THE CIRCLE
120    'K=Y-COORDINATE OF CENTER OF THE CIRCLE
130    'R=RADIUS
140    'N=NUMBER OF POINTS ON CIRCLE
150    'X() ARRAY CONTAINING THE X-COORDINATES OF POINTS ON CIRCLE
160    'Y() ARRAY CONTAINING THE Y-COORDINATES OF POINTS ON CIRCLE
170    LET P=2*3.14156/(N-1)              'CALC. INCREMENT IN THETA
180    LET C1=COS(P)                      'CALC. CONSTANTS
190    LET S1=SIN(P)
200    LET X(0)=H+R                       'CALC. INITIAL POINT
210    LET Y(0)=K
220    FOR M=1 TO N                       'INNER LOOP
230       LET X(M)=H+(X(M-1)-H)*C1-(Y(M-1)-K)*S1
240       LET Y(M)=K+(X(M-1)-H)*S1+(Y(M-1)-K)*C1
250    NEXT M
260 SUBEND
```

C-20 Parametric Ellipse Algorithm

The algorithm given below as a BASIC language subprogram generates an ellipse. It is based on Eqs. (4-38) and (4-39) of Sec. 4-8.

ELLIPSE1

```
100 SUB"ELLIPSE1":H,K,A,B,I,N,X(),Y()
110    'H=X-COORDINATE OF CENTER OF THE ELLIPSE
120    'K=Y-COORDINATE OF CENTER OF THE ELLIPSE
130    'A=LENGTH OF SEMI-MAJOR AXIS
140    'B=LENGTH OF SEMI-MINOR AXIS
150    'I=INCLINATION ANGLE OF MAJOR AXIS IN DEGREES
160    'N=NUMBER OF POINTS ON ELLIPSE
170    'X()=ARRAY CONTAINING THE X-COORDINATES OF POINTS ON ELLIPSE
180    'Y()=ARRAY CONTAINING THE Y-COORDINATES OF POINTS ON ELLIPSE
190    LET P=2*3.14156/(N-1)             'CALC. THE INCREMENT IN THE PARAMETER
200    LET I1=I/57.2957795               'CONVERT I TO RADIANS
210    LET C1=COS(I1)                    'CALC. THE COSINE AND
220    LET S1=SIN(I1)                    'SINE OF THE INCLINATION ANGLE
230    LET C2=COS(P)                     'CALC. THE INCREMENTS IN COSINE
240    LET S2=SIN(P)                     'AND SINE OF THE PARAMETER INCREMENT
250    LET C3=1                          'INITIALIZE THE ACCUMULATION
260    LET S3=0                          'VARIABLES
270    FOR M=1 TO N                      'BEGIN INNER LOOP
280       LET X1=A*C3                    'CALC. INCREMENTS IN X AND Y
290       LET Y1=B*S3
300       LET X(M)=H+X1*C1-Y1*S1         'CALC. NEW X AND Y
310       LET Y(M)=K+X1*S1+Y1*C1
320       LET T1=C3*C2-S3*S2             'CALC. NEW ANGLE FORMULAS
330       LET S3=S3*C2+C3*S2             'DOUBLE ANGLE FOR SINE
340       LET C3=T1                      'DOUBLE ANGLE FOR COSINE
350    NEXT M
360 SUBEND
```

C-21 An Algorithm for a Parametric Parabola

The algorithm for a parametric parabola given below as a BASIC language subprogram is based on Eqs. (4-54) and (4-55) of Sec. 4-9.

PARABOLA

```
100 SUB"PARABOLA":A,P1,N,X(),Y()      'PARAMETRIC PARABOLA
110    'A=DISTANCE FROM FOCUS TO VERTEX OF PARABOLA
120    'P1=MAXIMUM ANGLE (DEGREES) (CF. EQ. 4-45 OR 4-46)
130    'N=NUMBER OF POINTS ON PARABOLA
140    'X()=ARRAY CONTAINING THE X-COORDINATES OF POINTS ON PARABOLA
150    'Y()=ARRAY CONTAINING THE Y-COORDINATES OF POINTS ON PARABOLA
160    LET P=P1/((N-1)*57.295)7795)            'CALC. INCREMENT IN THETA
170    LET X(1)=0                 'INITIALIZE
180    LET Y(1)=0
190    LET A1=A*P*P
200    LET B1=2*A*P
210    FOR M=2 TO N                   'INNER LOOP
220       LET X(M)=A1+X(M-1)+P*Y(M-1)
230       LET Y(M)=B1+Y(M-1)
240    NEXT M
250 SUBEND
```

C-22 Algorithms For Parametric Hyperbolas

An algorithm which generates a parametric hyperbola is given below as a BASIC subprogram. The algorithm is based on Eqs. (4-57) and (4-58) of Sec. 4-10.

HYPERB1

```
100 SUB"HYPERB1":A,B,N,X(),Y()         'PARAMETRIC HYPERBOLA
110    'A=DISTANCE FROM CENTER OF HYPERBOLA TO VERTEX
120    'B=DETERMINES SLOPE FO ASYMPTOTES=+-B/A
130    'N=NUMBER OF POINTS ON HYPERBOLA
140    'X()=ARRAY CONTAINING X-COORDINATES OF POINTS ON HYPERBOLA
150    'Y()=ARRAY CONTAINING Y-COORDINATES OF POINTS ON HYPERBOLA
200    LET P=3.141592654/(2*(N-1))      'CALC. PARAMETER INCREMENT
210    LET C2=COS(P)                    'CALC. COSINE,SINE,TANGENT
220    LET S2=SIN(P)                    'OF PARAMETER INCREMENT
230    LET T2=TAN(P)
240    LET Q9=B*T2
250    LET S9=B*C2
260    LET X(1)=A                       'INITIALIZE
270    LET Y(1)=0
280    FOR M=2 TO N                     'INNER LOOP
290       LET X(M)=(B*X(M-1))/(S9-Y(M-1)*S2)
300       LET Y(M)=(B*(Y(M-1)+Q9))/(B-Y(M-1)*T2)
310    NEXT M
320 SUBEND
```

Another algorithm which generates a parametric hyperbola is given below as a BASIC subprogram. This algorithm is based on Eqs. (4-61) and (4-62) of

Sec. 4-10. This algorithm yields the portion of the hyperbola in the first quadrant. The portions in the other quadrants or nonorigin-centered hyperbolas can be obtained by appropriate rotation, reflection, and translation operations.

HYPERB2

```
100 SUB"HYPERB2":A,B,C,N,X(),Y()          'PARAMETRIC HYPERBOLA
110     'A=DISTANCE FROM CENTER OF HYPERBOLA TO VERTEX
120     'B=DETERMINES SLOPE FO ASYMPTOTES=+-B/A
130     'C=LIMIT OF X-COORDINATE
140     'N=NUMBER OF POINTS ON HYPERBOLA
150     'X()=ARRAY CONTAINING X-COORDINATES OF POINTS ON HYPERBOLA
160     'Y()=ARRAY CONTAINING Y-COORDINATES OF POINTS ON HYPERBOLA
170     LET P2=(A+C)/A                     'CALC. PARAMETER INCREMENT
180     LET P1=((LOG(1+P2)/LOG(10))-(LOG(P2-1)/LOG(10)))/(2*(N-1))
190     LET C2=(EXP(P1)+EXP(-P1))/2        'CALC. COSH P1
200     LET S2=(EXP(P1)-EXP(-P1))/2        'CALC. SINH P1
210     LET X(1)=A                         'INITIALIZE
220     LET Y(1)=0
230     FOR M=2 TO N                       'INNER LOOP
240         LET X(M)=C2*X(M-1)+(A/B)*S2*Y(M-1)
250         LET Y(M)=(B/A)*S2*X(M-1)+C2*Y(M-1)
260     NEXT M
270 SUBEND
```

C-23 AN ALGORITHM FOR A CIRCLE THROUGH THREE POINTS

The algorithm given below as a BASIC subprogram determines the circular arc passing through three points. It is based on the discussion of Sec. 4-11.

3PCIRARC

```
100 SUB"3PCIRARC":X(),Y(),N,H,K,R,S(),T()  'ARC THRU THREE POINTS
110     ' X(),Y()=COORDINATES OF THREE POINTS
120     ' N=NUMBER OF STRAIGHT LINES TO REPRESENT ARC
130     ' H,K=X,Y-COORDINATES OF CENTER (RETURNED)
140     ' R=RADIUS (RETURNED)
150     'S()=ARRAY CONTAINING X-COORDINATES OF CIRCLE
160     'T()=ARRAY CONTAINING Y-COORDINATES OF CIRCLE
170     MAT A=ZER(3)                        'DIM & SET EQUAL TO ZERO
180     MAT B=ZER(3)
190     FOR I=1 TO 3                        'COPY X() & Y() INTO A() & B()
200         LET A(I)=X(I)
210         LET B(I)=Y(I)
220     NEXT I
230     CALL"2DTRANS.":3,A(),B(),-A(1),-B(1)  'TRANS. 1ST POINT TO ORIGIN
240     CALL"SOLVE":A(),B(),H1,K1           'SOLVE FOR CENTER OF TRANS. ARC
250     LET H=X(1)+H1                       'CALC. CENTER-COORDINATES
260     LET K=Y(1)+K1
270     LET R=SQR(H1*H1+K1*K1)             'CALC. RADIUS
280     CALL"2DTRANS.":3,A(),B(),-H1,-K1   'TRANS. CIRCLE TO ORIGIN
290     CALL"ATAN":A(1),B(1),T1            'CALC. BEGINNING & ENDING ANGLES
300     CALL"ATAN":A(2),B(2),T2
310     CALL"ATAN":A(3),B(3),T3
320     LET T1=T1*57.29577951              'CHANGE RADIANS TO DEGREES
330     LET T2=T2*57.29577951
```

```
340     LET T3=T3*57.29577951
350     IF T1<T2 THEN 420                  'TEST FOR DIFFERENT CASES
360     IF T2>T3 THEN 470                  'T1>T2>T3
370     LET T3=T3-360                      'T1>T2<T3  CASE 1
380     IF ABS(T3-T1)<360 THEN 470         'TEST IF CASE 1 CORRECT
390     LET T3=T3+360                      'T1>T2<T3  CASE 2
400     LET T1=T1-360
410     GO TO 470
420     IF T2<T3 THEN 470                  'T1<T2<T3
430     LET T1=T1-360                      'T1<T2>T3  CASE 1
440     IF ABS(T3-T1)<360 THEN 470         'TEST IF CASE 1 CORRECT
450     LET T1=T1+360                      'T1<T2>T3 CASE 2
460     LET T3=T3-360
470     CALL"ARCA":H,K,R,T1,T3,N,S(),T() 'DRAW ARC THRU THE THREE POINTS
480 SUBEND
490 SUB"SOLVE":A(),B(),H1,K1               'SOLVE FOR CENTER OF CIRCLE
500     ' A(),B()=COOR OF 3 POINTS WHERE A(1)=B(1)=0
510     ' H1,K1=X,Y-COOR OF CENTER (RETURNED)
520     MAT C=ZER(2,2)
530     MAT D=ZER(2,1)
540     MAT E=ZER(2,2)
550     MAT F=ZER(2,1)
560     FOR I=2 TO 3                       'SET UP MATRIX
570        LET C(I-1,1)=2*A(I)
580        LET C(I-1,2)=2*B(I)
590        LET D(I-1,1)=A(I)*A(I)+B(I)*B(I)
600     NEXT I
610     MAT E=INV(C)                       'CALC. CENTER
620     MAT F=E*D
630     LET H1=F(1,1)                      'SET CENTER EQUAL TO H1,K1
640     LET K1=F(2,1)
650 SUBEND
660 SUB"ATAN":X,Y,A                        'TAN OF (YX)
670     ' X,Y=PROGRAM FINDS TANGENT OF (Y/X)
680     ' A=TANGENT OF (Y/X) IN RADIANS (RETURNED)
690     IF Y<0 THEN 780
700     IF X=0 THEN 740
710     IF X<0 THEN 760
720     LET A=ATN(Y/X)                     '0-90 DEG.
730     GO TO 850
740     LET A=1.570796327                  '90 DEG.
750     GO TO 850
760     LET A= 3.141592654-ATN(ABS(Y/X)) '90-180 DEG.
770     GO TO 850
780     IF X=0 THEN 840
790     IF X<0 THEN 820
800     LET A=6.283185308-ATN(ABS(Y/X))   '270-360 DEG.
810     GO TO 850
820     LET A= ATN(ABS(Y/X))+3.141592654 '180-270 DEG.
830     GO TO 850
840     LET A=4.712388981                  '270 DEG.
850 SUBEND
860 SUB"ARCA":X,Y,R,T1,T2,N,X(),Y()        'PARAMETRIC CIRCULAR ARC
870     'X=X-COORDINATE OF CENTER OF ARC
880     'Y=Y-COORDINATE OF CENTER OF ARC
890     'R=RADIUS OF ARC
900     'T1,T2=BEGINNING AND ENDING ANGLES IN DEGREES
910     'N=NUMBER OF POINTS TO REPRESENT ARC
920     'X()=ARRAY CONTAINING THE X-COORDINATES OF THE ARC
930     'Y()=ARRAY CONTAINING THE Y-COORDINATES OF THE ARC
```

```
940     LET T3=T1/57.3958              'CHANGE DEGREES TO RADIANS
950     LET P=(T2-T1)/(57.2958*(N-1))  'CALC. INCREME(N-1)T IN RADIA(N-1)S
960     LET C1=COS(P)                  'CALC. COS & SIN OF INCREMENT
970     LET S1=SIN(P)
980     LET X(1)=X+R*COS(T3)           'INITIALIZE THE ACCUMULATION
990     LET Y(1)=Y+R*SIN(T3)           'VARABLE
1000    FOR M=2 TO N                   'CALC. X,Y COOR.
1010        LET X(M)=X+(X(M-1)-X)*C1-(Y(M-1)-Y)*S1
1020        LET Y(M)=Y+(X(M-1)-X)*S1+(Y(M-1)-Y)*C1
1030    NEXT M
1040 SUBEND
```

C-24 An Algorithm For Generating Cubic Splines

An algorithm for generating cubic spline fits to n known data points with various end boundary conditions is given below as a BASIC language subprogram. The algorithm calculates the parameter range based upon chord distance between data points rather than using normalized splines.

SPLINE

```
100 SUB"SPLINE":S,N,P(,),C1,C2,N(,),B(,),L(),Z,U(,),C(,)
110     'S=CONTROL VARIABLE S=2 FOR 2-D CURVE, S=3 FOR 3-D CURVE
120     'N=NUMBER OF DATA POINTS
130     'P(,)=ARRAY CONTAINING DATA POINTS
140     'C1=INITIAL END CONDITION
150         '1=RELAXED
160         '2=CLAMPED
170         '3=CYCLIC
180         '4=ANTICYCLIC
190     'C2=FINAL END CONDITION
200         '1=RELAXED
210         '2=CLAMPED
220         'NOTE: IF A CYCLIC OR ANTICYCLIC INITIAL END CONDITION
230         'IS SPECIFIED THE FINAL END CONDITION IS ALSO SPECIFIED
240     'N(,)=NONZERO ELEMENTS OF M-MATRIX, SEE EQ. (5-33)
250         'N MUST HAVE DIMENSIONS OF (N,3)
260     'B(,)=ELEMENTS OF B-MATRIX, SEE EQ. (5-33)
270         'B MUST HAVE DIMENSIONS OF (2,N) OR (3,N)
280     'L()=SPAN CHORD LENGTHS
290         'L MUST HAVE DIMENSIONS OF (N-1)
300     'Z=NUMBER OF INTERMEDIATE POINTS PER SPAN
310     'U(,)=ELEMENTS IN TANGENT VECTOR MATRIX, SEE EQ. (5-33)
320         'U MUST HAVE DIMENSIONS OF (2,N) FOR 2-D AND (3,N) FOR 3-D
330         'U(1, )=X-COMPONENT
340         'U(2, )=Y-COMPONENT
350         'U(3, )=Z-COMPONENT IF APPROPRIATE
360         'NOTE: IF CLAMPED END CONDITIONS ARE SPECIFIED
370         'THEN THE VALUES FOR THE TANGENT VECTORS FOR
380         'THE FIRST END CONDITION MUST BE IN U(1,1), U(2,1), U(3,1)
390         'AND FOR THE LAST END CONDITION IN U(1,N), U(2,N), U(3,N)
400     'C(,)=ARRAY CONTAINING GENERATED POINTS ALONG CURVE
410         'C MUST HAVE DIMENSIONS OF (2,N+(N-1)*Z) OR (3,N+(N-1)*Z)
420         'C(1, )=X-COMPONENT
430         'C(2, )=Y-COMPONENT
440         'C(3, )=Z-COMPONENT IF APPROPRIATE
```

```
450     LET Z=Z+1                           'ADD ONE TO NO. INTERMEDIATE POINTS
460     IF C1>2 THEN 560
470     'GENERATE CHORD LENGTHS AND ELEMENTS IN B-,U-, AND M-MATRICES
480     'WHICH DEPEND UPON THE SPECIFIED END CONDITIONS.
490     CALL"ENDPNT":S,N,P(,),N(,),B(,),L(),Z,U(,),C1,C2
500     'IMPLEMENT GAUSSIAN ELIMINATION TO SOLVE FOR THE
510     'UNKNOWN TANGENT VECTORS.
520     CALL"GAUSS":S,N,P(,),N(,),B(,),L(),U(,)
530     GO TO 580
540     'INVERT MATRIX M AND SOLVE FOR UNKNOWN TANGENT VECTOR MATRIX U.
550     '(CYCLIC AND ANTICYCLIC SPLINES ONLY)
560     CALL"MATINV":S,N,P(,),N(,),B(,),L(),U(,),C1,Z
570     'GENERATE THE POINTS ON THE SPLINE CURVE
580     CALL"CURGEN":S,N,P(,),L(),Z,U(,),C(,)
590 SUBEND
600 SUB"ENDPNT":S,N,P(,),N(,),B(,),L(),Z,U(,),C1,C2
610     IF C1=1 THEN 680
620     LET N(1,2)=1                        'FIRST ROW OF M-MATRIX
630     LET N(1,3)=0                        'FOR CLAMPED INITIAL END CONDITION
640     FOR K=1 TO S
650        LET B(K,1)=U(K,1)               'SET B(K,1)=U(K,1) FOR CLAMPED END
660     NEXT K
670     GO TO 700
680     LET N(1,2)=1                        'FIRST ROW OF M-MATRIX
690     LET N(1,3)=.5                       'FOR RELAXED END CONDITION
700     FOR J=1 TO N-1
710        IF S=3 THEN 760
720        'CALCULATE THE 2-D SPAN CHORD LENGTHS
730        LET L(J)=SQR((P(1,J+1)-P(1,J))^2+(P(2,J+1)-P(2,J))^2)
740        GO TO 770
750        'CALCULATE THE 3-D SPAN CHORD LENGTHS
760        LET L(J)=SQR((P(1,J+1)-P(1,J))^2+(P(2,J+1)-P(2,J))^2+(P(3,J+1)-P(3,J))^2)
770     NEXT J
780     IF C1=2 THEN 820
790     FOR K=1 TO S                        'SET B(K,1) FOR RELAXED END
800        LET B(K,1)=(3/(2*L(1)))*(P(K,2)-P(K,1))
810     NEXT K
820     IF C2=1 THEN 890
830     LET N(N,1)=0                        'LAST ROW OF M-MATRIX
840     LET N(N,2)=1                        'FOR CLAMPED FINAL END CONDITION
850     FOR K=1 TO S
860        LET B(K,N)=U(K,N)               'SET B(K,N)=U(K,N) FOR CLAMPED END
870     NEXT K
880     GO TO 940
890     LET N(N,1)=2                        'LAST ROW OF M-MATRIX
900     LET N(N,2)=4                        'FOR RELAXED END CONDITION
910     FOR K=1 TO S                        'SET B(K,N) FOR RELAXED END
920        LET B(K,N)=(6/L(N-1))*(P(K,N)-P(K,N-1))
930     NEXT K
940 SUBEND
950 SUB"GAUSS":S,N,P(,),N(,),B(,),L(),U(,)
960     FOR J=2 TO N-1
970        LET N(J,1)=L(J)                 'CREATE NONZERO VALUES FOR
980        LET N(J,2)=2*(L(J)+L(J-1))      'INTERNAL ROWS OF M-MATRIX
990        LET N(J,3)=L(J-1)
1000          FOR K=1 TO S                 'CREATE ROWS 2 THROUGH N-1 OF B-MATRIX
1010             LET B(K,J)=3*(L(J-1)^2*(P(K,J+1)-P(K,J))+L(J)^2*(P(K,J)-P(K,J-1)))
1020             LET B(K,J)=B(K,J)/(L(J)*L(J-1))
1030          NEXT K
1040       NEXT J
```

```
1050      ' THE FOLLOWING IS THE GAUSSIAN ELIMINATION,
1060      FOR I=2 TO N
1070        IF N(I,1)=0 THEN 1180         'NORMALIZE
1080        LET D=N(I-1,2)/N(I,1)
1090        FOR K=1 TO 3
1100          LET N(I,K)=N(I,K)*D-N(I-1,K+1)  'REDUCE
1110          LET B(K,I)=B(K,I)*D-B(K,I-1)
1120        NEXT K
1130        LET Q=N(I,2)
1140        FOR K=1 TO 3
1150          LET N(I,K)=N(I,K)/Q          'NORMALIZE
1160          LET B(K,I)=B(K,I)/Q
1170        NEXT K
1180      NEXT I
1190      FOR K=1 TO S                    'SOLVE FOR UNKNOWN TANGENT VECTORS
1200        FOR J=0 TO N-1
1210          LET U(K,N-J)=(B(K,N-J)-N(N-J,3)*U(K,N+1-J))/N(N-J,2)
1220        NEXT J
1230      NEXT K
1240 SUBEND
1250 SUB"CURGEN":S,N,P(,),L(),Z,U(,),C(,)
1260      LET I=1
1270      FOR J=1 TO N-1
1280        FOR K=1 TO S                  'SOLVE FOR THE FOUR CUBIC SPLINE COEFF.
1290          LET F(1,K)=P(K,J)
1300          LET F(2,K)=U(K,J)
1310          LET F(3,K)=(3/L(J)^2)*(P(K,J+1)-P(K,J))-(1/L(J))*(U(K,J+1)+2*U(K,J))
1320          LET F(4,K)=(-2/L(J)^3)*(P(K,J+1)-P(K,J))+(1/L(J)^2)*(U(K,J+1)+U(K,J))
1330        NEXT K
1340        FOR T=0 TO L(J) STEP L(J)/Z
1350          IF J=1 THEN 1380
1360          IF T<>0 THEN 1380
1370          GO TO 1490
1380          FOR K=1 TO S                'CALC. POINTS ALONG CUBIC SPLINE
1390            LET R(K)=F(1,K)+F(2,K)*T+F(3,K)*(T^2)+F(4,K)*(T^3)
1400          NEXT K
1410          IF S=3 THEN 1450
1420          LET C(1,I)=R(1)             'CREATE C(,) MATRIX OF RESULTS
1430          LET C(2,I)=R(2)
1440          GO TO 1480
1450          LET C(1,I)=R(1)
1460          LET C(2,I)=R(2)
1470          LET C(3,I)=R(3)
1480          LET I=I+1
1490        NEXT T
1500      NEXT J
1510 SUBEND
1520 SUB"MATINV":S,N,P(,),N(,),B(,),L(),U(,),C1,Z
1530      DIM M(70,70),C(70),V(70,70),W(70)   'DIMENSION INTERNAL MATRICES
1540      MAT M=ZER(N-1,N-1)                'INITIALIZE AND REDIMENSION
1550      MAT C=ZER(N-1)                    'EACH INTERNAL MATRIX
1560      MAT W=ZER(N-1)
1570      MAT V=ZER(N-1,N-1)
1580      FOR J=1 TO N-1                    'CALC. SPAN CHORD LENGTHS
1590        IF S=3 THEN 1620
1600        LET L(J)=SQR((P(1,J+1)-P(1,J))^2+(P(2,J+1)-P(2,J))^2)
1610        GO TO 1630
1620        LET L(J)=SQR((P(1,J+1)-P(1,J))^2+(P(2,J+1)-P(2,J))^2+(P(3,J+1)-P(3,J))^2)
1630      NEXT J
1640      LET S3=L(N-1)/L(1)
```

```
1650    IF C1=4 THEN 1730
1660    LET M(1,1)=2+2*S3                  'FIRST ROW OF M-MATRIX
1670    LET M(1,2)=S3                      'FOR CYCLIC SPLINE
1680    LET M(1,N-1)=1
1690    FOR K=1 TO S                       'SET B(K,1) FOR CYCLIC SPLINE
1700       LET B(K,1)=(3/L(1))*(S3*(P(K,2)-P(K,1))+(1/S3)*(P(K,N)-P(K,N-1)))
1710    NEXT K
1720    GO TO 1800
1730    LET M(1,1)=2+2*S3                  'FIRST ROW OF M-MATRIX
1740    LET M(1,2)=S3                      'FOR ANTICYCLIC SPLINE
1750    LET M(1,N-1)=-1
1760    FOR K=1 TO S                       'SET B(K,1) FOR ANTICYCLIC SPLINE
1770       LET B(K,1)=(3/L(1))*(S3*(P(K,2)-P(K,1))-(1/S3)*(P(K,N)-P(K,N-1)))
1780    NEXT K
1790    '
1800    'SET UP INTERIOR MATRIX AND INVERT
1810    FOR J=2 TO N-1                     'CREATE NONZERO VALUES FOR
1820       LET M(J,J-1)=L(J)               'INTERNAL ROWS OF M-MATRIX
1830       LET M(J,J)=2*(L(J)+L(J-1))
1840       FOR K=1 TO S                    'CREATE ROWS OF B-MATRIX
1850          LET B(K,J)=3*(L(J-1)^2*(P(K,J+1)-P(K,J))+L(J)^2*(P(K,J)-P(K,J-1)))
1860          LET B(K,J)=B(K,J)/(L(J)*L(J-1))
1870       NEXT K
1880    NEXT J
1890    MAT V=INV(M)                       'INVERT M-MATRIX
1900    FOR K=1 TO S
1910       FOR J=1 TO N-1
1920          LET C(J)=B(K,J)              'CALC. SINGLE ROW C-MATRIX
1930       NEXT J
1940       MAT W=V*C                       'CALC. TANGENT VECTOR VALUES
1950       FOR J=1 TO N-1
1960          LET U(K,J)=W(J)              'CREATE TANGENT VECTOR MATRIX
1970       NEXT J
1980    NEXT K
1990    IF C1=4 THEN 2040
2000    FOR K=1 TO S
2010       LET U(K,N)=U(K,1)               'SET FINAL TANGENT=INITIAL TANGENT
2020    NEXT K
2030    GO TO 2070
2040    FOR K=1 TO S
2050       LET U(K,N)=-U(K,1)              'SET FINAL TANGENT=-INITIAL TANGENT
2060    NEXT K
2070 SUBEND
```

C-25 An Algorithm For Parabolic Blending

An algorithm which implements the parabolic blending technique described in Sec. 5-6 is given below as a BASIC language subprogram.

PARBLEND

```
100 SUB"PARBLEND":R(,),N,C(,)              'PARABOLIC BLENDING
110    'R(,)=ARRAY CONTAINING THE COORDINATES OF FOUR POINTS
120    'R(1, )=X-COORDINATES
130    'R(2, )=Y-COORDINATES
```

```
140    'R(3, )=Z-COORDINATES
150    'N=NUMBER OF POINTS ON CURVE
160    'C(,)=ARRAY CONTAINING POINTS ON BLENDED CURVE
170        'C(1, )=X-COORDINATES
180        'C(2, )=Y-COORDINATES
190        'C(3, )=Z-COORDINATES
200        'NOTE: C MUST HAVE DIMENSIONS OF (3,N)
210    DIM P(3,64),Q(3,64)              'ALLOWS UP TO 64 SEGMENTS
220    MAT S=ZER(3,3)                   'INITIALIZE AND DIMENSION
230    MAT T=ZER(3,3)
240    MAT P=ZER(3,N)
250    MAT Q=ZER(3,N)
260    LET TO=SQR((R(1,3)-R(1,2))^2+(R(2,3)-R(2,2))^2+(R(3,3)-R(3,2))^2)  'CALC. TO
270    FOR J=1 TO 3                     'SET UP TO GENERATE PARABOLAS
280        FOR I=1 TO 3
290            LET S(I,J)=R(I,J)        'THRU FIRST THREE POINTS
300            LET T(I,J)=R(I,J+1)      'THRU LAST THREE POINTS
310        NEXT I
320    NEXT J
330    CALL"GEN":S(,),1,TO,N,P(,)       'GENERATE PARABOLA THRU FIRST THREE POINTS
340    CALL"GEN":T(,),2,TO,N,Q(,)       'GENERATE PARABOLA THRU LAST THREE POINTS
350    LET K=0
360    FOR T=0 TO 1 STEP (1/(N-1))      'GENERATE BLENDED CURVE
370        LET K=K+1
380        FOR I=1 TO 3
390            LET C(I,K)=(1-T)*P(I,K)+T*Q(I,K)
400        NEXT I
410    NEXT T
420 SUBEND
430 SUB"GEN":P(,),S1,TO,N,X(,)
440    'P(,)=ARRAY CONTAINING THREE POINTS FOR PARABOLA
450    'P(1, )=X COMPONENT
460    'P(2, )=Y COMPONENT
470    'P(3, )=Z COMPONENT
480    'S1=CONTROL VARIABLE 1=FIRST PARABOLA, 2=SECOND PARABOLA
490    'N=NUMBER OF POINTS ON PARABOLA
500    'TO=CHORD LENGTH BETWEEN MIDDLE POINTS
510    'X(,)=ARRAY CONTAINING THE POINTS ON THE PARABOLA
520    'X(1, )=X-COMPONENT
530    'X(2, )=Y-COMPONENT
540    'X(3, )=Z-COMPONENT
550    MAT T=ZER(3)                     'INITIALIZE & DIMENSION
560    MAT S=ZER(3)
570    MAT M=ZER(3)
580    FOR I=1 TO 3                     'SET UP
590        LET T(I)=P(I,2)-P(I,1)       'P(SUB4)-P(SUB3)
600        LET S(I)=P(I,3)-P(I,1)       'P(SUB5)-P(SUB3)
610        LET M(I)=P(I,3)-P(I,2)       'P(SUB5)-P(SUB4)
620    NEXT I                           '(CF EQ. 5-54)
630    MAT U=S*S                        'CALC. D^2
640    LET D=SQR(U)                     'CALC. D
650    MAT V=T*S                        'CALC. THE DOT PRODUCT (CF EQ. 5-54)
660    LET X=V/U                        'CALC. X (CF EQ. 5-54)
670    LET A=1/(U*X*(1- X))              'CALC. ALPHA (CF EQ. 5-57)
680    IF S1=2 THEN 720
690    MAT W=M*S                        'CALC. COS(THETA) (CF EQ. 5-59)
700    LET T1=W/(TO*D)
710    GOTO 730
720    LET T1=V/(TO*D)                  'CALC. COS(THETA) (CF EQ. 5-59)
730    LET K=0
```

```
740     FOR T2=0 TO 1 STEP(1/(N-1))      'CALC. POINTS ON PARABOLA
750        LET K=K+1
760        LET T=T0*T2                   'CALC. T
770        LET R=T*T1
780        IF S1=2 THEN 800              'TEST FOR FIRST OR SECOND PARABOLA
790        LET R=R+X*D
800        FOR J=1 TO 3
810           LET X(J,K)=P(J,1)+(R/D)*S(J)+A*R*(D-R)*(T(J)-X*S(J))
820        NEXT J
830     NEXT T2
840  SUBEND
```

C-26 A Bezier Curve Algorithm

An algorithm which will generate Bezier curve segments is given below as a BASIC language subprogram. It is based on the discussion of Sec. 5-7.

BEZIER

```
100 SUB"BEZIER":N1,S,X(,),Y(,),Z(,),P,R(,)   'BEZIER CURVE
110     'N1=NUMBER OF VERTICES IN BEZIER POLYGON
120     'S=CONTROL VARIABLE 2=PLANE CURVE, 3=SPACE CURVE
130     'X( ,1)=ARRAY CONTAINING THE X-COMPONENT OF POLYGON VERTICES
140     'Y( ,1)=ARRAY CONTAINING THE Y-COMPONENT OF POLYGON VERTICES
150     'Z( ,1)=ARRAY CONTAINING THE Z-COMPONENT OF POLYGON VERTICES
160     'P=NUMBER OF POINTS ALONG BEZIER CURVE
170     'R( , )=ARRAY CONTAINING THE POINTS ALONG THE BEZIER CURVE
180          'R(1, )=X-COMPONENT
190          'R(2, )=Y-COMPONENT
200          'R(3, )=Z-COMPONENT
210     'INITIALIZE AND DIMENSION ALL MATRICES
220     'ASSUMES A MAXIMUM OF 10 POLYGON VERTICES
230     MAT J=ZER(1,N1)
240     MAT C=ZER(1,1)
250     MAT D=ZER(1,1)
260     MAT E=ZER(1,1)
270     LET N=N1-1
280     'DEFINE FUNCTION TO EVALUATE BINOMIAL EXPANSION (CF EQ. 5-65)
290     DEF FNF(X)
300        IF X=0 THEN 360
310        LET Y=1
320        LET Y=Y*X
330        LET X=X-1
340        IF X=0 THEN 380
350        GOTO 320
360        LET FNF=1
370        GOTO 390
380        LET FNF=Y
390     FNEND
400     LET K=1
410     FOR T=0 TO 1 STEP 1/(P-1)        'GENERATE BASIS FUNCTION (CF EQ. 5-64)
420        FOR I=0 TO N
430           LET J(1,I+1)=(FNF(N)/(FNF(I)*FNF(N-I)))*T^I*(1-T)^(N-I)
440        NEXT I
450        MAT C=J*X                     'GENERATE POINTS ALONG A
460        MAT D=J*Y                     '2-D OR 3-D BEZIER CURVE (CF EQ. 5-66)
```

```
470       LET R(1,K)=C(1,1)              'CREATE POINT RESULTS
480       LET R(2,K)=D(1,1)
490       IF S=2 THEN 520
500       MAT E=J*Z
510       LET R(3,K)=E(1,1)
520       LET K=K+1
530    NEXT T
540 SUBEND
```

C-27 B-spline Algorithm

Algorithms which will generate the required B-spline basis knot vectors and B-spline curves are given below as BASIC language subprograms. They are based on the discussion of Sec. 5-8. Note that the subprogram B-spline calls KNOT. The subprogram B-spline uses the Cox and de Boor algorithm to generate the B-spline curves of various order.

BSPLINE

```
100 SUB"BSPLINE":A,C,V(,),S,P,R(,)
110    'A=NUMBER OF POLYGON VERTICES MINUS ONE
120    'C=ORDER OF B-SPLINE BASIS
130    'V(,)=ARRAY CONTAINING DEFINING POLYGON VERTICES
140    'V(1, ) CONTAINS X-COORDINATES
150    'V(2, ) CONTAINS Y-COORDINATES
160    'V(3, ) CONTAINS Z-COORDINATES
165    'NOTE:THE FIRST POLYGON VERTEX MUST BE IN V(1,0),V(2,0),V(3,0)
170    'S=CONTROL VARIABLE S=2 FOR 2-D CURVE, S=3 FOR 3-D CURVE
180    'P=THE NUMBER OF POINTS GENERATED ALONG THE CURVE
185    'THE VALUE OF P WILL BE MODIFIED TO P=INT((P-1)/X(A+C))*X(A+C)+1
190    'R(,)=ARRAY CONTAINING THE RESULTING B-SPLINE CURVE
200    'R(1, ) CONTAINS X-COORDINATES
210    'R(2, ) CONTAINS Y-COORDINATES
220    'R(3, ) CONTAINS Z-COORDINATES
230    'N(,)=WEIGHTING FUNCTION (CF EQ. 5-78)
240    DIM N(25,25),X(100)
250    MAT N=ZER((A+C),(A+C))              'REDIMENSION N & FILL WITH ZEROS
260    LET B=A-C+2
270    CALL"KNOT":V(,),B,C,X(),S
280    FOR W=C-1 TO C+B
290       FOR I=0 TO B+(C-1)*2-1          'INCREMENT KNOT VECTOR SUBSCRIPT
300          IF I<>W THEN 340             'CHECK FOR A GEOMETRIC KNOT
310          IF X(I)=X(I+1)  THEN 340
320          LET N(I,1)=1                 'CALC. VALUES
330          GO TO 350                    'FOR N(I,1)
340          LET N(I,1)=0
350       NEXT I
360       FOR T=X(W) TO X(W+1)-X(A+C)/(P-1) STEP X(A+C)/(P-1)
370          LET L=L+1
380          FOR K=2 TO C                 'CALC. VALUES OF N(I,K) IN
390             FOR I=0 TO A              'LINES 380-580
400                IF N(I,K-1)<>0 THEN 430
410                LET D=0
420                GO TO 440
430                LET D=((T-X(I))*N(I,K-1))/(X(I+K-1)-X(I))   'FIRST TERM,
```

```
440             IF N(I+1,K-1) <>0 THEN 470   'EQ. (5-78)
450             LET E=0
460             GO TO 480
470             LET E=((X(I+K)-T)*N(I+1,K-1))/(X(I+K)-X(I+1))   'SECOND TERM,
480             LET N(I,K)=D+E        'EQ. (5-78)
490             LET G=V(1,I)*N(I,K)+G  'X-COMPONENT OF P(T)
500             LET H=V(2,I) *N(I,K)+H
510             IF S=2 THEN 530
520             LET Z=V(3,I)*N(I,K)+Z
530           NEXT I
540           IF K=C THEN 590
550           LET G=0
560           LET H=0
570           LET Z=0
580         NEXT K
590         LET R(1,L)=G
600         LET R(2,L)=H
610         IF S=2 THEN 630
620         LET R(3,L)=Z
630         LET G=0                     'RESET INITIAL X,Y,Z VALUES
640         LET H=0
650         LET Z=0
660       NEXT T
670     NEXT W
680     LET L=L+1
685     LET P=L
690     LET R(1,L)=V(1,A)
700     LET R(2,L)=V(2,A)
710     IF S=2 THEN 730
720     LET R(3,L)=V(3,A)
730 SUBEND
740 SUB"KNOT": V( , ),B,C,X(),S
750     ' V(,)=ARRAY CONTAINING DEFINING POLYGON VERTICES
760     ' B=MAXIMUM T VALUE=A-C+2
770     ' C=ORDER OF B-SPLINE BASIS
780     ' X()=ARRAY CONTAINING KNOT VECTORS GENERATED IN THIS SUBROUTINE
790     ' S=CONTROL VARIABLE  S=2 PLANE  S=3 SPACE CURVE
800     FOR I=0 TO B+(C-1)*2
810       IF I>C-1 THEN 840              'ASSURE MULTIPLICITY OF DEGREE C
820       LET X(I)=0                     'ASSIGN MULTIPLE END KNOT VECTORS
830       GO TO 960
840       IF I<B+C THEN 880              'CHECK IF END KNOT VECTORS REACHED
850       LET X(I)=X(I-1)                'ASSIGN MULTIPLE OR DUPLICATE KNOTS
860       GO TO 960
870       IF S=3 THEN 910
880       IF V(1,I-C)<>V(1,I-C+1) THEN 950  'CHECK FOR REPEATING VERTICES
890       IF V(2,I-C)<>V(2,I-C+1) THEN 950  'CHECK FOR REPEATING VERTICES
900       GO TO 850
910       IF V(1,I-C)<>V(1,I-C+1) THEN 950
920       IF V(2,I-C)<>V(2,I-C+1) THEN 950
930       IF V(3,I-C)<>V(3,I-C+1) THEN 950
940       GO TO 850
950       LET X(I)=X(I-1)+1              'ASSIGN SUCCESSIVE INTERNAL VECTORS
960     NEXT I
970 SUBEND
```

C-28 An Algorithm For a Bilinear Surface Patch

An algorithm which will create the bilinear surface patch described in
Eq. (6-19) is given below as a BASIC language subprogram.

BILINEAR

```
100 SUB"BILINEAR":N,M,P(,),Q(,)        'BILINEAR SURFACE
110    'N=NUMBER OF INCREMENTS OF U
120    'M=NUMBER OF INCREMENTS OF W
130    'P(,)=CONTAINS THE COORDINATES OF THE CORNER POINTS
140        'P HAS DIMENSIONS OF 4*3. FIRST COLUMN CONTAINS X-
150        'COMPONENTS, SECOND Y-COMPONENTS, THIRD Z-COMPONENTS
160        'OF THE CORNER POSITION VECTORS.
170    'Q(,)=CONTAINS THE COORDINATES OF THE INTERPOLATED SURFACE
180        'Q WILL HAVE DIMENSIONS OF (M+1)(N+1)*3
190        'THE FIRST M+1 COORDINATE PAIRS CORRESPOND TO U=0=CONSTANT
200        'THE SECOND M+1 COORDINATE PAIRS CORRESPOND TO U=1/N=CONSTANT
210        'THIRD M+1 COORDINATE PAIRS CORRESPOND TO U=2/N=CONSTANT
220        'NOTE: Q MUST BE DIMENSIONED IN DRIVER PROGRAM
230    MAT Q=ZER((N+1)*(M+1),3)        'REDIMENSION Q & FILL WITH ZEROS
240    FOR I=1 TO N+1                   'SET UP U=CONSTANT LOOP
250      LET U=(I-1)/(N)                'CALC. INCREMENT FOR U
260      FOR J=1 TO M+1                 'SET UP W LOOP
270        LET K=K+1                    'INCREMENT POINT COUNTER
280        LET W=(J-1)/M                'SET W
290        LET Q(K,1)=P(1,1)*(1-U)*(1-W)+P(2,1)*(1-U)*W+P(3,1)*U*(1-W)
300        LET Q(K,1)=Q(K,1)+P(4,1)*U*W  'CALC. X-COMPONENT
310        LET Q(K,2)=P(1,2)*(1-U)*(1-W)+P(2,2)*(1-U)*W+P(3,2)*U*(1-W)
320        LET Q(K,2)=Q(K,2)+P(4,2)*U*W  'CALC. Y-COMPONENT
330        LET Q(K,3)=P(1,3)*(1-U)*(1-W)+P(2,3)*(1-U)*W+P(3,3)*U*(1-W)
340        LET Q(K,3)=Q(K,3)+P(4,3)*U*W  'CALC. Z-COMPONENT
350      NEXT J
360    NEXT I
370 SUBEND
```

C-29 An Algorithm For Linear Coons Surface

An algorithm which will generate the linear Coons surface described by
Eq. (6-24) is given below as a BASIC language subprogram. The algorithm
assumes that the boundary curve can be described by equally spaced (in parameter
values) points on the boundary curves. The $P(u,0)$ and $P(u,1)$ curves are assumed
to be described by the same number of points as are the $P(0,w)$ and $P(1,w)$ curves.

COONSLIN

```
100 SUB"COONSLIN":N,M,A(,),B(,),C(,),D(,),Q(,)   'LINEAR COONS SURFACE
110    'N=NUMBER OF POINTS ON THE P(U,0) AND P(U,1) BOUNDARY CURVES
120    'M=NUMBER OF POINTS ON THE P(0,W) AND P(1,W) BOUNDARY CURVES
130    'A(,)=ARRAY CONTAINING THE POINTS ON THE P(U,0) CURVE
140        'HAS DIMENSIONS OF N*3
150    'B(,)=ARRAY CONTAINING THE POINTS ON THE P(U,1) CURVE
160        'HAS DIMENSIONS OF N*3
```

```
170     'C(,)=ARRAY CONTAINING THE POINTS ON THE P(O,W) CURVE
180         'HAS DIMENSIONS OF M*3
190     'D(,)=ARRAY CONTAINING THE POINTS ON THE P(1,W) CURVE
200         'HAS DIMENSIONS OF M*3
210     'Q(,)=ARRAY CONTAINING THE CURVES WHICH DESCRIBE THE SURFACE
220         'HAS DIMENSIONS OF (N*M)*3. THE FORMAT IS FOR A FIXED
230         'VALUE OF U. THE NEXT M ROWS OF THE Q MATRIX CONTAIN
240         'THE VALUES FOR VARIABLE W.
250         'NOTE: Q MUST BE DIMENSIONED IN DRIVER PROGRAM
260     MAT Q=ZER(N*M,3)                    'REDIMENION Q & FILL WITH ZEROS
270     FOR K=1 TO M                        'CALC. SURFACE
280        LET U=(K-1)/(M-1)
290        FOR J=1 TO N
300           LET W=(J-1)/(N-1)
310           LET S=S+1
320           FOR L=1 TO 3
330              LET Q(S,L)=A(K,L)*(1-W)+B(K,L)*W+C(J,L)*(1-U)+D(J,L)*U
340              LET Q(S,L)=Q(S,L)-A(1,L)*(1-U)*(1-W)-B(1,L)*(1-U)*W
350              LET Q(S,L)=Q(S,L)-A(N,L)*U*(1-W)-B(N,L)*U*W
360           NEXT L
370        NEXT J
380     NEXT K
390 SUBEND
```

C-30 An Algorithm For A Bicubic Surface Patch

An algorithm which will generate the bicubic surface patch described by Eq. (6-37) is given below as a BASIC language subprogram. The routine assumes that the boundary condition and the blending function matrices are known.

BICUBIC

```
100 SUB"BICUBIC":U1,W1,X(,),Y(,),Z(,),Q(,)  'BI-CUBIC SURFACE
110     'U1=NO OF INCREMENTS ALONG U-DIRECTION
120     'W1=NO OF INCREMENTS ALONG W-DIRECTION
130     'X(,)=4 X 4 ARRAY CONTAINING THE X-COMPONENTS OF THE
140         'P BOUNDARY CONDITION MATRIX EQ. (6-36)
150     'Y(,)=4 X 4 ARRAY CONTAINING THE Y-COMPONENTS OF THE
160         'P BOUNDARY CONDITION MATRIX EQ. (6-36)
170     'Z(,)=4 X 4 ARRAY CONTAINING THE Z-COMPONENTS OF THE
180         'P BOUNDARY CONDITION MATRIX EQ. (6-36)
190     'P(,)=4 X 4 BOUNDARY CONDITION MATRIX EQ. (6-36)
200     'N(,)=4 X 4 BLENDING FUNCTION MATRIX EQ. (6-31)
210     'U(,)=1 X 4 CUBIC BLENDING VECTOR EQ. (6-37)
220     'W(,)=4 X 1 CUBIC BLENDING VECTOR EQ. (6-37)
230     'Q(,)=MATRIX CONTAINING THE POSITION VECTORS FOR THE
240         'BICUBIC SURFACE, HAS DIMENSIONS OF (U1+1)*(W1+1) X 3
250         'FIRST COLUNM IS X-COMPONENT
260         'SECOND COLUMN IS Y-COMPONENT
270         'THIRD COLUMN IS Z-COMPONENT
280         'FIRST W1+1 ELEMENTS FOR U=0
290         'SECOND W1+1 ELEMENTS FOR U=1/U1, ETC.
300     MAT P=ZER(4,4)                      'REDIMENSION MATRICES &
310     MAT N=ZER(4,4)                      'FILL WITH ZEROS
320     MAT U=ZER(1,4)
330     MAT W=ZER(4,1)
```

```
340      MAT Q=ZER((U1+1)*(W1+1),3)
350      MAT A=ZER(4,1)
360      MAT B=ZER(4,1)
370      MAT C=ZER(4,1)
380      MAT D=ZER(1,1)
390      LET N(1,1)=2                    'SET UP N-MATRIX
400      LET N(1,2)=N(2,3)=-2
410      LET N(2,1)=-3
420      LET N(2,2)=3
430      LET N(1,3)=N(1,4)=N(3,3)=N(4,1)=1
440      LET N(2,4)=-1
450      MAT M=TRN(N)                    'CALC. TRANSPOSE OF N-MATRIX
460      MAT P=X                         'CALC. X-COMPONENTS OF
470      LET K=K+1                       'SURFACE ELEMENTS
480      FOR I=0 TO U1                   'SET UP U-MATRIX
490         LET U2=I/U1
500         LET U(1,1)=U2^3
510         LET U(1,2)=U2*U2
520         LET U(1,3)=U2
530         LET U(1,4)=1
540         FOR J=0 TO W1
550            LET L=L+1
560            LET W2=J/W1               'SET UP W-MATRIX
570            LET W(1,1)=W2^3
580            LET W(2,1)=W2*W2
590            LET W(3,1)=W2
600            LET W(4,1)=1
610            MAT A=M*W                 'CALC. SURFACE ELEMENT
620            MAT B=P*A
630            MAT C=N*B
640            MAT D=U*C
650            LET Q(L,K)=D(1,1)
660         NEXT J
670      NEXT I
680      IF K=2 THEN 720
690      IF K>2 THEN 740
700      MAT P=Y                         'CALC. Y-COMPONENTS OF
710      GO TO 470                       'SURFACE ELEMENTS
720      MAT P=Z                         'CALC. Z-COMPONENTS OF
730      GO TO 470                       'SURFACE ELEMENTS
740 SUBEND
```

C-31 Bezier Surface Generation Algorithm

An algorithm which will generate a cartesian product Bezier surface based on Eq. (6-48) is given below as a BASIC language subprogram. Bezier curves are used as the blending functions.

BEZSURF

```
100 SUB"BEZSURF":X(,),Y(,),Z(,),N,M,P,S(,)     'BEZIER SURFACE
110      'X(,)=ARRAY CONTAINING THE X-COMPONENTS OF THE POLYGON VERTICES
120      'Y(,)=ARRAY CONTAINING THE Y-COMPONENTS OF THE POLYGON VERTICES
130      'Z(,)=ARRAY CONTAINING THE Z-COMPONENTS OF THE POLYGON VERTICES
```

```
140          'NOTE: X,Y,Z HAVE DIMENSIONS OF N X M
150          'FORMAT IS THAT SHOWN IN FIGS. 6-12 & 6-13
160     'N=ORDER OF THE DEFINING BEZIER POLYGONS FOR U=0 AND U=1
170     'M=ORDER OF THE DEFINING BEZIER POLYGONS FOR W=0 AND W=1
180     'P=NUMBER OF GRID LINES FOR THE DEFINING SURFACE
190     'S(,)=POSITION VECTORS FOR SURFACE DEFINING GRID
200          'S(1, )=X-COMPONENTS
210          'S(2, )=Y-COMPONENTS
220          'S(3, )=Z-COMPONENTS
230          'FORMAT IS THAT FOR A FIXED VALUE OF U THE NEXT
240          'M ELEMENTS CONTAIN THE VALUES FOR THE CURVE Q(U(SUB I),W)
250          'S HAS DIMENSIONS OF 3 X P^2
260     MAT B=ZER(N,M)                'REDIMENSION & ZERO INTERNAL MATRIX
270     DEF FNF(X)                    'DEFINE FUNCTION TO CALC. FACTORIAL CF EQ.(5-65)
280        IF X=0 THEN 340
290        LET Y=1
300        LET Y=Y*X
310        LET X=X-1
320        IF X=0 THEN 360
330        GOTO 300
340        LET FNF=1
350        GOTO 370
360        LET FNF=Y
370     FNEND
380     FOR C=1 TO 3                  'FOR EACH COMPONENT CALC. SURFACE
390        LET W1=0                   'GRID POSITION VECTORS
400        ON C GOTO 410,430,450
410        MAT B=X                    'X-COMPONENT
420        GOTO 460
430        MAT B=Y                    'Y-COMPONENT
440        GOTO 460
450        MAT B=Z                    'Z-COMPONENT
460        FOR  U= 0 TO 1 STEP 1/(P-1) 'FOR FIXED U CALC. VARIOUS W'S
470          FOR W= 0 TO 1 STEP 1/(P-1)
480            LET W1=W1+1
490            FOR I=0 TO N
500               LET J1=(FNF(N)/(FNF(I)*FNF(N-I)))*U^I*(1-U)^(N-I)
510               FOR J= 0 TO M
520                  LET K1=(FNF(M)/(FNF(J)*FNF(M-J)))*W^J*(1-W)^(M-J)
530                  LET S(C,W1)=S(C,W1)+B(I+1,J+1)*J1*K1
540               NEXT J
550            NEXT I
560          NEXT W
570        NEXT U
580     NEXT C
590 SUBEND
```

INDEX